Theology as Autobiography

Theology as Autobiography

*The Centrality of Confession, Relationship,
and Prayer to the Life of Faith*

Colby Dickinson

CASCADE *Books* • Eugene, Oregon

THEOLOGY AS AUTOBIOGRAPHY
The Centrality of Confession, Relationship, and Prayer to the Life of Faith

Copyright © 2020 Colby Dickinson. All rights reserved. Except for brief quotations in critical publications or reviews, no part of this book may be reproduced in any manner without prior written permission from the publisher. Write: Permissions, Wipf and Stock Publishers, 199 W. 8th Ave., Suite 3, Eugene, OR 97401.

Cascade Books
An Imprint of Wipf and Stock Publishers
199 W. 8th Ave., Suite 3
Eugene, OR 97401

www.wipfandstock.com

PAPERBACK ISBN: 978-1-5326-8882-9
HARDCOVER ISBN: 978-1-5326-8883-6
EBOOK ISBN: 978-1-5326-8884-3

Cataloguing-in-Publication data:

Names: Dickinson, Colby, author.

Title: Theology as autobiography : the centrality of confession, relationship, and prayer to the life of faith / by Colby Dickinson.

Description: Eugene, OR: Cascade Books, 2020 | Includes bibliographical references and index.

Identifiers: ISBN 978-1-5326-8882-9 (paperback) | ISBN 978-1-5326-8883-6 (hardcover) | ISBN 978-1-5326-8884-3 (ebook)

Subjects: LCSH: Autobiography—Religious aspects—Christianity. | Autobiography—Authorship.

Classification: BL72 .D50 2020 (print) | BL72 .D50 (ebook)

Manufactured in the U.S.A. 03/13/20

*This book is dedicated to Maria Przada and Ben Asen,
true inspirations of what teachers of both theology
and faith should aspire to be*

Contents

Acknowledgments | ix

Introduction: Theology as Autobiography | 1

Chapter One
The Significance of (Auto)biography in the Christian Tradition | 21

Chapter Two
Augustine: Confession at the Foundations of Christian Theology | 46

Chapter Three
Mary Karr: Taking the Risk of Putting One's Faith into Life and One's Life into Faith | 63

Chapter Four
Christian Wiman: A Poetic Meditation on Life, Suffering, Faith, and Jesus Christ | 84

Chapter Five
Leo Tolstoy: Finding Faith Amidst the Tensions of the World | 105

Chapter Six
Rachel Held Evans and Dani Shapiro: Finding a Way Forward for Critical Faith Today | 122

Chapter Seven
Guibert of Nogent and Ignatius of Loyola: Errors, Pitfalls, and Reading Life in Light of Divine Activity in the World | 144

Chapter Eight
Teresa of Ávila : Living the Saintly Life | 161

Chapter Nine
Dorothy Day: Faith in the Context of Suffering and Marginalization | 179

Chapter Ten
Henri Nouwen: Locating a Contemporary Spirituality | 198

Chapter Eleven
Diana Eck: The O/other Already Before Us | 223

Conclusion | 239

Bibliography | 245
Subject Index | 257
Author Index | 261
Scripture index | 263

Acknowledgments

The present volume was initially conceived for a section of students I had just begun to teach at Loyola University, as part of a newly founded learning community on "Service and Faith" for incoming freshman. Bringing faith to life in the course was the single most important task I placed before myself and the students each semester, and giving this task an autobiographical focus in terms of its content was the crucial piece of the puzzle that I had previously been missing. I undertook this project as an attempt to make an introductory course in theology relevant and meaningful in the lives of college undergraduates, and I hope that I have somewhat succeeded in this task. In completing the multi-year project that this book since became, I tried to preserve the feel of the present material being part of a series of lectures intended to inspire students to take up for themselves a critical examination of their own lives of faith, whatever such a thing might in the end be. The argument I was building throughout the course was, for this reason, subtle in its declaration, though certainly not any less meaningful.

My intent in publishing this work was not just to preserve the record of a lecture course, but to push the boundaries of theological thinking through material that accumulated in the context of a university course, and which quickly expanded into making a statement in its own right. I very much hope that the reflections presented here push the reader into new domains of theological thought and methodology. Nonetheless, I am very grateful for the participation of each and every student who enrolled in the course, all of whom assisted me in shaping the present volume into its final form.

The energy and enthusiasm of the students I taught was always equally met by the faculty and staff who helped both to organize the group and to oversee the varied experiences the students would have throughout the years to come. We had many meetings before and throughout each semester and these times together inspired and focused my work in many ways. I want to thank Megan Barry, Jon Schmidt, April Gutierrez, and Marilyn Krogh for being part of these discussions and for offering meaningful support for iterations of a course that eventually gave shape to these lectures.

Many thanks are certainly also due to my wonderful colleagues in the Theology Department at Loyola University Chicago, who have provided invaluable assistance and insight throughout my time there. I could name every member of the department, but I would certainly like to single out Aana Vigen, Susan Ross, Hille Haker, John McCarthy, Mark Bosco, Mike Murphy, and Bob DiVito, in particular, for offering their support at key moments while I worked on and edited the present volume. I am also incredibly grateful for all of the administrative support from both Catherine Wolf and Joanne Brandstrader that was offered each time I taught the course.

I would like as well to extend a special thanks to the doctoral students who worked with me at various stages in this project, including Joseph Gulhaugen, Najeeb Haddad, Jacob Torbeck, Kathleen McNutt, and Marty Tomszak. Kathleen and Marty, especially, were instrumental in bringing this book closer to its final form, as they edited my lectures in order that they might cohere better with what was actually being taught in the course and offered helpful comments and suggestions as to content. I owe Marty a special thanks for drafting the brief biographical statements that precede each chapter, compiling bibliographic materials, and for his invaluable comments upon the manuscript as a whole.

Presenting lives of faith within the context of a course means that I have spent a fair amount of time contemplating those persons who have shaped my faith in the context of teaching theology. I cannot name them all, of course, but I would like to single out some individuals who have defined for me, over the years, what it means to encounter both one's life of faith and that which inspires such a faith outside of the self. My grateful thanks are due therefore to Harry Byrne, Cab Gutting, Anthony D'Agostino, Andrew Burkes, Danielle Harrison, Amy Laura Hall, Lieven Boeve, and Jacques Haers, among many others. This book is dedicated to two of those teachers, Maria Przada, one of the most inspiring "Women of the Word" I have ever known, and the late Ben Asen, whose memory continues to guide my every work in the field we shared.

"There is no clean intellectual coherence, no abstract ultimate meaning to be found, and if this is not recognized, then the compulsion to find such certainty becomes its own punishment. This realization is not the end of theology, but the beginning of it: trust no theory, no religious history or creed, in which the author's personal faith is not actively at risk."

—Christian Wiman, *My Bright Abyss: Meditation of a Modern Believer*

"So deeply do we care for you that we are determined to share with you not only the gospel of God but also our own selves, because you have become very dear to us."

—Saint Paul, 1 Thessalonians 2:8

"I would not speak about 'absolute' truths, even for believers. . . . Truth is a relationship. As such, each one of us receives the truth and expresses it from within, that is to say, according to one's own circumstances, culture, and situation in life."

—Pope Francis

Introduction

Theology as Autobiography

Theology is entering a period where a possible renewal of its traditional subject matter may be under significant revision. I stress the word *possible* because it is also possible that people, theologians especially, might miss it, might be looking the other direction and not see what has already been happening underneath their very noses. Or, perhaps worse, a certain academic snobbery might bring about the dismissal of a genre of writing that continues to impact and shape faith today in profound ways. These are the temptations we face at the moment because it has already been the case for a while now that such writings have not been taken as seriously as they deserve to be, and therefore critical engagement with these texts has frequently been muted in the field of theology. But missing the proper subject of theology, it should be said, is nothing new to the history of the terrain: as Gospel biblical accounts confirm, the biggest revelations often take place discretely, perhaps even amongst a few people, while most people are not looking in the right direction, and while only some can see the significance forming all around them.

There is no doubt that modern theologians have consistently felt the need to make their often dry and academic tomes comprehensible to a more general audience, though the success rates of such translations are often few and far between. It is with this struggle to articulate what matters to one's life of faith that I am proposing we might benefit from recontextualizing the arguments that sustain the life of faith, by moving determinately at times from the abstract and often speculative propositions of theological discourse as the primary subject matter of theology to the narratives of faith that speak of an original encounter with the divine that gave birth to a life of faith in the first place. Perhaps in shifting the focus of theological discussion as such, as well as its tone and accessibility, we might begin *another* journey to the center of the theological, one that takes the experiences of individuals, their struggles, and their hard-fought victories more centrally into account.

The subject I am explicitly referring to, the one that theology as a field needs to awaken more fully to, is the last century or so of tremendous *autobiographical* writings on faith that come not from the pens of theologians per se, but from the lives of ordinary persons whose struggles with faith are often lived at the margins of church, academy, and society, but which have the potential to reshape the ways in which each of those fields function.[1] I am thinking not only of the popular success of works like Elizabeth Gilbert's *Eat, Pray, Love*, Karen Armstrong's *The Spiral Staircase*, or Kathleen Norris's *The Cloister Walk*, but of so many writers who have chosen to tell their personal stories and struggles of faith within the context of various religious traditions and which are beginning to have an effect on the way in which we shape theological discourse. I would mention here writers as diverse as Anne Lamott, Greg Boyle, Sara Miles, Lauren Winner, Barbara Brown Taylor, Nadia Bolz-Weber, Scott Cairns, Nora Gallagher, Stephen Levine, and Roger Kamenetz, just to name some. Though these modern autobiographies and memoirs are not the first works to delve boldly into the realm of the autobiographical in matters of faith (C. S. Lewis's *Surprised by Joy* and Thomas Merton's *The Seven Storey Mountain* were earlier inspirational and, in many ways, ground-breaking works in the genre, for example), they are representative of a growing field that has captured the attention of persons far beyond any single religious institution.[2]

The author Jack Miles, himself formerly a Jesuit seminarian, was certainly onto something when he chose some years ago to rewrite the story of God as a biography and then to retell the story of Jesus as an intimate, personal "Crisis in the Life of God," as the book's subtitle would have it.[3] Conceiving of God's life, God's own story, as a biographical one, analogous to the unfolding of a human life, I would suggest, is a rather refreshing way to envision and enliven theological discourse. In fact, as I hope to argue in what follows, it is the *primary* thing we should be doing when we

---

1. Though there is a subtle distinction to be made between autobiography and memoir, as the former attempts to narrate an entire life history and the latter recounts a specific experience in a person's life, since both are first-person reflections, I am using them somewhat interchangeably in this book as I am placing stress upon self-reflection and self-narration as a whole. On the genre of memoir as a whole and its contemporary surge to the forefront of publishing houses, see, among others, Yagoda, *Memoir*.

2. There is some attention being given in a contemporary setting to the genre of spiritual autobiography, though systematic study of the field is not as fully developed as it might be. See, for example, Plekon, *Saints As They Really Are*, Leigh, *Circuitous Journeys*, Comstock, *Religious Autobiographies*, and McClendon, *Biography as Theology*.

3. Miles, *God* and *Christ*.

talk about faith: talking about *our* lives and the lives of others who have struggled with themselves, with others, and even with God, whenever we intend to perform an act that is even a little bit theological. It is only by introducing such a reframing of the conversation that we might achieve something like personal faith, which is really, in many ways, another word for *relationship*—a convenient and sensible substitution of terms that I will come back to again and again in this book.

Grasping the bulk of what this substitution implies, I want first to suggest that we need to understand how faith, like relationships, especially those involving persons we most love, is a *weak* thing, not a strong thing—one of the factors, I am guessing, that turns off a good many academics from autobiographical writings on the whole, in that such works might appear to somehow weaken the rigor of their critical, academic scholarship. Despite such fears, however, we have to admit that faith rests, as John Henry Newman once claimed, on weak claims rather than strong ones.[4] Faith, as Newman made clear, is grounded in a complex network of relations that undergird its existence; it is not determined, as in the sciences, through the strong claims of reason alone (and though reason most certainly does play a role in weak claims too). Faith develops organically through the many foundations that make up the people we are, and though such a foundation is in fact "weak" in a certain sense, *as is love*, it should never seek to be anything less than a movement closer to the source of our vulnerability.

As fragile and precarious as a relationship with another person can be, it can also be an extremely strong bond at the same time, something that a person is willing to give up one's own life for, for example. In another sense, we might imagine the mistaken effort involved in trying to "prove" (as in the sciences) to one's beloved that they are loved. It would be a ridiculous endeavor to do so, as if one could undertake proving such a thing within a court of law or as a mathematical proof.[5] Reason, to be sure, rests entirely upon strong claims, and this is as things should be. It is, after all, what undergirds the scientific achievements that allow enormous planes to take flight. Faith, however, and in a way that does not contradict reason (or science for that matter), rests upon much weaker evidence, and this is how things should be too. The "reasons" one might list that a particular friendship is a strong one are often difficult to produce, even more difficult to describe perhaps, but nonetheless powerful forces, despite the "weak" claims made on their behalf.

---

4. Newman, *An Essay in Aid of a Grammar of Assent*.
5. Latour, *Rejoicing*.

In the early church, to be sure, biographical and autobiographical narratives were frequently utilized in order to demonstrate how the life of faith had to be an embodied thing. You simply could not divorce who you were and the complexities of your life story from the theological nuances that brought faith to life within a given theological tradition. In the late modern world in which we live, however, we more often than not confuse the domains of reason, comprehended apart from any other factors within one's existence, and faith, thereby believing that the strong claims of reason should apply exclusively to matters of faith as well, even above all other claims made upon us. In short, this is a terrible site of confusion. Reason plays a role in developing one's life of faith, certainly, but it does not determine the entire scope of its applicability in one's life. Applying the claims of reason *alone* to a relationship, analogously for example, is the sure death of a relationship—a process of overanalyzing that quickly squelches any passionate fire that might have been otherwise smoldering.

Contrasted with this, a genuine love will almost always exceed the boundaries of reason in some manner. One often goes "out of one's head" in love, and this is as love should be too, though even such a force will necessarily have to be tempered with reason from time to time. Faith, I would argue, is little different than a relationship in this sense. There is so much that goes into the construction of one's faith and that brings it to life, as it were. We cannot neglect the claims of these various factors, no matter how much we may want to (over)rely upon one or two alone. There is, in fact, a *complexity* to faith that mirrors the complexity of the relationships we find ourselves in, and we should not be eager to reduce faith to a matter of reason or scientific (historical) fact alone.

Newman's view of the development of certainty in matters of faith, or other weak claims, was that it relied upon a complex series of probabilities that slowly, almost unconsciously, pushed us closer to faith, rather than be taken as (strong) absolutes, which really are not very helpful to building up one's faith in a genuine sense. Certainty can still be achieved, but it means something completely different than it would in the sciences. We intuit this truth immediately when someone asks us if we are certain we want to marry our beloved, a question that can only be answered while taking into account a large number of intimate and embodied factors, ones that, combined together, suffice to establish a specific sense of certainty, though in the weak terms I have been describing. This is no doubt why so many people also feel certain of being in love while the reality of their relationship is far more complex and may even, eventually, yield to doubts that undermine that same sense of certainty.

The manner in which I use the word *relationship* here is a deliberate and foundational one, and one that, I believe, further expands our awareness of just how important the growing body of autobiographical literature on faith can be for one's own personal reflection. I am thinking of the way in which Kathleen Norris uses the word *relationship* in her *Amazing Grace: A Vocabulary of Faith*, a book that is a testament to the way in which people of faith must reformulate their theological words and concepts so that they are meaningful in ever new senses, typically too in ways that exceed the definitions that were once given as abstracted from the embodied context of a life lived in faith. Norris learned from her grandmother, for example, "that this coming to my senses, this realigning of true relationship, might serve as a definition of the living faith. Not a list of 'things I believe,' but the continual process of learning (and relearning) what it means to love God, my neighbor, and myself."[6] Just as with relationships that grow and evolve over time, we are forced to provide new words and new meanings to describe just what it is that we are caught up in the midst of, this life of "faith" that makes a claim upon us as much as we make a claim upon it.

One of the biggest problems with faith in our world today, I believe, is that we are constantly trying to apply a child's vocabulary of faith, one limited in its diversity and expressiveness, to describe the complex matters that we are living as adults, as if the coordinates of friendship a person learned in primary school would adequately cover their adult life of friendship too. We have ceased at some point to translate the terms we learned in our youth into new contexts and situations, and we have perhaps, by doing so, missed the larger, much more complex development of faith that could have been ours all along. In some sense, of course, the words we use from childhood to adulthood will overlap; but in other cases (think of sexual intimacy, for example) they fall woefully short and do not, even should not, be used in the same way in both contexts.

Norris, in trying to evolve an adult faith along with her adult life, notes how returning to faith after having been forced to undergo it in her youth meant having to face some of the "scary" vocabulary of faith, words like *Trinity*, *mystic*, *exorcism*, *idolatry*, *incarnation*, *judgment*, *hell*, *dogma*, and *orthodoxy*. In her estimation, such words

> carried an enormous weight of emotional baggage from my own childhood and also from family history. For reasons I did not comprehend, church seemed a place I needed to be. But in order to inhabit it, to claim it as mine, I had to rebuild my

---

6. Norris, *Amazing Grace*, 2.

religious vocabulary. The words had to become real to me, in an existential sense.[7]

Sin, for example, is word many of us may need to rethink in order for it to have meaning in our current context, as it has generally been understood in a wholly negative sense, threatening people with damnation rather than introducing them into a complex discourse on the inherent fallibility and vulnerability of the human being.

For Norris, such words had to be transformed into a language that made sense to her within the life she was living in the present moment. They had to be felt viscerally and practically. This is, for all intents and purposes, a very realistic thing to do in order to find a place for faith within one's adult life, though the following question must also be asked: how many of us actually take the time and make the effort to relearn what these words might mean to us, what life they might be capable of giving to us if only we would strive to make an effort to understand and appropriate them anew?

Analogous to this line of inquiry, we might not be that surprised to ask the same question of relationships themselves, something on the minds of many who face a "crisis" in their friendships, marriages, or love life in general: after so many years of being with a significant other, how likely are we to make an effort to greet our beloved or friend anew, to relearn what they mean to us, to invigorate our life together by not taking them for granted any more, to realize that they have changed, are constantly changing in fact, and that we need to expand our understanding of their complexity as an individual if we are to remain relevant in their life? Far too many persons neglect such essential questions, ones that would clearly reinvigorate a relationship, but which, for whatever reason, remain unprovoked.

In many ways, it would seem that the problem we are facing in terms of the revitalization of faith is the same one many people face in revitalizing their love life. My belief, as I will maintain throughout the following study, is that this is not a coincidence, but rather reflects a loss of integrity central to the development of the human person.

Something similar, for example, underlies the problem of the existence of hypocrites in religious faith, as well as the problem of being "authentic" in the expression of one's faith, why it is so hard to maintain the genuineness of the relationship and sustain some sort of depth throughout time. To see the struggle in this way might help identify, not only those who feel like a hypocrite when they worship or pray or engage in some religious ritual that they might have had trouble translating from their childhood to their

---

7. Norris, *Amazing Grace*, 2–3.

adulthood, or from one religious tradition or community to another, but also those who are seemingly hypocrites in their relationships.

Think, for example, of those who are hypocrites in their love life perhaps without even fully realizing it. Thought-through reflections, such as "Am I faking it? Is this wrong? Am I aware of what I am doing when I say 'I love you' or 'I do'?" often reveal the serious depths we will go to in order to avoid having to face a "crisis of truth" that might bring about an "upending" of the ways in which we have constructed our lives and identities to that point in a relationship. The real truth here, and it is as true of relationships as it is of faith, is that almost all of us both *do* and *do not* do these things. We are all imposters and hypocrites at some level in order to "keep up appearances," as it were, but we might also know that we want to be in relationship with others too and that we cannot simply abandon such a desire as much as we might also be paralyzed by our inability to be as genuine or authentic as we might wish we were.

Faith, I am arguing, works with these same internal dynamics as one's love life, though we may not always be aware of the implications with which this "translation" presents us. First and foremost, as with relationships, faith is, for most of us, a messy, sticky, complex, and yet entirely desired and desirable affair. In these terms, we might begin to see how a person in a given religious community may be a complete hypocrite in the practicing of their faith, but this does not mean that the entire faith they seek to cultivate is somehow an endeavor to be wholly ignored. Would we be as willing to give up on our search for a beloved in our life simply because we were previously involved with a hypocrite or an imposter? On the contrary, despite how we may need some space apart from dating (or even religion!) for a while, our desires do not simply and fully evaporate. Realizing the way in which these things work, in their sheer complexity and messiness, I would add, is not just "normal"; this is the way in which a good many of us experience it most directly.

For Norris, the adult task of rebuilding her vocabulary of faith is directly invoked for her within the Christian faith because such faith is faith in a *living* person, the person of Jesus who is God and who is constantly changing with us. This does not necessarily exclude other religious traditions, of course, but it does make things that much more "personal" for her, as for many other people, when she realizes that faith is a living relationship with a living person, which Christianity in particular certainly draws to the fore of its commitments. We are forced in this sense, she imagines, to rethink our choice of words and the definitions we give them because we are evolving *with* God and changing our views of God accordingly. It is from this place specifically that she begins to rethink the meaning of the words about God in her life, and, from this place, as well, to draw important conclusions from such translations and the stories that continue to bring them *to* life for us. In her words,

> Language used truly, not mere talk, neither propaganda, nor chatter, has real power. Its words are allowed to be themselves, to bless or curse, wound or heal. They have the power of a "word made flesh," of ordinary speech that suddenly takes hold, causing listeners to pay close attention, and even to release bodily sighs—whether of recognition, delight, grief, or distress.[8]

In the Catholic tradition, this description resonates with the sacraments (originally *mysterion*, or "mysteries" in Greek)—and the Eucharist especially—which are the means by which grace is said to enter into our world. These are things we do not fully understand, according to the Christian tradition, but which are moments in which we recognize God's presence in our lives.

What Norris suggests is a familiar refrain we will hear again and again in many of the authors I want to look at more closely in the study that follows. The words that come to us from certain religious traditions have survived this long throughout history because they are words that know how to give life to us, help us deal with the complexities of life we might otherwise not know how to face, show us ways to connect with our embodied being and deal with life's messes in ways we might not have been suspecting. Trying to eradicate this religious language from our lives, this language of faith, is something we should be very loathe to do, then, as, in fact, it is really an impossible task, one that we would be devastated to find absent one day if ever it could be fully removed. Saying that life can be lived without faith is, I would suggest, the same thing as saying that one can live without relationships: you can do it, but you will be much worse off for it, and this is a truism not that difficult to prove.

I would suggest that each word within a given religious tradition must undergo a constant process of *translation* rather than a consistent focus on its *definition*, as translation implies an ongoing relationship, as well as the nature of movement and fluidity. It is dynamic, not static (though, to be sure, even definitions are not really so static either, as they too change over time). The words we hear in the Christian tradition that are often foreign to our ears need to be translated and retranslated into new contexts, taking on slightly different meanings and paying tribute to the powerful significance of the recontextualization of faith. This means, following Norris, that if we hear a theological word that has no meaning for us in our present circumstances,

---

8. Norris, *Amazing Grace*, 9.

we must seek such meaning out in a new way (a "new translation"), wresting the word from the context in which we heard it and reconfiguring it for usage in our lives anew. This does not mean that we reinvent the word entirely or make up a wholly new meaning previously unrelated to its other definitions. Rather, translation implies listening to the multiple resonances that a given word or concept implies and choosing from among them the one that best suits your current understanding and context, giving rise along the way to other perspectives and uses. For example, when the word *sin*, a common theological term, is invoked—a word heavy with centuries of meaning, and not all of it constructive—we might translate "sin," in certain contexts, into "brokenness," "failure," "wrong," "mistake," or the like, whatever allows us to read its meaning in our lives in a way that brings a renewed understanding of its impact upon our lives.

This does not mean that all of these possible translations are equal, theologically or doctrinally rigorous enough or should necessarily even be used. This also does not mean that we simply dismiss centuries of theological discussion on the relevance and meaning of a particular term. Some will have come from a religious background wherein one of these words will elicit a past trauma or a naively euphoric moment. Discerning which word is properly applicable to one's life, however, is an individual task of discernment and one that should be worked out with some diligence, discernment, and caution, in dialogue with centuries of other, more established definitions. "What is lost in making a translation and what is gained?" are real questions that any competent translator is apt to pose time and again, and, in fact, to never cease asking. Making translations from one religious tradition to another is also a difficult and tension-filled thing to do. What one word means in a given tradition where the word is linked explicitly to multiple other concepts and words is very likely not what it means in another tradition, even if we are in fact using the same word. This reality should not stop us, however, from making, as the philosopher Paul Ricoeur once put it, the *impossible* but *necessary* act of translation.[9] To discern the relevance of religious faith today, ceaseless acts of translation will be required.

The act of translation is first and foremost a relational process, one of learning a word's meaning within the context of other words and other languages. It is one of the main reasons too that I find the genres of spiritual and religious autobiography to be a meaningful place to begin the appropriation of a relevant theological viewpoint in one's life, for it is this genre that calls us most directly to translate what we are reading in the life of an individual of faith into our own lives and the contexts in which we are rooted. The

---

9. Ricoeur, *On Translation*.

autobiographical narrative, much like poetry, does not ask us to judge it based on whether or not it is true or false; it simply either resonates deeply with where we find ourselves in our lives or it does not. If it does, it lasts because it works; if it does not, it hopefully fades into the dark soon enough.[10]

Scripture, no matter one's opinion on the diverse stories that comprise whatever holy religious writing is under examination, is really no different. Scripture is a collection of texts that have resonated deeply with the experiences of billions of people throughout the ages, and *this* fact is what we should be focusing on when we read such writing, not just those seemingly ever-present red herrings like "did this actually happen?" or "did God say these things directly into the ear of the author?" These questions might be interesting to pursue under certain circumstances (and indeed we should in no way seek to limit such critical inquiries), but they are not the fundamental questions we should be asking of the text when seeking to cultivate the personal life of faith. (Both fundamentalism and the outright dismissal of religion are examples of the very modern category mistake of assuming that the biblical text ought to be historically verifiable and literally accurate.) Rather, the questions most deserving to be asked are more akin to "how does this story speak to the situation I find myself in right now?," "what relevance does this writing have for the development of my life of faith?," or "how have previous people of faith relied upon this text to instruct them in the forming of their lives?" These questions matter because they are intimately involved in the creation of meaning in a person's life. They are the stories we tell, the stories we "fabricate" even, because it is necessary to *have* a story that identifies us, and, in turn, through such stories, to find ourselves immersed in those other stories that make up the world around us.

It may be true *prima facie*, as the autobiographical writer Mary Karr has put it, that "any way I tell this story is a lie,"[11] but nonetheless, the words that surround us, that are given to us, that we string together and pass along, are essential to our lives and certainly to the possible development of anything we might call the "life of faith."

I find a deep resonance with these thoughts in the autobiographical story related by Eboo Patel in his memoir *Acts of Faith*. At one point in his

---

10. This is not to suggest that books claiming to be memoirs that have been in some way falsified are nonetheless worthy of our consideration (though, for whatever reason, they yet may be studied). Rather, I am suggesting that truth will always be "fictionalized" in some sense, though it may contain the closest approximation of truth that we are capable of as well. See Mary Karr's excellent reflections on this delicate quest for personal truth in her *The Art of Memoir*. On the moral nature of autobiography, see also Barbour, *The Conscience of the Autobiographer*. See also Yagoda, *Memoir*.

11. Karr, *Lit*, 1.

quest to merge his Muslim faith with his life's calling to understand how religious pluralism is needed in our world today, he relates his surprise at the comments made by his teacher at Oxford, Azim Nanji, who acknowledged that he himself became interested in his field of study for personal reasons: "So many of us begin our careers by studying our history and then locating ourselves within it."[12] This personal element is not wrong to locate as it guides us in our more "objective" pursuits; in fact, he is suggesting, it is the only way to begin a genuine study of human life that also takes seriously the fullness of the human person. We are all caught up in the midst of so many traditions and histories, nations and religions, some of which are held in great tension with each other, and we are forced by this circumstance to look at the stories that emerge from each and to decipher our place within them, or even between them. It is precisely for this reason that we must take the time to understand what a given tradition (or intersection of multiple traditions) means to us and how we might be able to relate to it. As Patel would learn in the midst of his own journey, a tradition is "a set of stories and principles and rules handed down over hundreds or thousands of years that each new generation has to wrestle with."[13] But, wonderfully, also:

> Under the guidance of Azim Nanji, I learned that Islam is best understood not as a set of rigid rules and a list of required rituals but as a story that began with Adam and continues through us; as a tradition of prophets and poets who raised great civilizations by seeking to give expression to the fundamental ethos of the faith.[14]

In a way too, you might say, it was his relationship with the person of Azim Nanji that most truly taught him, that enabled him to find this wisdom that tradition is not the rules, but is rather the stories and persons who comprise it and within which—in *relation* to which—one is able to situate oneself within the ethos of a given tradition.

As Patel came to grasp, so many of us fall into the trap of confusing God with other things: religious traditions, doctrines and dogmas, structures and rules, even various persons or experiences, rather than stepping back from all such things and trying to see God for who God is, in and of God's own self—whatever such a thing may or may not be in the end (and I'm afraid that I will say far too little about God's own qualities and characteristics in this book, mainly because this is an area that is, by definition, something very hard to talk about).

12. Patel, *Acts of Faith*, 105.
13. Patel, *Acts of Faith*, 58.
14. Patel, *Acts of Faith*, 111.

What does it mean for the life of faith, then, when the seeking individual steps back, stops confusing God with other things, and allows themselves to sit, often in great silence, before the mystery of the unknowable? This can often be the key question *and* quest that brings us to something that could be described as faith, a deep and lasting faith that fails even to find the words to express what is going on within us, though we try ceaselessly, and *should* try ceaselessly, to find those very words. In terms of one's relationships with others, this should make perfect sense: we will never fully know the other who stands before us, even those who are our beloved others, but we should never stop trying to express the depth and beauty and love that fills us when in their presence.

Patel's book is a story of finding his own faith, the faith of his family, about falling in love with both his faith and with a woman. It is therefore, I would suggest, about his desire for relationships, for significant persons in his life who could show him the paths he must take and how *this* is what constitutes not only his own personal story, but his ability to embrace the stories that make up his own religious, Muslim roots. Patel's story is one of becoming aware of how important faith is in one's life, and then, in turn, letting this newfound significance realign the other parts of one's life. Another way to describe such a process, I would wager, is one of self-awareness blossoming into a more fully formed process of self-critique, or seeing things from the other's point of view—which is what happens when we engage in serious relationship (or the ongoing acts of translation) with others. To see what is important, what matters most, is to see at the same time what does *not* matter as much as we once thought it did.

* * *

In the hopes of formulating a *self-critical* faith—which must flow from a realistic theological viewpoint these days, one I am here hoping to develop in some small measure—I want to contrast two recent memoirs, both of which aim to articulate the journey that leads toward a life of faith, one of which is not critical enough perhaps and the other almost too critical, though, I would hastily add, both are not "wrong" or "worthless" in any sense. These terms, in fact, do not really apply to the way in which we are trying to appropriate the meaning of faith in a person's life. It is terribly difficult to condemn someone's life when they share it with you, openly and honestly. I choose these two memoirs in particular because they offer us an excellent point of contrast yet visible through very similar life stories, illuminating at the same time how the quest to get to know oneself is not always something easily or rightly done.

Concerning the former, I will only briefly express what I felt at times to be a frustration in reading Lauren Winner's *Girl Meets God*, especially as this sentiment was formed in me at her not having, in my opinion, taken enough time to critically analyze her confusion of God with various men at this time in her life. The book describes a moving portrait of finding faith in the midst of life's other demanding relationships, and, as the title suggests, there is an attentiveness in her retelling of her life's story that resonates deeply with understanding faith as a relationship. Winner's own self-proclaimed "ridiculous jealousy" and "endless self-pity," both of which are developed explicitly as relational categories applicable to faith, are not just that which "sanctifies" her at the end of the book; they are also that which seems to prevent her from bridging the gap between her desires for a lover and her desires for God.[15] Both, in fact, are heavily cemented in her longing for a permanent identity—whether married or single, Jewish or Christian—that, however, is perhaps not as central to living the life of faith as one might think it is.

In many ways, this is one of the great problems we encounter in the development of the life of faith and that we have so much trouble letting go of: our personal and religious identity. We desire so badly to know whether we are really Christian or Muslim, a "true" believer or atheist, whether God or fate have picked the right person for us to love, whether there is a "master plan" for our lives that we need only tap into in order to live it out fully and which becomes the bedrock for some people's faith (i.e., if I only have enough faith then my life will fall into place, everything will be smooth sailing, I will amass fortune and friends, raise a happy family, etc.). Such ideas, I am afraid, say much about why we have, throughout the centuries, taken so much time and effort to preoccupy ourselves with ideas of God being omniscient, omnipotent, and the like, but they do very little to express any truth about a God who lives perhaps right before our eyes, seeking a personal relationship with us. There is no doubt that God lies beyond our very human projections of our desires and needs onto God, but so do those friends of ours whom we resist projecting ourselves onto as well. We do not need a God to be wholly removed from our world (e.g., omniscient, omnipotent, etc.) in order to preserve God's uniqueness and otherness. We simply need to enter into a more proper relationship with God, as ideally with a friend or lover.

---

15. Winner, *Girl Meets God*, 281.

In the Christian tradition, as we will see, Jesus becomes another way to read such images of God insofar as he is a permanent challenge to these categorical, distance-provoking labels we place upon God. Jesus, the weak human being who fails to be what so many of us envision God to be, is another way to read God, but also a deconstruction of who we might have thought God was. The centrality of this challenge to our vision for God is precisely why so many heresies were dispelled and rejected throughout the centuries, for Jesus was not just faking as if he was in pain: he was actually in pain, just as a human being feels pain.

Another approach, one that drifts perhaps too far in the critical direction, though is rooted in the same vein as Winner's memoir in that it merges the quest for the "right" man with God, is Sarah Sentilles's *Breaking Up With God*, where she rightly grasps the overlap between God and her desire to be loved by a human being, though, I would argue, she perhaps does not do enough to indicate how the fracturing of her image of God (as with a former lover) does leave open the possibility that there are other, perhaps more helpful notions of God (or lovers) out there. As the title of the work implies, this is a book about "breaking up with God," a conclusion that stresses most directly, to my mind, the essential translation of relationship for faith. Sentilles, for her part, is quick to demonstrate its resonance in our language: "It's the best love story ever told: God chooses you, sacrifices for you, kills for you, knows you, sees you, saves you. No wonder losing my religion felt like heartbreak."[16] It felt like heartbreak as well because her depiction of God throughout her life was one in which the overlap between divine being and an attractive male figure was pivotal: "I believed in a male God. I loved him. I needed him. Sometimes he was gentle and kind. Sometimes he frightened me."[17]

The dynamic between herself and God that Sentilles unfolds is certainly complex, and her honesty in depicting the difficulty of this overlap is much to her credit. What we witness, in this rendering of her story, is the confusion undergone in trying to confess the substitution of human beings for God that so many of us make, but which few of us are willing to acknowledge so forthrightly. Indeed, just how many persons fall headlong into the trap of confusing God with a parent, a loved one, a powerful persona, a charismatic religious figure or the like is difficult to tell, but probably more common than most "believers" would like to admit. This basic confusion is what, for the most part, drives Sentilles's narrative (and is also latent, but unrecognized for the most part, in Winner's), and it is

---

16. Sentilles, *Breaking Up With God*, 1.
17. Sentilles, *Breaking Up With God*, 2.

what allows us to perceive the powerful fog of relations between her and men in general, and her and God specifically.

For example, in a passage that reveals a good deal about her desires to know God at this point in her life, but also to hold God at a distance because this is where she feels safest, she declares:

> I'd never fallen in love with someone who was also in love with me. I always fell in love with men I didn't know or who told me again and again they were unavailable or who were dating other women or who couldn't remember my name or who didn't really know anything about me because I turned myself into the person I imagined they wanted me to be. I *loved* loving people who didn't love me. I loved trying to make them fall in love with me. I loved that they never did.[18]

How many people of faith become "before God" what they believe God wants them to be, and who relish being able to love this "God" precisely because they do not feel God's presence (or "love") in return? It is extraordinarily easy to become caught up in this drama of trying to obtain the inaccessible because it keeps us safe and we can control our fantasies about it. How difficult it is, on the contrary, to actually enter the fray, and put oneself at risk, as Christian Wiman will soon describe this process for us—to sift through the many layers of religious tradition in order to find the words that actually do speak to our lives and truly do assist us in realigning our narrative, if even in a purely "worldly" way that need not necessarily or frequently make use of God's name.[19] To be honest with ourselves in situations like this, where we project our deepest desires for relationship onto someone else, even onto God, is not an unusual thing at all: it takes a lifetime for many to even begin sorting such things out.

In terms of living a religious life, this confusion happens repeatedly, and religious persons are often horribly equipped to deal with these things. I have, for example, met women throughout my life who fall in love with God as with a man, or with the youth pastor or their priest, or with another man they mistake as a substitute for God. Yet despite such a thing being possible, it is a hard thing to tell someone: "You think you love this person, but you don't. You may even think you love God, but you don't. Stop fooling yourself and projecting your desires onto another." It is very difficult as well to talk to men about such things, for I have met many men who cannot abide the company of God because they are *competing with* God; for all intents and

---

18. Sentilles, *Breaking Up With God*, 84.
19. Wiman, *My Bright Abyss*.

purposes, practically speaking, they function *as* God and so cannot worship someone other than themselves.

Though these examples may sound somewhat extreme and are indeed very generalized, if we consider things from the standpoint of friendship, we might begin to see how these subtle truths play out in reality quite often, where a man has few actual friends, is an island unto himself, and does not need religion or God in his life, and a woman has many friends, realizes that she needs others in her life to get by, and finds religious community to be a source of comfort and even strength. I think here in pop culture terms of the way that Superman has been portrayed, doing things on his own, making his journey by himself to be a hero, and recent portrayals of Supergirl, who must rely upon her friends to be a "true" superhero, and so forth. These are, in many ways, the "gods" of today and ones that reflect our understanding of ourselves within an all-too-narrowly gendered world of relations.

But how do we begin to talk to such persons on either side of the gender divide (but also racial, class, and religious divides) about a God or a friend who might exist beyond all of these entirely human dynamics?

Sentilles is right to sense that certain "people of faith" who opposed certain other individuals, also rejected other people's faiths through relational reasons that they themselves were generally unable to articulate:

> Many of the people against the full inclusion of LGBT folks are also against the ordination of women. And the fact that Christian homophobia and misogyny are linked—that they depend on the same logic, use the same strategies—scared me, a woman seeking ordination in a church with some dioceses, even whole countries, that still didn't ordain women.[20]

She recognizes in this that church communities, as with most religious communities, are about people wanting to be with other people, people like themselves who hold the same values and principles, no matter what those values or principles actually are.[21] Hence, she illuminates their potential for containing a blind spot within the construction of their identities. She thereby establishes a perfectly valid critique of religious life shared in common, and one that needs to be shared with a good many religious communities, even though, in the end, this critique may say very little about the actual nature of religious truth or revelation or God (whatever these things end up being in reality). Whatever the divine reveals to humanity is in some measure at a remove from such human dynamics, even when it is entirely concerned with them and can only be explained in shared terms. Sentilles

20. Sentilles, *Breaking Up With God*, 148.
21. Sentilles, *Breaking Up With God*, 151.

is nonetheless brave to point out the scope and impact of these political dimensions, though we are still left wondering what kind of a God might there be yet lurking in the shadows, possibly even waiting for us beyond our own personal and psychological "hang-ups."

What Sentilles makes clear in her memoir in particular is that she struggles most to find an alternative way to view God beyond the patterned human relationships she knows because she still clings too tightly to the image of the male God she knew she could not let go of. It was too deeply ingrained in her to simply recognize as "wrong" and substitute with another perception of the divine. In her words,

> I criticized the father-figure God by day, but at night, when I was alone, I prayed to him, this man who thought I was special, who chose me, protected me, kept me safe, well, loved. My God was still a God who could hear me, a God with the power to make some sick and others well, to intervene in soccer matches, to influence the outcome of wars.[22]

Her language mirrors the pleas of distraught and distorted lovers who are unable to give up a particular image of their beloved in order to actually see their beloved as who they are in and of themselves, apart from what has been projected onto them. Again, and you might say "with a vengeance," this all-powerful, all-knowing God returns into her life, perhaps because she is unable, at this point in her life, to truly give him up: she wants to have such a God in her life because it grants her an identity that she does not want to part with, one sustained by a certain patriarchal inscription carved into her life.

We might, in this instance, recall a couple lines from earlier in the book: "I loved trying to make them fall in love with me. I loved that they never did." To be caught up in such a cycle is not a genuine life of faith, though it mirrors such a life, and even appears, at times, to be a critical reflection of such a life. What she is immersed in—and though she is even aware of the game she is playing with herself—is a childlike faith in a God-parent who will take away all of our problems: "I had believed in a God who loved me, and because he loved me, and because I was good, he would protect me. My faith was a kind of magic trick. My prayers were not much different from incantations. I might as well have been saying *abracadabra*."[23]

The difficult journey that she undergoes, that she propels herself toward, is one wherein she is able to give up on this God, to leave this God behind and stop projecting her desires, her frustrations, her pains, and her

22. Sentilles, *Breaking Up With God*, 163.
23. Sentilles, *Breaking Up With God*, 165.

longings onto this God. In her words, "Sometimes you break up with the person you love because you discover he isn't who you thought he was."[24] Her "breaking up with God," I would suggest at this point, is a good move, and also a very reasonable one, because she needs, as she herself acknowledges, to move beyond her vision of the divine, which had been confused for so long with the dynamics of boyfriends and the hopes of finally, at long last, being fulfilled once and for all by another being (of finding absolute, unchanging *definition* rather than engaging an unending act of *translation*). What she had been neglecting throughout, of course, was the peace and serenity that comes when you realize you are fine on your own and that you had been projecting so much of your own baggage onto someone else, God or a lover, it often matters little which one. As she will put it, "Sometimes you stay because you think you can fix him, because you think he'll change, because you remember the good times, the plans you made, everything you thought was possible."[25] Until you realize, eventually, "that everything you thought you loved about him is really everything you want to love about yourself."[26]

I would only add that there are those who are not strong enough to break up with God when they should. And there are those who are strong enough to break up with God, but not clever enough to realize that it was not really God in the first place who had brought such confusion into their lives. I think Sentilles remains still somewhat confused on the point at the end of her memoir, and deservedly so; it is not an easy thing to sort out in reality, in the context of our personal lives.

At times, however, she also seems to indicate that there might be another vision of God beyond what she had previously believed in, such as when she states that "I broke up with God that night. I broke up with the priesthood. I broke up with the river and the sky opening and the dove calling me beloved. I broke up with chosenness and salvation and belonging. And I imagined God held me while I cried."[27] This God who holds her after she lets go of God might be, in turn, the God she has been looking for, but unable to see; it might even be the "real" God so many of us long to gaze upon or be held by, the God who suffers with us in our weaknesses and in our failures rather than the omnipotent, omniscient God who simply appears to dictate the trajectory of our lives. But, of course, how many of us are willing to let go of this God of our own creation who seems to give us so much of what we are really longing for?

24. Sentilles, *Breaking Up With God*, 167.
25. Sentilles, *Breaking Up With God*, 167.
26. Sentilles, *Breaking Up With God*, 168.
27. Sentilles, *Breaking Up With God*, 169.

What Sentilles points us toward in a very direct manner through the breakdown of her image of God is a major theological issue that takes center stage for many of us, though a good portion of us are entirely unaware that there might be another way to view things. I am talking about the problem of theodicy, or the problem of evil and suffering in our world.

In its most basic form, we run up against the dangerous problematic of failing to comprehend why a God who could control everything in the world—again, the omnipotent, omniscient deity many of us were raised to believe in—would allow bad things to happen to good people. What we rarely consider, and this will form one of the major theological points I am trying to underscore in this book, is that it is perhaps our conception of God that is the problem, *not* the God who may yet exist beyond our projections onto God.[28] Learning to see a God who suffers *with* us, rather than a God who lifts us out of our suffering, is a terribly difficult thing to do, but it is a thing, I believe, that genuine faith often directly calls us to take up as a task well worth undergoing. Many of the authors I examine in the studies that follow will perform a similar act, a sign that tells us something quite profound about the nature of experiencing a God perhaps always yet *beyond* all our previous experiences of God, but close enough to us as to offer a presence that is there for the taking. It is also, within the Christian tradition, the very essence of the figure of Jesus—a radical reassessment of how we perceive the proximity of the divine in our lives.

Learning to love *herself* was the actual goal Sentilles had been after but could not see, and so, at the book's end, she tries to cultivate her life *without* God, perhaps even without the God who held her in her darkest places.[29] I am not entirely clear on the place she marks out for this possibility for another God, but that is also fine, since I think we have seen enough of her life at the conclusion to get a sense of the trajectory of where things are headed. Where she leaves us can be summed up briefly: "This is my faith: a fragile hope in what humanity might be able to do when we stop looking for someone else to save us."[30] Now, it is "Just us looking after each other." As I have been suggesting, turning to each other, to relationship itself, is not a turn away from faith, but directly toward it. Though God's name might be dropped from the conversation, the fact that her willingness to let go of a false notion of God in order to turn toward relationship means, to my mind, that she has opened another door, one that may eventually yield *another* vision of the divine.

28. Kearney, *The God Who May Be*.
29. Sentilles, *Breaking Up With God*, 189.
30. Sentilles, *Breaking Up With God*, 222.

Where we are left, however, is a fitting place to begin this study of lives of faith, for it is only in the brokenness of her image of God that we might be capable of finding a God beyond the God of strong identities, a God of weakness such as Saint Paul had talked about (see his comments in 1 Corinthians 1). It is a God who is there to hold us when the God we had imagined as being beside us for so long, a construction of God of our own making, suddenly falls apart. It is a God who appears when we stop looking to be saved by something outside of us, and start to look at where we have already fallen apart, for it is within such a brokenness that we might find too another source of healing.

CHAPTER ONE

The Significance of (Auto)biography in the Christian Tradition

I want to stress from the outset of my remarks on any biblical foundations for a theology rooted in the (auto)biographical a point that Mary Karr will later drive home to us, and which I have already noted: *translation* is just as important as *definition*—a maxim that might sound illogical, since a definition is often needed in order to make a convincing translation, but which, I hope, will make more sense when we realize how translation can also alter the usage of a given definition. I believe that this has been solid ground for biblical scholars for quite some time now, but I would like to take this statement a bit further in the context of the recent rise of spiritual and autobiographical writings.

In the context of autobiographical writings specifically this means that, despite the fact that autobiographical writing is a more or less obvious attempt to construct one's narrative *as* one's identity, the most genuine autobiographical accounts are typically those that draw our attention to the moments where what I am calling translation—instances where the attempt to master the narrative breaks down and finds alternative routes or means of expression—take precedence over the carefully defined narrative of the self that is otherwise presented. It is in such moments or events where the author finds new meaning through the loss of a previously well-defined life that precisely opens up the arc of the story toward transformation and conversion. These are the moments of translation that are so pivotal in conveying the authenticity of a life story.

Rather than invest ourselves and our vision for how one expresses faith in terms of definition, clarity, identity, and the conclusions we reach, I want to alter the stress that is more often than not placed upon the establishment of boundaries and limitations, and which frequently leads to the strong formation of personal, social, and religious identities, and place emphasis rather upon translation, or the movement that we make from one place to another—the very stuff of transformative encounters and conversion tales. Such an emphasis allows us to perceive a "fuller," though perhaps less "total," sense of identity that flows from this alternative focal point. What I am trying to access is something that becomes the location of imaginative and poetic play, where we stretch for a definition, but never really feel satisfied with what has been recorded, requiring, in practical terms, a new translation every so often, for new contexts and new languages.

Stressing this point does not mean that I think we should do away with all identities, once and for all. On the contrary, I am firmly convinced that identities are the substance of a shared cultural intelligibility, and that they will be with us for as long as we continue to utilize language. This is why we find autobiographical stories so fascinating as they portray the struggles inherent to defining and justifying any life. However, I believe too that taking identity as a relatively "fixed" or permanently defined matter often misses out on the permeable and fluid nature of definitions, something that is made abundantly clear by the evolutions and permutations that do exist historically within any language. It is in such fluid spaces that translation takes place, and where a life finds itself transformed into something at once familiar, but also previously unknown. Placing stress upon the act of translation, I hope, does not do away with the need for definitions, but it does loosen things up a bit, emphasizing how, no matter what definition we are working with, there is *another*, perhaps even more helpful way to read things, in a different language as it were, and behind every story of personal transformation.

In essence, my preference for translation over definition in order to emphasize a particular point of view is what might allow us, in the end, to see Scripture as itself a poetic, translational enterprise above all else, for translation is a task constantly searching for a resonance with its reader that is its hallmark—a movement from the life of the text to the life of the reader. It is not a top-down inscription of a subject within a matrix of fixed and unchanging representations. In this sense, the text is only "true" in the sense that, like a poem, it continues to resonate with the life of the one who sees their genuine self at once reflected in the words with which they are presented by the text. If the text cannot do this, it ceases to have any power and falls lifeless into the abyss of history. This is the main reason, moreover, that we never stop translating Scripture into new languages and into new historical contexts.

Another reason I want to lay stress upon the act of translation rather than on a conventionally more static sense of definition (which is often quickly subsumed under paradigms bearing headings with words like *doctrine* or *dogma*) is that I believe that this focus can open us up to the inherently relational nature of faith, as well as to the ways in which we convey faith through what is living rather than what is codified, totalized, or seemingly "dead." In this sense, as John Henry Newman had put it, tradition is a living, evolving thing, not a static, fixed mechanism imposed upon us, and it is something intimately connected to the autobiographical selves that we all are.[1] As such, I want to look briefly in this first chapter at the Bible as an ongoing project of translation, one that interacts with humanity in ever new ways, rather than as a collectively codified and prescriptive book. The lives that cross in the biblical narrative must come alive to us again, to "enliven" our faith within the century in which we now dwell, so that their faith might somehow become our faith—one of the most significant, but also misunderstood, biblical mandates.

Again, this insight should be nothing new to biblical scholars, or theologians in general, though such a perspectival shift does do something for the ways in which we reflect theologically. This is, in many ways, my real subject matter: when we look at the biblical narratives as a living translation of God into human contexts but also of humanity into divine ones, we might be able to see why the writing of such movements is central to a self-understanding of faith. More precisely, we might begin to discern how such writing of a life—the (auto)biographical point of view that is central to the biblical story—can, in turn, reshape the ways in which theology performs its services *to* faith, *in* faith, and *through* faith.

* * *

To see the importance of the stress that the biblical story places upon the autobiographical, perhaps we might focus on the biblical narrative and how it is different from other Ancient Near Eastern mythologies that sprung up around it at the time. There are many stories in such mythologies about impersonal gods who maintain a callous indifference to human welfare. There is a hierarchy between the gods and humanity, an order which marginalizes those on the bottom, much as we might perceive in a story of the Greek gods.

1. Newman, *An Essay on the Development of Christian Doctrine*. See also the commentary on Newman and the autobiographical in this context in Olney, *Metaphors of Self*, 12–13.

In contrast to this account, the biblical narratives of both the Hebrew ("Old Testament") and Christian ("New Testament") Scriptures make clear that the God whom they represent is concerned with personal relationships, moving between persons and peoples, even and especially the marginalized among them, and engaging them at their level, in whatever place they find themselves. In this sense, the biblical narrative inverts the normal hierarchy of social relations, focusing on those relationships of love that transcend hierarchical order. In this configuration of things, the lives of individual persons become the paramount and defining feature of Scripture.

The biblical story is one that emphasizes a God who reaches out to particular people and becomes known *through* those relations, to the extent that God is able to "translate" God's own self *into* those particular contexts. This defining action on the part of God is what marks the "chosenness" that Scripture often speaks of, and which is most helpfully understood as the particularity of all relationships, like being "chosen" for a sports team or as a dance partner in the school gym. Israel, for example, as the people of God, was chosen when they were, so to speak, the lowest of the low within Egyptian society. Chosenness subsequently becomes not only a preference for those on the margins of society, but also a way of saying, "This is the story we have chosen to tell," of a particular people. There are even several examples of Old Testament figures (Melchizedek and Balaam, to name two more prominent ones) who are not part of the Jewish people, but who nonetheless have relationships with the same God as the Israelites, demonstrating that the relationships that this God holds dear are not limited to one particular people alone.

Part of what is fascinating about the chosenness of those who are least among society, who are in fact among the most vulnerable, is that, as we realize we are chosen and loved, our vulnerability is also revealed to us, but in different ways.

As God describes God's own self to Moses, one of the central figures at the root of the Israelite story, and as detailed at the outset of the formation of Israel itself: "I am the God of your father, the God of Abraham, the God of Isaac and the God of Jacob" (Exodus 3:6). The significance of this personal relationship—of a God who defines the divine being in relation to specific human persons, as demonstrated numerous times in the earliest Hebrew stories (e.g., Jacob's wrestling with God)—eventually carries over into the Christian understanding of who God is as well, never negating the previous relationship, we must add, but still standing in relationship to it.

As Jesus will state when confronted with a question about the resurrection, this personal understanding of God is still present in relation to those same persons who are now, in some sense yet to be comprehended, not even considered to be dead:

> The same day some Sadducees came to him, saying there is no resurrection; and they asked him a question, saying, "Teacher, Moses said, "If a man dies childless, his brother shall marry the widow, and raise up children for his brother." Now there were seven brothers among us; the first married, and died childless, leaving the widow to his brother. The second did the same, so also the third, down to the seventh. Last of all, the woman herself died. In the resurrection, then, whose wife of the seven will she be? For all of them had married her." Jesus answered them, "You are wrong, because you know neither the scriptures nor the power of God. For in the resurrection they neither marry nor are given in marriage, but are like angels in heaven. And as for the resurrection of the dead, have you not read what was said to you by God, 'I am the God of Abraham, the God of Isaac, and the God of Jacob'? He is God not of the dead, but of the living." And when the crowd heard it, they were astounded at his teaching. (Matthew 22:23–33[2])

Jesus' answer to a question about the reality of relations (particularly concerning marriage in this context) posed by a Jewish sect at the time, the Sadducees, opens the centrality of relationships that much wider, moving beyond the ways in which we have circumscribed relationships in social and political terms (i.e., the categories of married, single, divorced, widowed, etc.) and toward a much broader consideration, one "like the angels," which we can hardly even fathom, of course. Just what such a form of relations might be exactly, he does not say, though he does point to a possible horizon where we might gather an answer: a God "of the living" who moves beyond the labels we attach to ourselves.

When God refers to Abraham, Isaac, and Jacob—whether with Moses or in the context of Jesus' life—it is as if those persons are still living, and not deceased. This is a most interesting thing to contemplate as well since we would typically consider such persons as being no longer among the living. This is normally how we understand the boundary that separates the living and the dead (a presupposition that also often centers a good deal of misplaced emphasis on the afterlife, I would add). What Jesus (re)focuses his questioners on is the manner in which these persons long since labeled as "dead" could yet be said to be still living, still being called upon to translate this God's name into a new idiom, pushing all traditional notions of

---

2. All biblical quotations are taken from the NRSV translation.

relationship into new territory and rendering his listeners perhaps more perplexed than before they had asked the question.

When we more fully encounter the Christian story, the story of the Christ, things are no different. We are still looking to translate God's name into a new context, and there is as much continuity with God's previous names as there is with the many new names God is given. To comprehend this complex act of ongoing translation is to comprehend the "living life" that Peter, in the New Testament, will refer to explicitly in the book of Acts after he heals a crippled beggar, a moment centered on the same phrase I have been examining thus far:

> The God of Abraham, the God of Isaac, and the God of Jacob, the God of our ancestors has glorified his servant Jesus, whom you handed over and rejected in the presence of Pilate, though he had decided to release him. But you rejected the Holy and Righteous One and asked to have a murderer given to you, and you killed the Author of life, whom God raised from the dead. To this we are witnesses. (Acts 3:13–15)

Not only is the role of the witness essential here—which is a position that the genre of (auto)biography stresses in some ways perhaps above all else—but the passage also refers to Jesus as the "Author of Life" (Acts 3:15), the one who inextricably links *bios* ("life") to *graphe* ("writing") in order to stake out what exactly is to be described upon the terrain of faith, its proclamation and personal expression. In Peter's eyes, Jesus is not only equated with God, the Creator, the "author of life" in this sense, but he is also linked explicitly to the writing of one's life as the writing of one's faith. Jesus is rewritten into the ongoing project of naming a God who continues to lead a "chosen," beloved people, which is not fixed once and for all either.

In many ways, this quest for a permanent unfolding of diversity in God's relations with humanity is why the church rejected the early "heretic" Marcion's attempt to excise the Hebrew Scriptures from the Christian texts in the second century. Rather than choose one Gospel and dispense with the Hebrew Scriptures, the church canonized what had rather been slowly passed down to it over the centuries from among the various churches who recognized their God in stories they had been prayerfully and liturgically reading: the different, broken narratives of all four Gospels as the most "authentic" representation of the Christian story.

Something very central to the Christian understanding of the self develops in relation to the divine that cannot be overlooked or downplayed in this regard. The autobiographical context matters tremendously for the determination of faith, as I will try to unpack in what follows. There is something within the very selves that we are, selves formed in relationships of faith that transcend traditional social and political bonds (as the earliest Christian communities testified through their somewhat atypical relations with each other), that causes faith to be transmitted through the lives we live and in no other way. As Paul would put it to an early church in Thessalonica, Greece, in a way that would inextricably link the life of faith with the lives of the people who live it: "So deeply do we care for you that we are determined to share with you not only the gospel of God but also our own selves, because you have become very dear to us" (1 Thessalonians 2:8). His emphasis on the nature of this sharing perhaps only underscores the early church witness of Justin Martyr, who frequently translated the term *Gospels* as the "memoirs of the apostles."[3]

If we step backward into the lives of the ancestors that brought such a faith to life, as it were, we see moving tales of near despair, loss and death, but also of joy, hope, and love. Abraham, Moses, David, Job, Jeremiah, Jesus, Paul, Peter: it is the lives that they lived, as much as the teachings they asserted about the God who loved them, that is conveyed through the Scriptures, a fact that should give us pause to consider how important the stories of these persons' lives were. The telling of one's life *is* the telling of faith, even when the person whose story is being told denies the faith that lives in them (e.g., Peter's denial of Jesus). It is a vital act of translation that brings writing to life as much as a life is put into writing. The very act of reading about these lives, and of making *their* stories *our* stories—the process of writing oneself into Scripture, if you will[4]—is an act of spiritual translation, and it is what makes the life of faith a living one. Beyond simply causing us to wonder, time and again, how and why such biographical tales were transformed into institutionalized structures and doctrinal claims, we should come first to the realization that it is this spiritual, prayerful act of translation that shapes the narrative ("writing") of the lives of faith in which we subsist.

For the moment, it might help us simply to stop and consider how the lives of certain people of faith recorded in Scripture have had a tremendous impact upon the lives of faith that we live, and how they have charted a deep undercurrent in Scripture that is often misplaced or ignored. I want to highlight this aspect of the scriptural story because I believe it might introduce us to another perspective on why spiritual autobiographical writings today matter so much: such memoirs and autobiographies are part of a scriptural legacy that is only now perhaps receiving its due influence upon literature and writing as a whole, as the attentiveness of the linkage of *bios* and *graphe*,

---

3. Martyr, *First Apology* and *Dialogue with Trypho*.
4. Boitani, *The Bible and Its Rewritings*.

life and writing, that is present in the biblical account is mirrored in the autobiographical records of lives of faith that we see sold in bookstores today. In this sense, I believe that our attentiveness to this biblical legacy can actually have a significant effect upon the practice and teaching of theology far beyond what it has already achieved, when it takes this connection of life and writing into sharper focus.

Take, for example, the book of Ruth, which is little more than a short four-chapter account of a relationship between a non-Israelite woman, Ruth, and a Jewish man, Boaz. After losing her first husband, Ruth goes with her mother-in-law Naomi in search of food, but also of a new life and a new husband, one of the only means of support for a woman in this time and place in history. Naomi, for her part, tries to convince Ruth that her fortunes would be better if she traveled apart from her, going back to her own people. But Ruth, in a passage so emphatic in its description of relationships that it has been used liturgically for both conversions and wedding vows, tells her:

> Do not press me to leave you
>   or to turn back from following you!
> Where you go, I will go;
>   where you lodge, I will lodge;
> your people shall be my people,
>   and your God my God.
> Where you die, I will die—
>   there will I be buried.
> May the LORD do thus and so to me,
>   and more as well,
> if even death parts me from you! (Ruth 1:16–17)

Underscoring the significance of relationships within Scripture in general, I want to stress a singular point about this conversion narrative: Ruth becomes a Jew because she feels bound to Naomi. Seemingly this familial bond, even beyond the death of Ruth's first husband, Naomi's son, is *the* major consideration undertaken before her conversion. Faith is understood, for Ruth, as a relationship to a person, an act of being faithful established through the language of lovers as much as through religious creed, a notion central to both the book of Ruth and the highly erotic love poem within the Bible, the Song of Songs. For her part, Ruth will become the great grandmother of the legendary King David, celebrated in the genealogy of Matthew as an ancestor of Jesus. But her story is also, quite simply, a love story (though not necessarily in the traditional sense of falling in love with one's future spouse). It is a story of choosing to remain with those whom she feels bound to, and of finding security in life and faith through her devotion to

Naomi. Though this is not a typical "love story" per se, it is one that stresses how central relationships are to the identity of those seeking to be part of this particular faith. The book of Ruth, viewed from this angle, is more central to our understanding of the message that Scripture presents us with as a whole than has perhaps been acknowledged.

The question I want to ask at this point is a deceptively simple one: what does it mean that an entire book of Scripture is devoted to a woman who becomes a part of the religion (and its Scripture, including her inclusion in Jesus' genealogy in the Gospel of Matthew) simply because she is in some sort of a relationship with her mother-in-law? Moreover, what does this mean for our understanding of Scripture itself, which is often taken to be something akin to a law book, or a set of moral standards and prophetic visions? And what are we to make of this reality in terms of our understanding of the development of a person's life of faith vis-à-vis their relationship to the Scriptures as a whole?

To try to grasp what is going on here, and as part of any possible answer we might give to these questions, I want first to step back into the significance of a single person's life in weaving together the tapestry of faith. On this point as well, the Hebrew Scriptures were often quite clear, and in clear contradistinction to those religions of the ancient Near East that would consistently marginalize certain members of their own community. Keep in mind that in Roman lore, Romulus kills his brother Remus and founds the ancient city of Rome, but when Cain kills Abel in the biblical account, God judges this action as wrong (Genesis 4). Another example of this marginalization is the contrast between Ancient Near Eastern child sacrifice and the story of Abraham and Isaac, in which God calls for, but then stops, the sacrifice of the son. God takes the side of the unjustly victimized, time and again, as too when he apparently sends the prophet Nathan to chastise David when David has Uriah killed in order to marry his widow. Likewise, God dies in Christ, God saves Isaac, God uplifts Joseph when he is cast out among his brother, and so forth.[5]

In a provocative passage that seems to indicate the depths that this God is willing to go to in order to take an individual life seriously—in this case a particular prophet whom God has chosen—we hear these words:

> Now the word of the Lord came to me saying,
>
> > "Before I formed you in the womb I knew you,
> > and before you were born I consecrated you;
> > I appointed you a prophet to the nations."

---

5. See the commentary on such acts of scapegoating and violence in Girard, *Violence and the Sacred*.

Then I said, "Ah, Lord God! Truly I do not know how to speak, for I am only a boy." But the Lord said to me,

> "Do not say, 'I am only a boy';
> for you shall go to all to whom I send you,
> and you shall speak whatever I command you.
> Do not be afraid of them,
> for I am with you to deliver you,
> says the Lord."

Then the Lord put out his hand and touched my mouth; and the Lord said to me,

> "Now I have put my words in your mouth.
> See, today I appoint you over nations and over kingdoms,
> to pluck up and to pull down,
> to destroy and to overthrow,
> to build and to plant." (Jeremiah 1:4–10)

Here we have the calling of the Israelite prophet Jeremiah laid out for us in a narrative of early origin. God chooses Jeremiah to proclaim a specific message to the people of Israel, but also to other nations. God chooses Jeremiah as a "chosen one" among his "chosen people," though this does not necessarily exclude others from receiving a call from God as well (e.g., the foreign prophet Balaam in Numbers, or Melchizedek in the book of Genesis are "non-Jews," but are already in relation to the God of the Jews who works with them as well, as I have already noted). The implications of this call for Jeremiah are that God consecrates him, anoints him, as a prophet, to speak God's words to the people, and in this sense to be a conduit of the divine Word. God descends to the level of the individual life and cares about this life, has a plan for this life, and does not vainly sacrifice or discard such a life. The ultimate significance of this passage, however, is clear: God cares about the individual life, the seemingly insignificant person, perhaps even the most insignificant person in the world. Each person has a potential to "pluck up and pull down" nations and kingdoms. This is the God we are dealing with here, and the divergence of this God from a variety of mythological deities is quite astounding.

What this also means is that the individual person who has faith in such a personal God finds that they are elevated as well in terms of the dignity and respect that they are shown on an individual basis and despite how insignificant they might otherwise appear to be. Suddenly, we begin to understand why there is an emphasis on social justice in the Hebrew world, and why the "alien, the orphan and the widow," but also the poor and those who are suffering in general, become not just marginalized groups within a larger collective that ignores them, but social subgroups to be cared for and seen within the center of society (cf. Deuteronomy 10:18; Zechariah 7:10). For quite some time now, Catholic social teaching, similarly, has placed its focus on social justice, worded as a "preferential option for the poor."[6]

Essentially what we witness here is a God who enters into relationship with us through our vulnerability, and through, in fact, *God's own vulnerability*—the only authentic way for a relationship to take place between two parties. We do not relate to a God who simply reigns over us as supreme. We do not relate to a God who has no point through which we can access that God, move into the depths of God's being and find a relationship present as an actual possibility. This attentiveness to the significance of relationships, but also to how they are most truly established when we enter into them through our most vulnerable moments, is what the biblical narrative is mainly concerned with. In the language of lovers that will be a hallmark for us throughout this study, it is when you open up and share in your vulnerability, even though the other person in the relationship could certainly use such a vulnerability against you, but instead chooses to open up to you and holds your story lightly in their hands, that you truly enter into a state of relationship and intimacy. In many ways, the central focus of the Christian story seems to be that we are able to open up to a relationship with God when God, in God's own self, is vulnerable with us, to the point of death even. In the figure of Jesus, for example, we witness the dissolution of our identities in a form of weakness and vulnerability that, in reality, opens us up to a more genuine sharing of ourselves, our brokenness even, through which something like love has a chance to flourish in us.[7]

We can note as well, in this vein of thought, how, much later in early Christian writings, Paul addresses the members of the church in Thessalonica, telling them:

> As for us, brothers and sisters, when, for a short time, we were made orphans by being separated from you—in person, not in heart—we longed with great eagerness to see you face to face. For we wanted to come to you—certainly I, Paul, wanted to again and again—but Satan blocked our way. For what is our hope or joy or

---

6. See the documents published by the Pontifical Council for Justice and Peace in the *Compendium of the Social Doctrine of the Church*.

7. Conversely, when a person does not share their vulnerability and seeks only to maintain their power over another, intimacy is never truly achieved. Sadly, this is often a tactic to maintain control over others, one that men, speaking very generally of course, have been far too comfortable with in relational terms over the centuries.

crown of boasting before our Lord Jesus at his coming? Is it not you? Yes, you are our glory and joy! (1 Thessalonians 2:17–20)

The people whose names we will never know have become a source of glory and joy for Paul, an integral part of *his* life of faith. We also see in this passage the possibility of restoring one's faith through a face-to-face encounter with another person of faith (see 1 Thessalonians 3:10). As with Jesus' encounter with two disciples on the road to Emmaus after his resurrection (Luke 24:13–35), it is the breaking of bread together, a time of intimacy and communion, that allows one's heart to burn as if on fire and to see a person for who they truly are. What Jesus conveyed to those two disciples was the story of God's people, from Abel to Jesus, the story of suffering and of a God who cares for those living on the margins of the world (and in the case of Abel, of being scapegoated and falsely killed).

It is doubly intriguing that the resurrection narratives of Jesus, as Henri Nouwen, one of the subjects of this book, will make clear, are intimate affairs amongst friends. They are not universal, global proclamations of Jesus' conquering of death and anything else that stands in his way as one might typically assume. Nor are they something that is presented to us as if we must factually verify them in order to believe in them. In this sense, we would do well to think as Nouwen does: if the resurrection of Jesus bothers you (or so many other miracles or extraordinary stories often told in the context of faith), do not worry about it. It was, and is, meant for Jesus' closest friends, those whom he loved. It was an intimate confirmation of his willingness to be with them beyond his death, not some otherworldly message from the beyond that merely confirms his lordship over life. Even the resurrection, this story would seem to suggest, needs to be translated into a new idiom today.

What we witness in such an act of translation is the construction of a self through faith that is central to the Jewish and Christian traditions, and which implies a certain connection to those who are marginalized in the world. That is, even the seemingly insignificant stories of the marginalized matter, just as one's autobiographical context matters in the establishment of one's faith. The stress laid upon the individual life, and the intimacy of God's making an appearance to these persons even beyond their supposed death seems to confirm such an understanding. We cannot, and should not want to, transcend or abstract ourselves in any way from these highly personalized contexts. In many ways, this is why the Gospel accounts of Jesus' life and death are so very significant. Not only do they provide another perspective on the significance of biography within the life of faith, but they also delve into the "death" of the self that Christianity promotes as a form of permanent self-critique, often translated as "new life" or "conversion"—a point that I will return to on numerous occasions.

Lifting up the details of the lives of the holy and righteous ones, as Peter had put it, means allowing their stories to come to the foreground of the establishment of one's faith. We see this, among other places, in the Christian book of Hebrews, where the letter demonstrates multiple models of living life in the faith of Jesus (11:4—12:13): Abel, Enoch, Noah, Abraham, and Moses, but also Gideon, Barak, Samson, Jephthah, David, and Samuel, as well as the prophets, are all lauded as exemplary lives of faith whose stories need only be told and retold throughout history in order for faith to take root in the individual person.

> Therefore, since we are surrounded by so great a cloud of witnesses, let us also lay aside every weight and the sin that clings so closely, and let us run with perseverance the race that is set before us, looking to Jesus the pioneer and perfecter of our faith, who for the sake of the joy that was set before him endured the cross, disregarding its shame, and has taken his seat at the right hand of the throne of God. Consider him who endured such hostility against himself from sinners, so that you may not grow weary or lose heart. In your struggle against sin you have not yet resisted to the point of shedding your blood. And you have forgotten the exhortation that addresses you as children—
>
> "My child, do not regard lightly the discipline of the Lord,
>   or lose heart when you are punished by him;
> for the Lord disciplines those whom he loves,
>   and chastises every child whom he accepts."
> (Hebrews 12:1–6)

As the author of Hebrews makes clear, the examples that are worthy of lifting up are those who have suffered, who have been unjustly treated, but whose case the Lord is willing to pick up and defend (in fact, this is the definition of the Holy Spirit, the *Paraclete*, or "defender"). Living a life of faith becomes a willingness to suffer, but also to endure, a suffering confronted in life and therefore capable of helping others through their own suffering: "Because he himself was tested by what he suffered, he is able to help those who are being tested" (Hebrews 2:18). I would wager, moreover, that this, and not necessarily some prophetic foreshadowing of the figure of Jesus, is why the "songs of the suffering servant" in Isaiah are so significant in conveying the message that is central to the Christian narrative (especially as in Isaiah 58:5–9).

The Gospels portray the life and death that Jesus embodied, not just the miracles and teachings that characterized his ministry, and which are, if we are to be honest, all found in the Hebrew scriptural narratives, most prominently in the stories of Elijah and Elisha, and in the words of the prophets (cf. Luke 6:17–49). In the face of this fact, we are forced to ask: What makes Jesus and his story unique in all of this? In some measure, it must be his passion and death, his resurrection and the promise of new life (see Mark 14—16). It must be concerned with his unnecessary suffering, and the lifting up of the human element in life (which is what the incarnation is all about!). In other words, it must be about the fullness of being in relationship with life, with God and with each other—something that, paradoxically, can only be experienced through the death of Christ (as I will unfold more fully in a moment).

If we can see the basis of faith and of Jesus' uniqueness as really being about relationship, and its importance, we can begin to see why the incarnation matters so much for Christians, because the incarnation is the defining movement of God's entering into a profoundly concrete relationship with humanity. God *becomes* flesh. God becomes human in the sense that God wants to enter into relationship with humanity by pouring Godself out into human form, crossing the boundaries of the human and the divine in order, precisely, to be closer to us. Israel certainly had a profound relationship with God before God became flesh, and this is not something negated by the incarnation. The incarnation merely points toward the significance of the message already contained within Judaism: God wants to be in relationship with humanity, and relationship is inseparable from faith. God's autobiographical act as witnessed in the story of Jesus brings faith *to* life and, as a consequence, it embodies both.

I believe that this is what Jesus' life and death and resurrection are as examples of his ministry: they can only be embodied acts, not just symbols, but embodied acts, especially if understood *sacramentally*. And this point may also help us understand why the doctrine of transubstantiation was such a big deal for Catholics throughout history, as it is a teaching that claims that God is actually *in* physical matter. God is not just an abstract idea about the divine, but a material reality in our daily lives. What we hear in the Christian story is that God yearns for a deeper relationship with humanity, to the point that God enters into flesh, God is here before us, walking amongst us, in the midst of us, even when we did not know it—and this is so not just during the biblical times, but in the midst of the messiest of everyday human affairs. To suggest this is to point toward the sacramental presence of God in our world.

What Paul mirrors at the end of the book of Acts, which gathers together the stories of the apostles and the early church after Jesus had ascended into heaven, is the passion of Jesus at the end of the Gospels, but without his having actually to die in the way that Jesus did, a sign that Jesus' horrific death need not be done to any individual ever again. I take this ending to mean too that the lie that allows us to negate the significance of the individual life before us—to enslave, reify, victimize, or inherently dismiss or exclude the intimate details of the life of the person who is standing before us, or, conversely, to project our desires onto them in order to avoid them as well—is the lie that has been discarded by Jesus' death. It is a lie that is now permanently discarded and we are better off in its absence.

In other words, we must take seriously the life before us, in all of its particularity and messiness. This, above all else, is what the biblical story is about and why its autobiographical element rings so loudly in our ears to this day—a fact that I believe the current genre of autobiographical literature testifies to quite boldly.

Toward the end of Richard Rodriguez's memoir *Darling*, he speaks about how the Catholic Church has stressed that its Creed is not one's faith, but is that which points toward the person who helped us to believe: in this case, the person of Jesus. Yet, Rodriguez points out, "[B]efore we get to Jesus (or Abraham or Moses or the Prophet Mohammad or Buddha) there is probably someone else. Mama. Papi. Miss Nowik. Nibs. Rabbi Heschel. Brother James."[8] The list might truly go on forever, and be likewise different for every person. The point he takes from this—the conclusion that Rodriguez draws, which is really, I would argue, a translation of one person's faith to another's—is that each person matters for the life of faith that one has, and the life of faith within a given individual underscores how each person truly matters. Not only is such a pledge a matter of pursuing social justice, which it undoubtedly is, but it is likewise a matter of seeing faith as inextricably bound up with the many particular lives lived in faith all around us. Faith can be seen at work through such lives and by turning to those very lives in order to translate them into *our* lives.

The call to imitate the faith of another person is the way in which we are to understand the formation of our own life of faith. It was for this reason that Paul had stressed the role of imitation in the development of faith in his First Letter to the Corinthians: "I appeal to you, then, be imitators of me" (4:16) and, driving the point home still further, "Be imitators of me, as I am of Christ" (11:1; cf. Philippians 3:17). Paul's point, which would become almost synonymous in the fifteenth century with Thomas

---

8. Rodriguez, *Darling*, 224.

à Kempis's spiritual classic *The Imitation of Christ*, makes manifest the singular principle guiding these reflections: it is in the persons we know and the relationships we foster that we come to encounter faith in our own lives. It is this lasting legacy of the individual's significance that makes the (auto)biographical narrative so central to the development of one's faith, and the reason too why the genre of (auto)biography has remained so important in the Christian traditions.

The early church is so littered with hagiographical accounts of the early saints and martyrs that one can almost miss the significance of such works within the tradition and what it intended, and still intends, to pass along to us. We have unfortunately become so accustomed in the modern age to criticizing the rather fantastical and miraculous accounts of faith that such hagiographies present us with, that we often casually neglect the much more significant reality: that it is the life and story of faith of the individual believer or saint that brings others to faith in its complexity, rich with nuances and even apparent contradictions.

In the short few centuries that arose after the scriptural account had been recorded, there arose a vast and flourishing trade in writings that focused on the lives of the faithful, often in dramatic detail and significance. We have no less than Athanasius's *Life of Anthony*, Gregory the Great's *Life of Benedict*, Gregory of Nyssa's *The Life of Macrina*, Sulpicius Severus's *Life of Martin of Tours*, and a series of biographies by Jerome on both holy men and holy women, all testifying to how studying the life of a saint might bring one into contact with the saintly within one's own self.[9] Such biographies were given in a context wherein one of the greatest means of conveying the faith, and again stressing the importance of relationship, was through letter writing—an inherently relational medium of writing and a genre that had become canonized through the efforts of Paul, Peter, James, and others, which had only gained strength through the efforts of early Christians such as Ignatius, Clement, Polycarp, and Barnabas, to name only a few.

Though much of what follows in this book relies upon more contemporary writers who may or may not sense the significance that the (auto) biographical plays within the history of the passing on of faith within the Christian tradition, I turn to their works because I believe that they summon this precarious embodiment of faith within the individual life, the only real way of guaranteeing that the faith is preserved, but also challenged and pushed to evolve, or be translated, into ever new and renewing forms. I turn to these particular lives too because I believe they represent

---

9. See, among others, the writings anthologized in White, ed., *Early Christian Lives* and *Lives of Roman Christian Women*.

for us a clear and concise picture of what it means to embrace our brokenness as a movement toward faith, which is central to the story we find in the Christian narrative.

* * *

The history of Christianity is littered with people taking their desires for control, power, security, and life after death—all of these being taken up as issues surrounding the establishment and defense of a particular identity—and projecting those onto, and in some sense corrupting, a religious tradition and its image of the divine. Such activity often leads people to come up with an idea of God as an all-powerful person who controls everything and provides an ultimate security. (And this is why critiques of religion that focus on these things are so powerful as well as so greatly needed.) Such ideas of God give us our identity and make us feel secure. When our identity gets challenged, our God gets challenged; when our God gets challenged, our identity gets challenged. If God is vulnerable, we are vulnerable too. One of the most important parts of the Christian message therefore is that the notion of a God who is completely powerful and who will solve all our problems and give us complete security is an idol; this God does not exist.

When Jesus dies on a cross and is buried like a criminal, you can understand why he was so disappointing. A sign was placed above his head that said "King of the Jews" in order to mock him because he looked nothing like a king. You cannot, so the thinking went, claim to be a deity and then simply die as a great disappointment to people's hopes and dreams. Jesus' story, however, is one that almost goes out of its way to emphasize how he is helpless and weak; even the disciples sensed this toward the end of his life. The story of Jesus is the opposite of what many people thought, and still think, God should be. A weak God such as portrayed in the Gospels challenges our sense of identity, even though it remains at the heart of the biblical message and continues to probe the depths of our misunderstandings. The biblical narrative, from the exilic life of Israel to Jesus' death on the cross, continuously asks us: What does it mean to experience the loss of one's identity, of one's own self? What does it mean, moreover, to die to the self? And how are we supposed to go on living once something so vital to our identity has appeared to leave us once and for all?

What I want to take a look at, however, is what might appear as problematic to some when contemplating the significance of the Christian self—the autobiography of faith—that is, the death of the self that Saint Paul speaks of, and that Jesus embodies through his own death. The question we have to ask ourselves is: how can we talk about taking the self seriously when the "old self" we were born with is supposed to die? How do we do theology *as* autobiography if the self is something we die to? This is nothing if not a highly significant question throughout the history of Christian theology and one that must certainly play a central role in a book committed to investigating a variety of selves immersed in their various spiritual quests for self-understanding.

In many ways, to ask about the death of the self—the ultimate way of phrasing the failure of identity—is to provoke a deeply religious inquiry that moves beyond simply Christianity, but, as I have been saying, is not really understandable unless you are looking at it from within a particular religious tradition, from within a relationship to the self that you already are in, and are asked to take account of. In many ways, this death of the self, as a revealing of the "fiction" of the self that we all maintain, is one that we need to learn to work with, in our constructions of it, and this realization may make all the difference.

In short, the strong sense of self we crave is more or less a fiction—a stress upon definition over any act of translation that would undo us. The stories we tell about ourselves more typically get contradicted by reality. As such, sometimes we know we are lying, but we want to identify with our lie in order to be something we are not. We create a narrative of someone who appears to be powerful and in control, but that eventually breaks down when confronted in certain circumstances with reality. Saint Paul, among other things, tells us a story of welcoming the breakdown, and of finding out that Jesus was already ahead of us in grasping the significance of this breakdown for the life of faith.

Let us begin at the beginning for Christians, not only at the death of Jesus on the cross, but in the words of Paul who interprets this event for us as he characterizes the old self that is crucified with Christ:

> For if we have been united with him in a death like his, we will certainly be united with him in a resurrection like his. We know that our old self was crucified with him so that the body of sin might be destroyed, and we might no longer be enslaved to sin. For whoever has died is freed from sin. But if we have died with Christ, we believe that we will also live with him. We know that Christ, being raised from the dead, will never die again; death no longer has dominion over him. The death he died, he died to sin, once for all; but the life he lives, he lives to God. So you also must consider yourselves dead to sin and alive to God in Christ Jesus. (Romans 6:5–11)

In a modern context, we might think, for example, of sin as a state of being broken and without direction, but also of not being willing to show or to admit to anyone that you are broken or lost. The impression Paul gives of this death of the self is distinct, and the reason why many Christians throughout history have disregarded the selves that they are, giving themselves up to martyrdom—even acts of self-imposed distancing from themselves—in order to live their calling to a "higher" form of life. This call has an echo, at least on the surface, in something Jesus once said, and which still carries a lot of weight behind it within certain theological contexts:

> If any want to become my followers, let them deny themselves and take up their cross daily and follow me. For those who want to save their life will lose it, and those who lose their life for my sake will save it. What does it profit them if they gain the whole world, but lose or forfeit themselves? (Luke 9:23–25)

Taking up one's cross and following Christ to their own death is the command that those who follow after this Jesus are called to assume. Such a call runs in radical contrast to the ordinary, everyday sense of how we construct our lives and identities.

More typically, people can work so hard to achieve a more or less "perfect" identity or sense of self that they could be said to lose their own soul. We often want to know what we will "get" if we give up our life, for example, but the words we hear from both Jesus and Paul counsel strongly against such a reading of this death of the self. This particular death to the self cannot be approached that way. Jesus simply dies, with no guarantees of something better to come—yet another sign of why the apostles were so wholly disappointed and willing to flee from the foot of the cross. (It is also a wonderful reminder that the women who stayed by his side until his death were there because of the relationship they had with him, not something that they felt he could offer to them!) It is not until three days later that he shows up again. In the meantime, the hope is that something better will come, *perhaps*, but we cannot know what that will look like, or really anticipate much of anything of what it will look like. We simply stare at the cross, at the death that calls us to imitate it, and have no idea what will happen after we take our first steps towards following in Jesus' footsteps.

The question that remains, however, is a profound one too: does this death that Paul speaks of lead to a complete renunciation of the autobiographical, as if one's story were nothing in light of the call to follow Jesus? And if so, how exactly is one to go about living such a reality?

To be clear, Jesus speaks here of not forfeiting one's self, it is true. But how are we to understand this in relation to Paul's desire to know nothing except Jesus Christ crucified (1 Corinthians 2:2)? Does he not want to know himself, his desires, his actions, or those others who give him such glory and joy?

I believe that what is being expressed here by Paul, and it is a logic that we must be carefully attentive to, is that the selves that we are, the representations of our selves that we give, are permanently divided from within. They are cracked at the foundation, as it were (the result of what tradition has called "original sin"), and comprehending this fractured nature, this particular theology suggests, is the only way we can actually, paradoxically, come to peace with ourselves. In his Letter to the Romans, Paul talks about being a Jew (or any identity, for that matter) as being divided within. He introduces a fundamental distinction between being a Jew "in the flesh" and being a Jew "in the Spirit." Such a split applies as such to any identity. It is the translational element or moment within any given definition that opens us up to the transformative encounter with the other (as friend, lover, or God perhaps) who allows us to see ourselves in a way that we could not see on our own. Paul argues in this vein, to be clear, that Gentiles who were like Jews "in the spirit" could be part of the Christian movement, which had initially only wanted to accept Jews "in the flesh" into its ranks, because they had been transformed through the failure of their (defined) identities but in such a way as not to entirely lose them either. In the transformative encounter, something had opened up a possibility for conversion (or translation) that brought new elements into play and into the lives of those who were able to see through the cracks in their own façades and beyond themselves.

Likewise, recognizing this fractured self is where Christianity, at least in its Pauline form, begins to promote a type of self-critique that is absolutely essential to understanding what it means to be a Christian. That is, a Christian will be a subject who is critical of itself, of its own identity as anything that can be yet divided from within. This is the reality of the spirit/flesh divide that Pauline thought introduces to us in very stark terms:

> Live by the Spirit, I say, and do not gratify the desires of the flesh. For what the flesh desires is opposed to the Spirit, and what the Spirit desires is opposed to the flesh; for these are opposed to each other, to prevent you from doing what you want. But if you are led by the Spirit, you are not subject to the law. Now the works of the flesh are obvious: fornication, impurity, licentiousness, idolatry, sorcery, enmities, strife, jealousy, anger, quarrels, dissensions, factions, envy, drunkenness, carousing, and things like these. I am warning you, as I warned you before: those who do such things will not inherit the kingdom of God. By contrast, the fruit of the Spirit is love, joy, peace, patience,

kindness, generosity, faithfulness, gentleness, and self-control. There is no law against such things. And those who belong to Christ Jesus have crucified the flesh with its passions and desires. If we live by the Spirit, let us also be guided by the Spirit. Let us not become conceited, competing against one another, envying one another. (Galatians 5:16–26)

Paul lays out this logic in a number of places in his letters, and it seems to be a central pivot upon which his theology turns.[10] He acknowledges, at this juncture in particular, just how much of a "fiction" we are to ourselves: we can even be split into categories and divisions that we had no idea identified us. As should be clear to us, even the Christian can be subdivided just as the Jew was from Paul's point of view: there are Christians "in the flesh" and Christians "in the spirit" and we often do not see the difference between them, though knowing the difference is the essential thing we are supposed to strive after.

Paul goes on to describe the difference between living a new spiritual life and a human one:

And so, brothers and sisters, I could not speak to you as spiritual people, but rather as people of the flesh, as infants in Christ. I fed you with milk, not solid food, for you were not ready for solid food. Even now you are still not ready, for you are still of the flesh. For as long as there is jealousy and quarreling among you, are you not of the flesh, and behaving according to human inclinations? For when one says, "I belong to Paul," and another, "I belong to Apollos," are you not merely human? What then is Apollos? What is Paul? Servants through whom you came to believe, as the Lord assigned to each. I planted, Apollos watered, but God gave the growth. (1 Corinthians 3:1–6)

In essence, this logic unfolds as such: there are certain representations that we use in our world to define the subjects that we all already are, but which are capable of being divided from within, revealed as "nothing" before God (i.e., as in Galatians 3:28, Jew/Greek, slave/free, male/female, being only the most pronounced ones at his time of writing). Patriarchy has proceeded throughout the centuries by men not wanting to give up their power, by not being willing to admit they are fractured, and yet here is Paul pointing out the brokenness of that particular way of seeing the world, among others.

Paul is willing to suggest moreover that each of these representations is divided from within into another division, one between the spirit (of being a Jew, for example) and the flesh (i.e., a "division of division itself" then).

---

10. See Agamben, *The Time that Remains*.

This is what will prompt him to eventually say that he can act as a Jew while with Jews, and a Gentile while with Gentiles—a logic that throws quite a few people off balance perhaps, maybe even leaving some to suspect Paul of being relativistic—but helps him to better explain what Jesus was up to hanging out with tax collectors and prostitutes.

> For though I am free with respect to all, I have made myself a slave to all, so that I might win more of them. To the Jews I became as a Jew, in order to win Jews. To those under the law I became as one under the law (though I myself am not under the law) so that I might win those under the law. To those outside the law I became as one outside the law (though I am not free from God's law but am under Christ's law) so that I might win those outside the law. To the weak I became weak, so that I might win the weak. I have become all things to all people, that I might by all means save some. I do it all for the sake of the gospel, so that I may share in its blessings. (1 Corinthians 9:19–23)

Paul's logic here, though we will find it repeated throughout the chapters that follow in numerous ways, is one that we must listen to very carefully: Paul is not merely suggesting that he is being clever in order to win converts to Christianity, acting "as if" he was a Gentile in order to convert Gentiles. He was actually becoming "weak" with each socially identified weakness, with each socially marginalized person. He recognizes how each of these socially and politically constituted identities somehow fails to be the strong identity that we wish it to be, and in this fractured space of being not exactly what we want to be, Paul sees Jesus' movement towards his own brokenness, and therefore towards the fullness of his own humanity. Paul seizes this moment of translation possible through transformative encounter to move downward with those on the margins of society, those with fractured identities and exilic lives, in order to demonstrate how we are precisely capable of exhibiting relationship (or *faith*) best when in such situations.

As should be clear from even the most cursory readings of the Gospels, Jesus spent time with those on the margins of society. He saw each social representation that meant, and still often means, so much to each human being (like the male/female divide) and yet he acknowledged that each representation can still be divided from within. Every identity can be split from the inside, causing the "old self," the former identity, to fracture, though not to go away completely either. It still remains, but it is as if cancelled out, not to be taken as seriously as we once thought it had to be (for self-definition).[11] Our weakness is now ever before us, reminding us that we

---

11. See the central argument made in Agamben, *The Time that Remains*.

do not exist as we once thought we did. We are no longer the people we had thought ourselves to be.

The key to making the transition from seeing one's identity as fractured to a new identity beyond the social representations imposed upon us is to be found only within the ability of the person to see their own limitations, that is, the failure of their representations of themselves, and thereby, through seeing this failure, to make the trek from identity to non-identity, and from non-identity to a new identity once again. That is, we are able to see how our institutionalized identities fail to live up to the experiences we have, and we therefore allow more experience to creep in and redefine us—again, as profound moments of *translation*. In other words, we see how limited our experiences really are, and start allowing the great depths of other voices, throughout ages of tradition and of the people who stand before us in the present, to speak to us still. We are caught in such a way within a delicate balance of relations between past persons (often collected as the traditions we live within) and present persons living new forms of life.

Another way to view this flow from traditions and structures to experiences is to refocus on other terms that are synonymous in this context: *works* and *faith*. This is where I would look at the interesting position of the book of James, the book that the great Protestant Reformer Martin Luther once wanted removed from the Christian Bible, as it lays significant stress upon the inherent relationship of faith and works—that is, the idea that any faith must also be put into action, or embodied. This is another way to say that any notion of faith must be rooted in an embodied context, or the position of the autobiographical, as I have been calling it. In the words of James,

> But be doers of the word, and not merely hearers who deceive themselves. For if any are hearers of the word and not doers, they are like those who look at themselves in a mirror; for they look at themselves and, on going away, immediately forget what they were like. But those who look into the perfect law, the law of liberty, and persevere, being not hearers who forget but doers who act—they will be blessed in their doing. If any think they are religious, and do not bridle their tongues but deceive their hearts, their religion is worthless. Religion that is pure and undefiled before God, the Father, is this: to care for orphans and widows in their distress, and to keep oneself unstained by the world. (James 1:22–27)

Notice how, again, those who are "weak" in social terms, who are tread upon by society, are inherently connected to this tension between faith and works. This is so because it is only through a discovery of our own "weaknesses"—our own failures to be the identities we want to be—that we are able to take up the call of Christ to embrace our failures, to take up our cross and follow him.

> What good is it, my brothers and sisters, if you say you have faith but do not have works? Can faith save you? If a brother or sister is naked and lacks daily food, and one of you says to them, "Go in peace; keep warm and eat your fill," and yet you do not supply their bodily needs, what is the good of that? So faith by itself, if it has no works, is dead. But someone will say, "You have faith and I have works." Show me your faith apart from your works, and I by my works will show you my faith. You believe that God is one; you do well. Even the demons believe—and shudder. Do you want to be shown, you senseless person, that faith apart from works is barren? Was not our ancestor Abraham justified by works when he offered his son Isaac on the altar? You see that faith was active along with his works, and faith was brought to completion by the works. Thus the scripture was fulfilled that says, "Abraham believed God, and it was reckoned to him as righteousness," and he was called the friend of God. You see that a person is justified by works and not by faith alone. Likewise, was not Rahab the prostitute also justified by works when she welcomed the messengers and sent them out by another road? For just as the body without the spirit is dead, so faith without works is also dead. (James 2:14–26)

Faith protects us from being self-engrossed or narcissistic. It points to the larger picture of things—to God and to others. Yet it can also be a complete abstraction if not rooted in the particularities of life, our experiences and "works." It is true that works can be a form of self-absorption, as Luther correctly claimed. Yet James emphasizes both so that the corrective to a possible self-absorption in works is one's faith; and, in turn, we see how the corrective to an abstracted faith is an embodied life, the works that we live out. The two must maintain their unending and unresolvable tension in order to give rise to the selves that we strive to be, and in whatever context we find ourselves.

When Paul says he only wants to know "Christ crucified" (1 Corinthians 2:2), he is speaking about the failure of our identities as well as the failure of Christ to be the idea of God we had previously maintained. Paul contrasts this sharply with the Jews (who want to see signs) and the Greeks (who want arguments, knowledge, wisdom) (1 Corinthians 1:22–23). Though these groupings are certainly not exhaustive of all attempts to avoid having to face the brokenness of our selves, there are many people today, to be sure (not just "Jews" and "Greeks," which are really just generic types in this sense) who would rather base their faith upon a miraculous event or a reasoned argument than face the brokenness of their identity as the way toward faith. But, as Paul reminds us, this is the only way we can actually discover the truth of what Jesus was up to, in his life and in his death and resurrection.

In this permanent state of things, we find ourselves continuously thrust into a tension between structural, even institutionalized works and the experiential faith that cannot be entirely subsumed under a given religious banner.[12] This tension, moreover, is why we can only look to the pulsating, vibrant *life* of faith as it is lived out in the individuals who embody it for our own guidance and benefit. The relationships that we undertake within such a context as the imitation of those who have gone before us, and who have struggled intensely with the faith that they were called to live out, is precisely the only way in which to engage faith in our own lives. It is this activity of biblical witness, with its increasing and fervent stress on the (auto)biographical contours of faith, that we must pay attention to, again and again, throughout the entire process that is the passing on or translation of faith.

By turning to the stories of individuals who bring this tension to life in our world today, as well as in the history of Christianity, I hope to illustrate in what follows how the act of "dying with Christ" still speaks to us profoundly and with great meaning and depth. Though we may often feel as if the story of religious faith has no room within the secular world in which we live, I believe that a closer reading of particular lives of faith might actually show us something different, an alternative narrative that may open us up to a vulnerability within that can actually connect us intimately to others.

---

12. Malabou, *Plasticity at the Dusk of Writing*.

CHAPTER TWO

Augustine

Confession at the Foundations of Christian Theology

In 354 CE, the North African village of Tagaste witnessed the birth of a child who would go on to be arguably the most influential figure in the history of Western Christianity. Reared by a devoutly Christian mother, Monica, Augustine's education took a more formal turn when he was sent to Carthage at the age of seventeen to prepare for a career in public service by studying rhetoric. His academic career led to an increased interest in the structure, eloquence, and logic present within the rhetorical field and caused him to question the faith that he had been brought up with. Furthermore, a growing collection of sexual exploits, including the fathering of a child with his concubine, began to torment Augustine and his understanding of an omnibenevolent God, the goodness of creation, and the nature of sin. He would find momentary solace in various competing ideologies, including Manichaeism and Neoplatonism, before being permanently struck by the beauty, truth, and eloquence of Bishop Ambrose's sermons during a stay in Milan.

This momentous return to his Christian roots and his scholarly aptitude eventually led to Augustine's ordination in 391 and his election to the bishopric of Hippo in 395. He would spend his ministerial career combatting the various heretical movements that had tickled his fancy years earlier, as well as dedicating volumes upon volumes of his work to quashing the rise of Pelagianism and its rejection of original sin. Aside from this work's discussion of his Confessions, *the reader should be aware of Augustine's* City of God, *a semi-autobiographical work in its own right. A response to the final sacking of Rome in 410 by the Visigoths,* City of God *attempted to explain the fall of the world's most powerful Empire through a lens that did not reject the Christian ethos that pervaded its borders. Augustine would continue to fight various heresies and apostasy until his death in 430, leaving behind a corpus that would lay the foundations for Western Christianity as we know it.*

Augustine's life story opens up a source of inquiry that is centered on one of the oldest questions to permeate the Christian tradition, a question that also lies at the heart of autobiographical writing: What does it mean to confess? Typically, the word *confess* means to articulate one's beliefs, as when one professes their faith or recites a creed, but it can also mean to reveal one's sins, as in the Catholic sacrament of reconciliation or in the admission of a crime. In either case, it is a matter of disclosing something that had not previously been known, acknowledging that which was there all along, but had not been stated; that is, it is an act revealing what had been hidden from plain sight.

There is much to say about the role of "confession" within a theological setting, as the practice certainly has a long history. Confessions of faith have often been seen as litmus tests of where a person stands politically or religiously—consequently as somewhat coherent markers of a person's identity. Such markers become highly personal too when we consider how confessing one's sins really does "reveal" the person who lies underneath whatever representation of the self they provide to those around them. I may socially appear to be such and such, but when the "truth" of my actions is revealed, when my ugly sins are shown, here is who I really am, we might say.[1]

Sin is a difficult word to comprehend these days, but there is no doubt that it lies at the foundations of Christian thought and practice. The state of "original sin" that defines the "fractured" human being is an essential understanding of the human state of existence imparted by the Judeo-Christian traditions. Its condensed message is that, at our core, we are not who we often think and say we are. Sin has distorted our self-perception, and we are consequently unable to do the things we wish we could do. Though we are fundamentally good, so to speak, we are yet tainted by a brokenness that is somehow also constitutive of us, no matter how much we would like to deny the reality of this truth. To suggest as much is not

---

1. It should be noted too that confession has played, and continues to play, a large social role in terms of defining the individual's relationship to the community through the disclosure of who they are, what acts they have engaged in, what they believe, and so forth. Though a modern autobiographical sensibility often tends to downplay the communal and social aspects of confession, a certain communal identity is often made present, or disclosed, at the same moment as the individual confesses their own story.

to say that we are incapable of getting things "right"; indeed, this is where words like *salvation* and *redemption* take on a very specific resonance in formulating one's faith. But making this claim *is* to suggest that we are in need of a fundamental experience of a grace that comes from *beyond* us, but also somehow from *within* us, in order to find that goodness completed in us. As Christianity would come to teach, grace, as such, becomes a perception of ourselves given to us by God that goes beyond our broken limitations. This grace can comfort us or it can sting, because it comes from without and tells us the truth about ourselves. Such grace, or mercy, comes in many ways from our willingness to acknowledge our brokenness, that is, it stems from the confession of our sins.

What will it mean, in light of such reflections, for Augustine to offer us his confessions? What is it exactly that he is planning to confess to us? Will this be about faith, or will it be about his private, hidden, and sinful life? The answer is clear from the start: the two are, or at least should be, inseparable: to confess your faith is to confess who you really are deep down, and there is no way to present one without the other. Insofar as we are able to demonstrate our failure to accurately represent ourselves, we present our "genuine" selves by showing the cracks and fault lines of our true nature. We are broken people, and this is what we must show to each other.

What Augustine realizes about the simultaneous presentation of our confession of faith and our confession of sin is that both are inextricably linked to our desires. This linkage is what in turn will propel his analysis of his own life and faith into the central platform of Christian theological understandings of the self, not to mention just basically what it means to be a Christian. As he famously opens his *Confessions*, "to praise you is the desire of man, a little piece of your creation. You stir man to take pleasure in praising you, because you have made us for yourself, and our heart is restless until it rests in you."[2] What he is pointing out is not just the inevitability of God finding a place within each person's heart, but the necessarily intertwined nature of our confessions: everything must fit together in one place, our desires as well as our faith. The focused integrity of the self that is established in relation to the development of one's faith must be determined as *the* subject of theological inquiry. As Augustine himself will formulate this thought later in his *Confessions*, "To hear you speaking about oneself is to know oneself."[3] This relationship is, moreover, the reason he will later put such an emphasis on maintaining the integrity of one's will, even when it seeks out that which is not good:

2. Augustine, *Confessions*, 3.
3. Augustine, *Confessions*, 180.

No one is doing right if he is acting against his will, even when what he is doing is good. Those who put compulsion on me were not doing right either; the good was done to me by you, my God. They gave no consideration to the use that I might make of the things they forced me to learn. The objective they had in view was merely to satisfy the appetite for wealth and for glory, though the appetite is insatiable, the wealth is in reality destitution of spirit, and the glory something to be ashamed of.[4]

The naturalness of the inclination of our desire for God should resonate loudly within this description, and it highlights how a good many religiously inclined persons would be guilty of such wrongful coercion of other people's wills. The main thing I want to stress, however, is that Augustine places his emphasis upon the integrity of the individual's will above all else—a point that will be echoed centuries later by John Henry Newman's formulation of the role of conscience in a person's life. For Newman, as for Augustine, one must follow one's conscience above all else, which is certainly shaped in part by religious traditions and many other elements in one's life, when one chooses to dissent from a given doctrine or teaching of a religious institution.[5] Or, in other cases, one's conscience is bolstered by one's adherence to the truth encountered in one's life. In summation of the power of such a process, Augustine provides another path to behold: "This experience sufficiently illuminates the truth that free curiosity has greater power to stimulate learning than rigorous coercion."[6] Making an allowance for such curiosity is not tangential to the search for God—it is the cornerstone of such a search made in freedom toward an unknown God. As we will find to be the case in Mary Karr's stumbling toward prayer and a God she could not name because she did not know, and which was a result of her own freedom to explore the presence of God in her own way, we find

---

4. Augustine, *Confessions*, 14–15.
5. Newman, *A Letter Addressed to the Duke of Norfolk*.
6. Augustine, *Confessions*, 17. Yet, such a "free curiosity," he quickly concedes, must be tempered: "Nevertheless, the free-ranging flux of curiosity is channelled by discipline under your laws, God. By your laws we are disciplined, from the canes of schoolmasters to the ordeals of martyrs. Your laws have the power to temper bitter experiences in a constructive way, recalling us to yourself from the pestilential life of easy comforts which have taken us away from you" (Augustine, *Confessions*, 17). Just what such "laws" given by God are remains somewhat unclear. One might be tempted in reading this passage to note how the insertion of "natural law" into his theology remains problematic throughout his theological formulations, as such positions can also be used to justify the degrading of women, or the condemnation of anything that appears to be "unnatural" (e.g., his condemnation of "sodomy" as always deplorable—see Augustine, *Confessions*, 46). It also will let corporal punishment have its reign, when it might in fact be part of the coercion he is so opposed to.

Augustine declaring himself at the same problematic juncture that he is unable to pray to a God he can't conceive of, but also unable to conceive of God unless he prays to God first:

> "Grant me Lord to know and understand" which comes first—to call upon you or to praise you, and whether knowing you precedes calling upon you. But who calls upon you when he does not know you? For an ignorant person might call upon someone else instead of the right one. But surely you may be called upon in prayer that you may be known.[7]

The question here is not "which God is the right God?" but the more essential question: "if you are God, how are we to know you? How are we to achieve intimacy with you?" Confirming what we will see in the next chapter as Karr's ultimate decision to first seek out God and only then to find and know God, Augustine develops this logic in its most simplistic, incremental form: "In seeking him they find him, and in finding they will praise him. Lord, I would seek you, calling upon you—and calling upon you is an act of believing in you."[8] In such a way, we stand before a God whom we want to have faith in, indeed must have faith in, in some sense, before we even get to know who this God is—as paradoxical as such a viewpoint might at first glance appear to us.

My inclination here is to suggest that this is precisely why we must learn to view religion itself as a traditional path toward getting to know God, not the end goal after determining that it contains some form of an "absolute truth." The liturgies, prayers, rituals, and creeds that embody the faith and its practices are intended to help someone locate the presence of the divine, not to coerce them or to "beat it out of them" in some manner, and as Augustine so helpfully reminds us. This is a truth we often forget when we look at these things in the church today, and this point is no minor one: religious liturgies, for example, are intended to be a seamless interaction between one's lived life and the life of others who come together to admit their brokenness and to find a grace that is capable of permeating their entire life. They are not merely, as is often the misperception, something we are obliged to do, as a "duty" to God or the church.

Augustine, with a blunt honesty that is refreshing to behold, is unafraid to ask the question which his desires prompt him to pose: "Who then are you, my God? What, I ask, but God who is Lord?"[9] It is at this point, however, that Augustine finds himself confronting an abyss of thought and

---

7. Augustine, *Confessions*, 3.
8. Augustine, *Confessions*, 3.
9. Augustine, *Confessions*, 4.

so slips in a series of Greek conceptualizations, no doubt borrowed from thinkers such as Plotinus (and his Platonic theological speculations), that fill up his conceptual identifications of the divine, but which, I would argue, also create a certain tension within his theology, as these Greek concepts are often at odds with the humanity of the person of Jesus the Scriptures present us with. In a series of abstractions, Augustine, however, proceeds to name the God he does not know with a high degree of certainty:

> Most high, utterly good, utterly powerful, most omnipotent, most merciful and most just, deeply hidden, yet most intimately present, perfection of both beauty and strength, stable and incomprehensible, immutable and yet changing all things, never new, never old, making everything new and "leading" the proud "to be old without their knowledge"; always active, always in repose, gathering to yourself but not in need, supporting and filling and protecting, creating and nurturing and bringing to maturity, searching even though to you nothing is lacking: you love without burning, you are jealous in a way that is free of anxiety, you "repent" without the pain of regret, you are wrathful and remain tranquil.[10]

Unlike a lot of the authors whom we will turn to later in this book who are willing to surrender even their conceptions of God so that they might encounter a God beyond what they had known or experienced, Augustine immediately provides a platform of common metaphysical traits of the presumed divinity, and this will become highly problematic, I would suggest, when it conflicts with his other visions of God as presented in the person of Jesus—a person he does not spend nearly as much time, in this context, describing.

Indeed, there is often a conflict between the traditional terms used to characterize God's being, such as *omniscience, omnipotence,* and the rest, and the grace of God which takes precedence over these, and either merging or disentangling the former from the latter is not an easy task. Yet as Cardinal Walter Kasper has more recently claimed, and I believe we must take this subtle twist on God's being very seriously, looking at God's mercy as the fundamental lens through which to read God's other attributes is a most necessary thing to do.[11]

Augustine, for his part, has a view of God as an all-powerful and especially incorruptible, pure, holy being, qualities that he perhaps wrongly projects onto the divine because he wants the divine to hold such attributes

---

10. Augustine, *Confessions*, 4–5.
11. Kasper, *Mercy*.

as a sign of God's power and majesty. There is in this a sharp contrast present with another image of God, one that relates to the person before them in an intimate manner and who actually enters into one's life: the person of Jesus. This tension between the abstract deity in the clouds, an all-powerful, all-knowing being, and the person of Jesus is played out in *Confessions* on multiple levels, demonstrating how Augustine holds both distant and intimate views of God but does not explicitly bring them together, which is a central task for Christian thought. Thus, in many ways, this part of his thought is underdeveloped in the *Confessions*.

What Augustine does acknowledge, however, is the difficulty and complexity we encounter when we do try to name the being who is God, thereby implicating and critiquing even his own projected ideas of God: "But in these words what have I said, my God, my life, my holy sweetness? What has anyone achieved in words when he speaks about you? Yet woe to those who are silent about you because, though loquacious with verbosity, they have nothing to say."[12] What Augustine touches upon here is a permanent, in-built tension within theological discourse: a tension within one's notion of God that recognizes the limitations of being able to say anything about God, but which also realizes that one must yet say *something* about God. In the language of lovers that I will repeatedly turn to in this book, one will never fully know their beloved, but one must not stop trying to know them. This tension has traditionally been described as an ongoing feud between negative and positive theologies, or what we *cannot* say about God and must cross out (*apophatic* theology) and what we *do* say about God in order to have some idea or representation of who this God is (*kataphatic* theology).

What Augustine adds to this problematic situation of our being caught within language, at least, is his recognition that only God can provide him with a sense of who God is to him: "In your mercies, Lord God, tell me what you are to me."[13] In other words, understanding anything of God must begin with the humility of not projecting one's conceptualizations of God onto God, something that Augustine himself struggled with in multiple ways, as I have already noted. Augustine's notion of God has not left God room to be something beyond his projections, as with a friend or lover who might bristle when too many expectations or identities are foisted upon them. But this is a point too that Augustine seems to recognize does take place at some level. Or, as he succinctly renders this formulation himself: "let him rejoice and

---

12. Augustine, *Confessions*, 5.
13. Augustine, *Confessions*, 5.

delight in finding you who are beyond discovery rather than fail to find you by supposing you to be discoverable."[14]

Humility by this count is everything, even if Augustine himself fails at it on occasion (as do we all to be sure). This is a point we will encounter again later in other authors, and which Augustine will eventually recount in somewhat proverbial fashion: "the controlled modesty of a mind that admits limitations is more beautiful than the things I was anxious to know about."[15] His striving for humility before God certainly tempers some of the potential tensions within his conceptualization of God, and it also leads him to acknowledge a fuller dimension of God's being, one that exhibits just this humility: "But you may smile at me for putting these questions. Your command that I praise you and confess you may be limited to that which I know."[16] He refrains thus at this point from speculating further on things he does not know, like where he came from before he was born.[17] In many ways, he issues a caution to all those theologies (and theologians) who would speculate on many abstruse and abstracted matters.

Augustine does, however, seek to develop a way to know of God, and he believes he has achieved it through the analogy one can posit between humanity and the divine, despite the fact that this is, and remains, a heavily contested thing to do. The "analogy of being," as it has come to be known, that Augustine develops here has its scriptural correlate in Romans 1:20, where Paul declared that "the invisible things of God are understood and seen through the things which are made."[18] As Augustine puts it, "You have also given mankind the capacity to understand oneself by analogy with others, and to believe much about oneself on the authority of weak women."[19] I think we can interpret his reference to "weak women," despite its sexist context,[20] as a general acknowledgement that the "weakness" found within humanity can yet lead to authentic insight about the divine, including Augustine's own propositions, which exhibit, to his mind, the strength of using analogical reasoning to understand something of God. Yet to reason like this is also a little more than problematic, since we really have no absolute basis for drawing such analogous formulations, as what appears at one point

14. Augustine, *Confessions*, 8.
15. Augustine, *Confessions*, 79.
16. Augustine, *Confessions*, 8.
17. Augustine, *Confessions*, 7–8.
18. See Augustine, *Confessions*, 184.
19. Augustine, *Confessions*, 8.
20. See, e.g., his comments on women's naturally "submissive" bodies, Augustine, *Confessions*, 302.

to be analogous, may later appear to not be so.[21] And yet we continue, as we must, to posit such analogies.

What does seem clear is that Augustine needs this form of analogy in order to "correct" what he sees as "wrong" with his ancient context, where human life was devalued to the point of a person's getting more upset about an error in language pronunciation than about the death of a human being (and though this problem still persists in our world today in many sad and tragic ways).[22] Augustine himself illustrates what he finds to be the most problematic aspect of trying to locate truth: "My sin consisted in this, that I sought pleasure, sublimity, and truth not in God but in his creatures, in myself and other created beings. So it was that I plunged into miseries, confusions, and errors."[23] Feeling his way through his own past yet in relation to God's being, Augustine begins to recount his errors, to confess them aloud, for, as he will put it a bit later, "Nothing is nearer to your ears than a confessing heart and a life grounded in faith."[24]

As such, he undertakes a deliberate course of confession in order to render himself vulnerable before God, and thereby to move closer through intimacy and relationship with God.

> I intend to remind myself of my past foulnesses and carnal corruptions, not because I love them but so that I may love you, my God. It is from love of your love that I make the act of recollection.... You gathered me together from the state of disintegration in which I had been fruitlessly divided. I turned from unity in you to be lost in multiplicity.[25]

The multiplicity he is referring to in this context is the lack of the integrity or unity that a person of faith seeks after when they try to unite the various disparate aspects of their life into one place, where a confession of faith and a confession of one's sins become the same thing. This is the task, you might say, to which all humans are called, but to which few respond. It is not God's responsibility to "wake us" from our slumber to how such an integrity can change our lives forever. Augustine too recognizes as much when he claims that "I travelled very far from you, and you did not stop me."[26] It is not God's responsibility we are talking of here, but ours. In such ways, we create our own hell within us: "I went astray from you, my God, far from your

21. White, ed., *The Analogy of Being*.
22. See Augustine, *Confessions*, 21.
23. Augustine, *Confessions*, 22–23.
24. Augustine, *Confessions*, 26.
25. Augustine, *Confessions*, 24.
26. Augustine, *Confessions*, 24.

unmoved stability. I became a region of destitution."[27] This is the precise sentiment that will cause him to seek eventually to flee from himself as he had become repugnant to himself: "I had become to myself a place of unhappiness in which I could not bear to be; but I could not escape from myself. Where should my heart flee to in escaping from my heart? Where is there where I cannot pursue myself?"[28] The answer, of course, is nowhere if not in God—nowhere if not in relationship, and so in faith as well.

At the same time, however, God is involved in the equation because, according to Augustine, it is God who lies at the base of our desires. God is the love that we seek after, but God is also a love that does not coerce us into loving God in return. This reality is the real freedom and the beauty, but also the subtlety and the frustration, of the relationship, and, I would only add, of all relationships in our lives. Love cannot be controlled in any sense, and it is precisely this fragile nature of love that causes so many of our relationships to be so maddeningly frustrating. In Augustine's wording, "The single desire that dominated my search for delight was simply to love and to be loved."[29] But, as he will later describe this desire more clearly, it was not a pure love dwelling in such freedom. It was rather an illusion of what appeared to be love to him, a type of love that he thought he could manipulate at will. "I was in love with love, and I hated safety and a path free of snares."[30] What we see in these reflections, at least, was that he was not yet in that place of loving God that would allow him to pose the question "But when I love you, what do I love?"[31]

Augustine was consequently distracted and confused as to how he might go about fulfilling that desire, especially when such pleasurable temptations drove him far from the truth of his desire for love, that is, the truth of how only God and true relationship could fulfill such desires.

> The bubbling impulses of puberty befogged and obscured my heart so that it could not see the difference between love's serenity and lust's darkness. Confusion of the two things boiled within me. It seized hold of my youthful weakness sweeping me through the precipitous rocks of desire to submerge me in a whirlpool of vice.[32]

27. Augustine, *Confessions*, 34.
28. Augustine, *Confessions*, 60.
29. Augustine, *Confessions*, 24.
30. Augustine, *Confessions*, 35.
31. Augustine, *Confessions*, 183.
32. Augustine, *Confessions*, 24.

In fact, this misguided desire was so strong in him that even when he finally realized that God is calling him elsewhere, to a holy life of faith as relationship, he will still maintain enough pleasurable confusion as to declare that he sees the need for proper relations, but is not yet ready to receive them: "Grant me chastity and continence, but not yet."[33] If ever there was an articulation of an honest collaboration between one's desires and one's quest for truth, this may perhaps be it.

What the young Augustine had discovered was the almost absolute pleasure in confusing the end goals of one's desire, substituting human ends for divine ones. In his words, "My desire was to enjoy not what I sought by stealing but merely the excitement of thieving and the doing of what was wrong."[34] At this point, he even goes so far as to steal a pear from a neighbor's garden just to experience the delights of stealing a pear, even though he had better ones waiting for him at home.

> I had no motive for my wickedness except wickedness itself. It was foul, and I loved it. I loved the self-destruction, I loved my fall, not the object for which I had fallen but my fall itself. My depraved soul leaped down from your firmament to ruin. I was seeking not to gain anything by shameful means, but shame for its own sake.[35]

This is, in many ways, why it is so difficult to determine what exactly is a concrete manifestation of sin and what is not. We might think, for example, and in the context of the "language of lovers," of those persons who enter into relationships with others when they know that it probably won't work out in the long run. What is it exactly that they are after? A temporary reprieve from loneliness? What feels like the thrill of "illicit" sex? Someone to fill the gaping wound of an absent or abusive parent? This list could certainly go on and on.

What Augustine is drawing us to see, however, is that there is often a much deeper motive for our sinful ways than we might at first glance perceive, but which we must get hold of if we are to make any spiritual or material progress toward becoming more aware of ourselves (self-critique) and our desires.

In ways that greatly foreshadow later psychological insights about the decisions we (wrongly) make "for love" and the consequences which such misguided efforts yield, Augustine describes how he sought out love from among those who would return his love and yet bind him to a terrible form of

---

33. Augustine, *Confessions*, 145.
34. Augustine, *Confessions*, 29.
35. Augustine, *Confessions*, 29.

(a grossly inverted) "joy": "I was glad to be in bondage, tied with troublesome chains, with the result that I was flogged with the red-hot iron rods of jealousy, suspicion, fear, anger, and contention."[36] He was led on, he tells us, by the tragedies and love stories coming from the theater, as they provoked him with their misdirected representations of love. "That was my kind of life. Surely, my God, it was no real life at all?"[37] The deception and illusion that permeated the representations he saw before his eyes, and which entered into his heart, were too much for him to bear as his life began to veer off course and his actions moved seemingly beyond his ability to control them.

For a variety of reasons, and primarily because he began to search out something different in his life that might actually give him life, he turns to the study of the biblical texts, which he describes as such: "And this is what met me: something neither open to the proud nor laid bare to mere children; a text lowly to the beginner but, on further reading, of mountainous difficulty and enveloped in mysteries."[38] He discovers more mystery there than he at first comprehended, and so, from the beginning of his quest for a faith, he concerns himself with asking questions of the text that he will later discard as a distraction: "In my ignorance I was disturbed by these questions, and while travelling away from the truth I thought I was going towards it."[39]

What he discerns is that the customs and practices "of different regions and periods were adapted to their places and times, while that law itself remains unaltered everywhere and always."[40] Hence he becomes particularly inclined toward the "spiritual" reading of texts instead of their "literal" version, which, he finds, "kills." In the context of listening to Saint Ambrose's sermons, in fact, he remarks "Those texts which, taken literally, seemed to contain perverse teaching he would expound spiritually, removing the mystical veil."[41] What he comes to realize is that his quest

36. Augustine, *Confessions*, 35.
37. Augustine, *Confessions*, 37.
38. Augustine, *Confessions*, 40.
39. Augustine, *Confessions*, 43.
40. Augustine, *Confessions*, 44.
41. Augustine, *Confessions*, 94. Extending this form of interpretation, Augustine goes on to provide a radical multiplicity of interpretations when he claims that "So what difficulty is it for me when these words can be interpreted in various ways, provided only that the interpretations are true? What difficulty is it for me, I say, if I understand the text in a way different from someone else, who understands the scriptural author in another sense? In Bible study all of us are trying to find and grasp the meaning of the author we are reading, and when we believe him to be revealing truth, we do not dare to think he said anything which we either know or think to be incorrect. As long as each interpreter is endeavouring to find in the holy scriptures the meaning of the author who

for "certainty" in biblical and faith matters was what actually kept him from real belief, and "By believing I could have been healed."[42] Instead of pursuing this path, however,

> I wanted to be as certain about things I could not see as I am certain that seven and three are ten. I was not so mad as to think that I could consider even that to be something unknowable. But I desired other things to be as certain as this truth, whether physical objects which were not immediately accessible to my senses, or spiritual matters which I knew no way of thinking about except in physical terms.[43]

And yet he has to concede that he does trust and believe in a good many things that he can't himself prove, such as what existed before he was born, the identity of his parents, and so on, things "which I could not know unless I believed what I had heard."[44] This does not mean that he falls headlong into an absolute certainty of the Christian faith—no, he actually oscillates between his faith being "sometimes stronger, sometimes weaker. But at least I always retained belief both that you are and that you care for us, even if I did not know what to think about your substantial nature or what way would lead, or lead me back, to you."[45] He judges that we are too weak to discover the truth by reason alone, and that we must fall back upon the revealed nature of Scripture in order to ascertain the truth of our lives. Augustine sees a connection that his desire for certainty was related to his desire to love and be loved in return. His openness to a sense of mystery that

---

wrote it, what evil is it if an exegesis he gives is one shown to be true by you, light of all sincere souls, even if the author whom he is reading did not have that idea and, though he had grasped a truth, had not discerned that seen by the interpreter"? (259–60). And, continuing on this train of thought, he suggests concerning those who claim to have a singular, "right" reading of a text that they are "proud" and "have no knowledge" of the Scriptures, "but love their own opinion not because it is true, but because it is their own. Otherwise they would equally respect another true interpretation as valid, just as I respect what they say when their affirmation is true, not because it is theirs, but because it is true. And indeed if it is true, it cannot be merely their private property. If they respect an affirmation because it is true, then it is already both theirs and mine, shared by all lovers of the truth" (264). And this reveals the true principle that Augustine is after here: "Anyone who claims for his own property what you offer for all to enjoy, and wishes to have exclusive rights to what belongs to everyone, is driven from the common truth to his own private ideas, that is from truth to a lie" (265). And this is one of the major reasons why Christianity is not a cult; the knowledge it contains is common property, meant for all, and not just for a reserved group of special persons.

42. Augustine, *Confessions*, 95.
43. Augustine, *Confessions*, 95.
44. Augustine, *Confessions*, 95.
45. Augustine, *Confessions*, 96.

comes about through his reading the Bible in a sense stops him from the compulsion to have to search for certainty in a way that will never actually arrive. As we will see develop throughout several of the life stories we will later turn to, this renunciation of certainty and the capacity to sit in a mystery that cannot be named is one of the most pronounced religious insights one can gain in their life.

Sin, for Augustine, can now be seen for what it is, as a disordered desire: craving things and people with the desire that should be reserved for the love of, or desire for, God, as well as an attempt to make certain things that cannot be so. Augustine himself, at this stage in his development, felt in bondage to these disordered desires, and at times unable to control them to any degree. Even once he knows this to be the case, he felt that he could not really stop. He traces this back to what Paul writes in his Letter to the Romans, as I pointed to in the last chapter: doing the thing you do not want to do (7:15). The world Augustine inhabits in his slavery to desire is thus incredibly shallow; there is no respect for complexity or mystery. The quest for certainty, as Christian Wiman will later put it, becomes a compulsion and a punishment at the same time. In reading the Bible, however, Augustine finds a sense of mystery and complexity that is respected and fostered, not done away with or replaced with a superficial sense of certainty. The literal sense of Scripture, as noted above, can kill. What Augustine sees, and what ultimately gives him life, is that there is a connection between how we handle our everyday desires and how we handle our spiritual desires, and so the ability to respect the dimensions of one must learn to overlap with the other.

Through all of these meanderings, Augustine eventually comes to understand that revelation means that something is being shown to us that we did not know before. In this way, the biblical text served as a source of revelation: not because someone told him it was revelation, but because it actually revealed something to him in his life, showing him something beyond himself—that the mystery of God was one that did not subscribe to the measures of certitude that we normally search for in this world. What really comes to him in his reading of the Bible is a mystery so deep that I believe it continues to haunt his theology, which I alluded to a moment ago: the tension present there, and in Christian doctrine, between an ephemeral, transcendent and highly philosophically speculative "higher being" and the "enfleshed" human person of Jesus Christ. This is a tension that historically constitutes Christianity in many ways, especially in the doctrine of the Trinity.

For the Augustine who had once been part of the Manichees, a fiercely dualistic group that shunned the flesh in order to access the spiritual, the notion of a God in human form was initially repulsive: "I was afraid to believe him incarnate lest I had to believe him defiled by the flesh."[46] Indeed, when he does invoke the "Word" who is Jesus Christ, he immediately refrains from the name of Jesus, but goes into a discussion of his eternal being.[47] This is perhaps because, as he will state toward the end of his *Confessions*, "Formless spiritual being is superior to formed body," a point the existence of Jesus seems to contest in many ways.[48] Even in the resurrection, we must remember, Jesus retained his wounds.

I want, however, to question this assumption about the problematic nature of that which can be corrupted, or that which can be changed. It is this same fear of corruption and change that causes people to want to explain and find answers for suffering and death. In contrast to this, many religious and spiritual communities have a tradition of being at peace with death and not explaining it away, simply providing witness to the suffering of the other person and not trying to reason it out. I want to show this difference because it seems that not even Augustine knows why he believes this to be a more proper formulation of things: "Although I did not know why and how, it was clear to me and certain that what is corruptible is inferior to that which cannot be corrupted; what is immune from injury I unhesitatingly put above that which is not immune; what suffers no change is better than that which can change."[49] So begins for Augustine at this point in his text a long series of abstract theological reflections on the nature of God. These seem to culminate when he later inquires "But when I love you, what do I love?"[50] And he concludes:

> [T]here is a light I love, and a food, and a kind of embrace when I love my god—a light, voice, odour, food, embrace of my inner man, where my soul is floodlit by light which space cannot contain, where there is sound that time cannot seize, where there is a perfume which no breeze disperses, where there is a taste for food no amount of eating can lessen, and where there is a bond of union that no satiety can part. That is what I love when I love my God.[51]

In this poetically vague passage, Augustine points to the infinite capacity and complexity of desire. But, we are forced to ask, in contradistinction

46. Augustine, *Confessions*, 86.
47. Augustine, *Confessions*, 226.
48. Augustine, *Confessions*, 274.
49. Augustine, *Confessions*, 111.
50. Augustine, *Confessions*, 183.
51. Augustine, *Confessions*, 183.

to the cataloging of abstract speculations on the divine he had earlier listed, what is *this* image of God? How would it differ from, say, Mary Karr eventually experiences with various Alcoholics Anonymous members who looked to a vague "higher power" to guide them out of themselves? Is this not an experience of the "numinous" that pushes one toward that which is beyond them, and which can, as Augustine seems to illustrate, be merged with the Christian tradition, no matter how vague it may seem at first glance?

What Augustine is reaching toward in his wonderfully poetic depiction of God, I believe, is an experience that seems to transcend the ordinary understanding of things: a light that extends beyond all space, a sweet smell that cannot be blown away, a hunger that cannot be satisfied but which also does not go away. These are attempts to grasp something far beyond what humanity can comprehend on its own terms. Indeed, this God seems to shatter the very capacity for understanding that we rest upon so frequently. It is also, if we can see it for what it is, a highly personal experience that informs our idea of God directly, even if it is an experience that must also be put into dialogue with centuries of speculation on other experiences of the divine.

I believe that what we encounter in his personal reflections on his experience of God indicate too that, perhaps, Augustine struggled with his own body, and with the very existence of all bodies. Concerning his own body, for example, we notice how he struggles a good deal to directly mourn his mother's death, a very strange, and no doubt cultural contextual moment, but one that says too a good deal about how he held his ability to mourn, even physically mourn, in check. We also notice how his body reacts in ways that reveal a deeper truth of his struggles, and which he himself seems to note, but also perhaps misses the significance of. As he recognizes in the midst of his inner struggle to articulate what he believes, "For I sounded very strange. My uttered words said less about the state of my mind than my forehead, cheeks, eyes, colour, and tone of voice."[52] In many ways, his very body speaks a truth that his words cannot follow—and yet he continues to place the mind above the body, the abstract speculations on God above the humanity of Jesus, again and again.[53] I think what goes on in his *Confessions* is that the unresolved tension between an abstract, philosophical (somewhat Platonic) deity—no doubt very much a product of Greek philosophical thought—has trouble coinciding with an embodied, incarnate God found in the person of Jesus. In many ways, Christian history has and continues to play out this tension (analogously) as one between

---

52. Augustine, *Confessions*, 146.
53. See the comments on the mind/body relation in Augustine, *Confessions*, 147.

the Christian taking up an "ideal" life of abstracted holiness and the messy reality in which we actually live.

What we see in Augustine's narration of his life story, the first real confessional autobiographical writing in the Christian tradition, is how one makes the movement from personal confession to the formulation of theology as an abstract speculation, because, as he himself says, he wants to say *something* about God, and also so that he doesn't fall back into the errors of many non-Christian or heretical groups. The fact that Augustine's influence upon the history of Christian thought has been so incredibly deep has nearly cemented the preference for the abstract characteristics of God over the vulnerability of God as displayed in the person of Jesus. And yet his willingness to ask the deeper questions about his experience of God within the context of his own life not only cements the command of Christianity to take the individual life seriously, but also challenges his own understanding of God, opening us up to new interpretations of how God might interact with our vulnerability and longing for relationship. What he initiates, then, is a trend within Christian literature to take seriously the life of the individual person that has only grown more pronounced over time.

CHAPTER THREE

Mary Karr

Taking the Risk of Putting One's Faith into Life and One's Life into Faith

Born on January 16, 1955 in east Texas, Mary Karr knew, even as a child, that writing was her true vocation. Speaking of poetry specifically, Karr remembers "from a very early age, when I read a poem, it was as if the poet's burning taper touched some charred filament in my rib cage to set me alight." Her initial forays into the world of published writing would take the form of poetry volumes, including Abacus *(1987) and* The Devil's Tour *(1993), before her memoir* The Liars' Club *(1995) would earn her critical acclaim and revolutionize the contemporary memoir scene. That work would spend more than a year at the top of the* New York Times *best seller list and earned plaudits from* The New Yorker, People, *and* Time, *opening the door for her to continue expanding the genre in* Cherry *(2000),* Lit *(2009), and* The Art of Memoir *(2015). Most recently, Karr has transformed a commencement address she delivered at Syracuse University in 2015 into* Now Go Out There and Get Curious *(2016), elevating her typical raw emotion into a uniquely crafted work of advice for the next generation. Karr is also a Guggenheim fellow in poetry, regularly contributes to* The New Yorker *and* The Atlantic, *and teaches at Syracuse University where she holds the Peck Professor of Literature Chair.*

Mary Karr's fairly recent memoir of her conversion story takes a form very similar to Augustine's *Confessions*, from what he would call sin and she would call brokenness, to a place of searching, to crawling toward something like faith within their lives. Though it may seem to some like a stretch of the imagination to place toward the beginning of a book dedicated to uncovering the life of faith and its transmissions someone who seems to be at times irreverent, cantankerous, and so bluntly honest that one wonders whether she would even be allowed into certain churches, let alone into a communion of saints, this is just what I intend to do. In fact, as we will see become steadfastly clearer as I continue to unfold what constitutes the life of faith, is that the story of Karr's life is not something unfamiliar to the development of a "living saint": hers is rather more like its precondition. Her ability to string her life into a coherent series of words, engaged through a brutally honest scrutiny of herself and her actions, is what, to my mind, makes her autobiography *Lit* a perfect place to begin.

Karr's entire life seems to have been formed under the sign of language, of putting oneself into words—a point very dear to the history of theology, ever since John's gospel proclaimed the *logos*, or Word, made flesh the center of all creation. But what does this mean, to have a Word made flesh and to see such a Word as generative of all created matter? Is this Word the order latent within the entire universe, the cosmos brought into human form that we are contemplating? How would such a thing affect how we understand our own relationship to language? What might such a relationship look like? And how might such a relationship work its way into Karr's life and its retelling?

Recalling the impact that a single line of the German thinker Ernst Cassier's *The Philosophy of Symbolic Forms* had upon her in college, Karr notes early in her story how words shape "our realities, our perceptions, giving them an authority God had for other generations."[1] This is an interesting thought to register, that words have taken the place of the divine within the modern world (we might think, for example, of Cervantes or Shakespeare and their creations of particular subjectivities in the modern period). Karr seems to intuit the significance of this as she tries to put her life into words: "Words warranted my devotion—not drugs, not boys. That's why I clung to the myth that poetry could somehow magically still my scrambled innards."[2] Even early in her years, as she recalls, there was a sense that words can provide an order or a foundation to her life. The inquiry she raises is how poetry could do this, how it could heal her in a way that the divine appeared not to—a quest for identity through language that has often sought to supplant the place of the religious in our modern world.

It is noteworthy as well that she uses the word *myth* in this context to describe her relationship to language, for we will have to ask if this is or was a myth that she harbored. Was it a false one, or an accurate one destined to

---

1. Karr, *Lit*, 40.
2. Karr, *Lit*, 40.

give her the stability and identity she was searching for? If her understanding of poetry was that it could heal, why was she so alone and broken until she discovered faith? And just what kind of faith was it that she found? Certainly, I would note, even such a discovery of faith does not preclude the possibility that she ultimately does find redemption and faith in words, though perhaps after returning to them from an altogether different point of view.

The turn that Karr takes from abstract poetry and novel writing to memoir—the basis for her writing in general[3]—is founded upon a shift in determining what is ultimately important to her, as well as what she knows best. Recalling some advice given to her from a mentor long ago concerning her poetry writing, she relates: "When I bristled that I'd been a philosophy major in college, he said, And that's all you're telling anybody. What you took in college. You're pointing right back at your own head, telling everybody how smart it is. Write what you know."[4] And this is the irony of her search for what was already within her: she is committed to clinging to the power of the myth of words in her life rather than some sort of a god, and yet she is not actually able to put her genuine self into words. As she highlights in the introduction, "Any way I tell this story is a lie."[5] She is almost obsessed with the act of confession, of trying to figure out what is true and what is not. What she signals through this struggle is how our capacity for self-deception permeates our experience of confession. Learning that you have been in error is a lengthy process.

At an early point in her life, however, she does not write about her life in a meaningful way; she merely repeats what sounds "smart" to others. She becomes, as such, completely subject to "other" traditions that define her in ways she is unable to escape. And, in many ways, *this* is the reality of the all-too-modern predicament that we have such trouble facing: in the absence of religion, we believe ourselves to be "free," when, in reality, we become trapped by other traditions that are so difficult for some of us to even recognize as present. And their hold upon us, for that very reason, becomes doubly ensnaring. We believe that maintaining the free use of our words means that we are free, and we fail to notice how those words are actually given to us by others outside of us, often imposed upon us in ways that we would normally reject.[6] In Karr's case, her mother, her upbringing, and her

---

3. See her more recent *The Art of Memoir*.
4. Karr, *Lit*, 57.
5. Karr, *Lit*, 1.
6. One might think here of the more recent rise of certain non-denominational churches that claim to be "doctrine free," when, in truth, they are often highly concerned about people believing particular things in particular ways. What this represents, in many ways, is the fundamental reforming ("Protestant") urge to purify things which

alcohol abuse all have a hold on her that she will spend the rest of the book trying to come to terms with.

Despite the presence of this particular "myth" in her life, however, Karr begins to stumble into what will eventually become an acceptance of a more or less "traditional" faith (in this case, the Catholic Church), and her language begins to record such shifts throughout her memoir. In the midst of her failing marriage, one that she had sought to fill in the wound of her own family's lack of love (as she'll later say: "Why hasn't his love filled the black hole I've been pouring booze into?"[7]), Karr observes of her tendency toward drinking heavily that "Slurping these spirits is soul preparation, a warped communion, myself serving as god, priest, and congregation".[8] The substitution of words for God has resulted in the substitution of herself and her actions for God, and this leaves her in a certain state of destitution, though she is not sure how to extricate herself from it, or how to revisit her connection to words in light of it. What she demonstrates, if I can put things this way, is how we often want to be the master of our own narrative, a task that refuses any act of translation, as I have described it, and rather seeks to establish a definitive account of the self once and for all.

She maintains throughout her presentation of her life's story, however, a deep ironic detachment from traditions—one that, I would suggest, keeps her at a certain remove from religious traditions in her youth, but which also safeguards her from making some false steps. In a specific sense, an ironic distance appears as the only way to establish a clearly defined sense of self apart from the traditions that tried to claim her. She acknowledges at the same time having been subject, as are many of us, to the "myth of autonomy," of "breaking free" from such traditions. In the case of someone obsessed with breaking free from their parents and not being influenced by them, for example, they become almost obsessed with their parents; the myth of autonomy can bind them even further. In this context, in attempting *not* to become her mother, Karr is becoming *just like* her mother. Karr's story is therefore a journey from the myth of autonomy to the realization that you are bound up in relationships that have a claim on you. Her irony and humor are defense mechanisms, to be sure, but they are also critical tools to discern where reality lies and to aid in the construction of a self when such a task had seemed so precarious. Going beyond this, she will

---

has become internalized to such a degree that we do not even recognize its hold upon us. This phenomenon, it should be noted, arises in any given institutional structure (Catholic and Orthodox included) and is an internal impulse for an authentic "experience" that can run to extremes in many ways.

7. Karr, *Lit*, 222.
8. Karr, *Lit*, 159.

eventually be able to achieve a sort of substitutionary logic, or translation, of one concept for another that will aid the development within her of something like a faith that enables her to find the fractures within her narrative as possible moments of transformative encounter.

In a parenthetical comment, she notes how "You could say I needed God then, which notion would've gagged me like a maggot. But if you're a nonbeliever, replace the word God with truth or mercy."[9] As such, she extends the logic of substitution in the other direction. Instead of exchanging God or religion for words or herself, she mobilizes the very notion of God into something else: truth or mercy. She starts to observe a new logic in which old religious "traditions" begin to reveal the deeper, foundational relations at work within them. In essence, her willingness to translate God into other paradigms and terminologies will assist her in discerning the role that religious thought has played in the life of human beings—in the service of truth and not apart from it—and this will, in the end, as she herself will recognize, save her from herself.

This simple act of translation, I argue, is what allows her to realize later on that she had killed off the possibility of God's presence in her life without even realizing it, for she had denied the role that "God" or "truth" or "mercy" plays within the sphere of human life:

> To kill truth to defend my fear was—in one way—to kill God. Oedipus wound up murdering his father because he ignored the divine warning that he would. When he learned the truth, his guilt so ruined him, he stabbed out his own eyes. Without truth, I was blind, worshipping my own fear-driven thoughts, and the ground beneath me never stopped heaving.[10]

In many ways, this is akin to asking yourself if you have ever had someone tell you something true, and argued against it, because of your fear. To do such a thing, you kill something, *truth* in fact, in that instance. You can't claim you know God and fight against truth at the same time. Any place in your life where truth is present, accepting that truth is another way of accepting the presence of God. This is, among other things, a wonderful critique of religious people who deny truth but claim they love God. In Karr's formulation, to preserve "God" was to open the door to truth in her life in whatever way it presented itself, and likewise to heed its revealing of the ways she had been serving only her own fears. To not "kill God" in her life, she has likewise first to take stock of the vision of God she did have, even

---

9. Karr, *Lit*, 184.
10. Karr, *Lit*, 184–85.

though she had had an irreligious upbringing and felt that she truly had no conception of God to work with in the first place.

As another member of AA puts the implicit but unasked question to her eventually: "First off—can't you see this?—you have a concept of God already. It's one who's pissed at you."[11] To which she responds, "Which is oddly true, given my godless upbringing. Where had that come from?"[12] What she comes to realize is that "It's like you have to break up with the guy who's beating the crap out of you before you can scan the room and find the nice guy who's got a crush on you."[13] This formulation sounds very much like Augustine when he says, "God, I drifted far from you, and you did not stop me." This is the language of lovers, but this time not emphasizing the fantasy of romance, but the often pathetic "weakness" of real love, that which is reflective, I would add, of the "weakness" of God.[14] To love anyone is to be weak. If God is love, to know love is to likewise know God in some measure, and this love too makes one weak. Simply put, the "weakness of God" means that we are not going to get hit over the head with God's action, not the real God at any rate, the one we should expect or wait upon. Augustine's efforts against himself to construct an all-powerful, all-knowing deity that could control all aspects of life (what he meant through his use of the term *predestination*) will not work here. Karr's discovery was rather that God patiently waits for us to realize that God has been in love with us since we were born, since we were conceived in our mother's womb, as the prophet Jeremiah had put it. In many ways, this is generally true of parents and their children, in that they will give the child a sometimes free rein to hurt themselves, but they will be there when they are needed after the child has hurt themselves.

This reworking of her idea of God is not easily done, however, not least because of the cultural difficulties that Christians and other religious believers have set before her. In fact, one of Karr's greatest struggles with adopting some form of faith in her life is taking seriously the narrative of God that Christians themselves often present to the world. This is no small matter, too, since it is precisely the relationships we have with those around us that does bring us a sense of what a given life of faith is about, for better or for worse. As she described her own struggle to appropriate belief in God at one point in her life: "I'm trying to start hearing the word *God* without some reflexive flinch that coughs out the word *idiot*. Maybe, as somebody suggested, I'd have to practice internally repeating God-specific sentences to hear them in my

---

11. Karr, *Lit*, 217.
12. Karr, *Lit*, 217.
13. Karr, *Lit*, 217.
14. Caputo, *The Weakness of God*.

own voice."[15] And practice, especially in the Catholic variance she discovers, will become, in the end, what allows her to see God in a wholly new light within her life. Though it may sound strange to suggest something so oriented toward the practical and the everyday, the sheer discipline of routinely trying to access a space to even talk about the divine can actually lead one to God. This is precisely the route by which Karr more or less successfully encounters God: she first makes space for God, and only then is she able to let God enter her life. A significant take-away from this insight is that, in relationships too, it is similarly important to cultivate and foster space for one another, without any projections being forced upon one another, otherwise there really is no relationship—as in an obsessive "relationship" or in a marriage that has fallen into a rut of codependency.

One of the reasons that Alcoholics Anonymous (AA) has been so popular and helpful to many over the years, and why pastors often seek to replicate its successes in churches (though, I believe, many people in the pews often fail to see exactly why it has been so successful), is that it takes things "one day at a time"; it tries to see nothing but the very up-close and personal within life, not getting bogged down with unhelpful abstractions or speculations on the nature of that which we don't fully know. Such a focus, and also *release*, aids the individual who submits to its program in forming the personal discipline needed to find what had been lacking in their life, not by abstracting into one's own mind, but in very practical terms: by having to confess to the group itself what you have been up to, and in having to confront people you have wronged, actually confess to them as well the various misdeeds you have done to them.

Religion, for the most part, can't get close to this kind of honesty, precisely because it is too painful for most people to accept as a necessary step in the process of coming closer to others in their life. Religion, for far too long, in many ways, has been about keeping people distant from one another, abstracted even from their own selves—transcendent, then, in the wrong sense of the word. If this insight is on to something, we should perhaps leave "transcendence" up to the sciences that dazzle us with their ability to make the unknown known to us, and start taking a look at the intimate details of our lives that we already know all too well, but have generally gotten entirely wrong.[16]

15. Karr, *Lit*, 217–18.

16. The philosopher of science Bruno Latour has, in fact, claimed that the difference between religion and science is that, as counterintuitive as it might sound, religion deals with that which is up-close and personal, that which is near to us and often very underwhelming, but very, very real (the immanent), and science deals with that which is far away, almost impossible to observe up close and which therefore inspires a very

The main point I want to emphasize through Karr's work is that "truth" is often taken to refer to a contextual location or place, one that reflects our embodied position in this world. There are "truths" that we encounter on a daily basis and that do not appear to us as "transcendent" of our world. That is, they are "embodied" (i.e., involve even our bodies).[17] In contrast, when we speak of "Truth," we are often referring to an abstract, transcendent reality (i.e., God, the divine, or the Good, etc.). These are often very difficult to conceptualize precisely because they often lack a body that we can see, touch, taste, hear, etc. This is traditionally why "Truth" often becomes too heavily equated with the mind and also with reason—as Augustine seems to have fallen victim to as well.

Karr challenges this division between Truth/truth and Mind/body when she talks about how they have to go together, and how you can't kill off the "truth" without also killing off the "Truth." Yet, in the history of theology and in churches even today, there are people who would rather talk about "Truth," but don't want to talk about the "truths" before their eyes (e.g., unequal gender roles, poverty issues, what's really going on in unhealthy relationships, the desires of one's body, etc.). These are yet precisely the places where "truth" needs to be merged with "Truth" so that our picture of truth becomes entirely one with the context of our own lives. To engage this focal point is to address directly what so many addictions try to get away from (e.g., eating disorders): the reality of the body itself.

Trying to locate God within the everyday discipline she is seeking, Karr attempts to perceive what this "God" might actually look like to her. As someone in AA advises her, and which she takes to heart as a helpful instructive needing to be implemented in her life: "You can make up your own concept of what to revere. Like nature . . . some Great Spirit, like the Native Americans have. Talk to it. Practice reverence at it. Attend it the way you've been attending these fears of yours."[18] From this perspective, she has to learn a new type of language to move from the myth of autonomy and of worshipping her own fears to finding something else beyond her fears and learning to relate to herself (and others) in an entirely new way. And so, quite plainly and boldly, she does, though the attempt seems to her, at the beginning, as an almost impossibly insincere effort: "Higher power,

---

real awe in us when we finally observe what it sees (the transcendent). For Latour, whose lead I follow in this, religion is the "language of lovers" (of relationship, then) and science a very specific discourse of discovery of that which is extra-ordinary. See Latour, *Rejoicing*. See also Miller, *Speculative Grace*.

17. On the role of the body in women's autobiographical writings, in particular, see Smith, *Subjectivity, Identity, and the Body*.

18. Karr, *Lit*, 219.

I say snidely. Where the fuck have you been?"[19] But, then, despite her irreverence, she immediately begins to sense something else taking place in her initiative to let the dialogue begin, something that opens her up to a dialogue and movement beyond the narrative she had constructed of her autonomous self and her "warped" faith that had actually denied relationship rather than be open to it:

> The silence envelops me. There's something scary there, some blanket of dread around me that feels like God's perennial absence, his abandonment, if he does exist. (Now I'd call it my deliberately practiced refusal of his presence.) It's hard to sit in. A few seconds later, I say: Thanks for keeping me sober today. Then I get up.[20]

The singular effort somehow moves her, you might say, and she tries to leave the space she is barely keeping open for herself; though suddenly she wants more of whatever it was she began to sense moving through the moment. In other words, she isn't willing to give up so easily on herself or on this God she is searching for, and this is the case despite what she actually thinks about herself and her own unwillingness to take any such experience of prayer seriously: "I flop back on my knees. And help me. Help. Me. Help me to feel better so I can believe in you, you subtle bastard."[21]

What Karr emphasizes through her reticence to pray, but also her willingness to work at times against herself so that she might actually formulate the words that will comprise her prayer (in my words, to allow some *translation* to permeate her *definition* of herself), is what should be the very essence of prayer, but is often lacking: it is first and foremost the recognition of a relationship taking place, the creation of a space for acknowledging one another that is capable of blossoming into something like friendship. She senses a blank space and enters into it. In this way, facing the silence is the only way to have a relationship with something beyond oneself. As such, we often don't know who people are when we first meet them; we must only initially be willing to access a blank space. Rather than trying to fill up the blank space with phones or chatter (e.g., to project something into this space), we have to learn to live in the silence, and this is as true in relationships as it is in prayer. One enters into prayer, whether or not they believe in God, in order to begin the relationship, and, as times passes, to watch the relationship grow. Such is what Karr will come to realize the moment after

---

19. Karr, *Lit*, 219.
20. Karr, *Lit*, 219–20.
21. Karr, *Lit*, 220.

the words leave her mouth: "This is my first prayer—a peevish start, tight-lipped, mean of spirit, but a prayer nonetheless."[22]

When her prayers start to become a sort of foundation for something new in her life, a process that takes some time to unfold, she is even willing to concede that maybe it's her convincing herself of something beyond her fears, or maybe it's God—she calls it a "draw" between them.[23] What was really transpiring, we might say, was a deepening and securing of her desire *for* God, for relationship itself then, something that can be held onto even without God's presence always being detected, something which is essential to the development of one's faith, as I have been indicating so far.

One of the last prayers of Jesus before his death in fact is: "why have you abandoned me?" What such a prayer demonstrates is how we often have a fantasy that prayer is something more than this recognition of an absence, of the silence. But what prayer actually becomes is a search and a crying out, a sitting in the emptiness or nothingness that allows one to access something beyond themselves. This notion, of course, is not as strange as it might sound, for why should the human being, with its very limited capacity to detect anything like an immaterial or supernatural presence—whatever these things are or are not—be able to suddenly know when it is in the presence of the divine? The Scriptures are simply full of moments where an individual misrecognizes the divine and must be told, in fact, that God is somewhere close, much closer to them in reality than they had anticipated (as with Samuel mishearing God's voice and thinking that it is the priest Eli's in 1 Samuel 3).

These situations are, however, what mainly constitute the beginnings of a revelation from God to an individual: misrecognition, being corrected by someone who has experience with this sort of thing, going back and trying to listen again, and then discerning for oneself what one is hearing. This is in many ways the vital role that religious community and tradition can, and do, play in a person's life, and, as such, is often the first critique against the mythology of the autonomous self, as Karr had described it.

As paradoxical as it might sound, what Karr discovers is an essential insight for the development of faith, and one which mirrors Augustine: you have to want God before you find God. As she describes this struggle with desire in the context of her friend's insight, "This faint yearning was not belief itself, but wanting to believe. Willingness, it was which for months Joan had been telling me I lacked."[24] Such a willingness will even be present later on when she prays prayers she "hardly" believes, as she puts it, but

---

22. Karr, *Lit*, 220.
23. Karr, *Lit*, 225.
24. Karr, *Lit*, 226.

that she takes "blind comfort from."²⁵ To be sure, from her perspective, this "blind comfort" isn't necessarily a bad thing at times either, though it may sound like such prayers are indeed the "opium of the masses," as Karl Marx had once put it. Such a dismissal of faith or of religion, however, misses the essential dialectic within the life of faith between faith and doubt (or uncertainty), as between that which provides comfort and that which afflicts us. Lest we forget how important this dynamic is to the life of faith, we might recall how even the Roman soldier in the Gospel had once cried out to Jesus, "Lord, I believe. Help my unbelief" (Mark 9:24). This oscillation between belief and unbelief, strange as it may sound—between not recognizing or knowing the presence of the divine in our lives, but in searching for it nonetheless—is what Christianity underscores to the world as part of the nature of faith itself, something that is often heightened in certain persons who struggle with such paradoxes in their lives.

Karr's struggle with alcoholism, I would argue, is a moment of such apparent contradiction that actually pushes her towards faith in a genuine manner not readily available to many people, at least not those unwilling to fight against themselves and the ways in which they are dominated by an imbalanced perspective. Her addiction to alcohol becomes, for that reason, both a good thing and a bad thing, a blessing and curse alike. One could argue that it is a good thing, as she herself will, insofar as she is somewhat unable to resist the truth that appears before her in her life: "*One day at a time* forces you to reckon with the instant you actually occupy, rather than living in fantasy la-la that never arrives."²⁶ This disciplined practice will ring true despite the fact that her disease can also threaten to bring her down, time and again. This is of course the trap of her "disease" that is alcoholism, but also a dark turn toward herself alone, her blindness and her ability to deceive herself, the severing of any chance for relationship (or love) to flourish in her life. This is, in other words, the dark myth of autonomy that causes us to turn away from the depths of relationship offered to us at various points in our lives.

At one point, after she catches herself in a deliberate lie to cover up her drinking abuses, she defines her condition as such: "I have a disease whose defining symptom is believing you don't have a disease . . . but I'm not ready to stop listening to the screwed-up inner voice that's been ordering me around for a lifetime. My head thinks it can kill me . . . and go on living without me."²⁷ What she is highlighting is the sheer and perplexing difficulty

---

25. Karr, *Lit*, 300.
26. Karr, *Lit*, 208, emphasis in the original.
27. Karr, *Lit*, 196, de-emphasized from the original.

of trying to cure something that you don't believe you have in the first place. I would wager, in addition to this, that such a blindness is a major part of the problem in considering the role of faith within today's world: we have diseases that we don't even consider as diseases (like affluence, for example, or the domination of reason over the real complexity of the human person), and which prevent us from embracing a much more multifaceted domain of faith. By disregarding religion or the life of faith entirely, we have no idea what we actually lose, and no idea what it could do for us. Religious persons, far from seeing the difference, for the most part, often make matters even worse, for themselves and for others.

What Karr comes to realize about herself is that there is a certain (non) rational conclusion she has been heading toward, and it is one that I think a fair number of us struggle with without fully knowing it: the head seeks to go on living without the fullness of herself, including her body—which was at the time being occasionally ravished by alcohol—promoting a kind of "disembodied" life. This is precisely the kind of rejection of the fullness of the human person that I am gesturing toward directly, one that is committed to ignoring the ways in which we are much more than just our brains and the rational arguments that tell us not to look deeper than what we see on the surface of things, because we cannot detect that which we cannot see at work. This is the very condition that undermines any movement toward the divine in our lives.

As John Henry Newman had already pointed out, there are a complex series of networks and probabilities that truly make up the life of faith. By relying solely on reason, Karr eventually came to realize that she had been neglecting the other parts of herself—the fullness of her own humanity. Her struggles with alcoholism hence, almost ironically, reminded her of the other parts of herself that she needed in order to embrace her own humanity. In this, the body made itself known to her, as it makes itself known to all of us, through the impulses and desires we feel. Missing the fullness of her own life, we can now see, was the main reason why she had missed the presence of God in her life, as the intimacy God (*or* a lover *or* a friend) works in a person's life as it moves through one's entire, embodied existence.

This problematic ignorance of the wholeness of the human person seen in relation to God becomes clearer to Karr as she holds a conversation with another AA member, who tells her: "You have to start giving the higher-power thing a try—it's the one suggestion you skirted. You didn't pray."[28] And, as her friend continues, "Faith is not a feeling, she says. It's a set of actions. By taking the actions, you demonstrate more faith than someone who

---

28. Karr, *Lit*, 217.

actually has experienced the rewards of prayer and so feels hope. Fake it till you make it. Didn't you fake half your life drinking?"[29] What this person is pointing Karr toward are the practices that are embodied, working thus *with* one's body—not just mental exercises that one assents to.

This insight is what makes liturgical practices in a faith community such a significant piece in the puzzle of faith. In taking the embodiment of faith more seriously than she had ever done, Karr is pointing toward the importance of engaging in practices of faith rather than just talking or thinking about it. Later, in fact, another AA participant will even go so far as to say that the prayers and meditations are really another way to remind the mind that it has a body: "You do it to teach yourself something. When my disease has ahold of me, it tells me my suffering is special or unique, but it's the same as everybody's. I kneel to put my body in that place, because otherwise, my mind can't grasp it."[30]

As Karr herself will experience while in prayer, a sentiment not of minor significance to the development of one's self in faith: "I feel small, kneeling there. Small and needy and inadequate. Pathetic, even. Like somebody who can't handle things."[31] In essence, our bodily actions remind us that we are vulnerable. This practice in particular allows Karr to realize her own vulnerability and smallness, which are the things that allow all of us to connect with others, ourselves, *and* God. Jean Vanier, for example, has said that being a Christian is a process of becoming little—a point that Henri Nouwen will reiterate later for us. This smallness, you might say, is a form of poverty that should become the cornerstone of one's life of faith. What we often miss in such reflections, however, is that it is precisely these embodied practices that move us deeply and allow us to see how we are intended to be both a body and a mind, inseparably together, though we often have little understanding of either, let alone how they work together.

Despite not having a very fixed notion of the divine, of God, Karr tries to discover the merits of prayer. Though this may sound highly paradoxical to those of us who struggle with the distance we feel from ourselves and so search out a reconciliation through reason alone, I think that this approach to prayer is not such a bad idea to contemplate, for how are we to know anything of God unless we enter into a relationship with God, unless we first hold open a space for relationship, and so faith, to take place? Moreover, even for those within a given faith tradition, so again says Christianity, you oscillate at times between various conceptualizations of

---

29. Karr, *Lit*, 217.
30. Karr, *Lit*, 241.
31. Karr, *Lit*, 275.

God. A person's resistance to prayer, and so to God as well, becomes, in this sense, another way of seeing only our own failure to reach out for that which lies beyond us, and thus it becomes too a key to our fermenting unhappiness with ourselves:

> Leaves aren't yet tumbling from the trees, but for me, all color is leaching from the landscape. I'm blunted, muted, starved, yet stubbornly refusing the one suggestion everyone sober for very long makes: prayer. I recoil from any talk of spiritual crap, though I can't fail to notice that the happier, less angry ex-drunks talk about such matters without any strapped-on, phony-sounding zeal. Joan the Bone claims some nonbelievers use the group as a higher power.[32]

Prayer, from this point of view, is a willingness to be open. What Karr simply wants is what she sees in the people around her who have achieved some semblance of inner peace, and, to be honest, this *is* a very appealing thing—the radiant peace with oneself that one finds occasionally among those who live a life of faith to the fullest, without fear and without hesitation to admit of their "smallness." It is also another profound indicator of the truth we touch when we conceive of faith as a form of relationality. And so Karr begins to move toward a life of prayer as a form of dialogue with a God she doesn't even know. The advice from a friend that she follows, when experiencing a moment of financial struggle in her life, is: "Just pray every day for ninety days and see if your life gets better. Call it a scientific experiment. You might not get the money, but you might find relief from anxiety about money. What do you have to lose?"[33] Yet, and this is what we should be attentive to here, does this suggestion mean to Karr, or to anyone else for that matter, that her prayers will receive a direct answer? Quite to the contrary. "As Emile Zola once noted: The road to Lourdes is littered with crutches, but not one wooden leg," she admits.[34] Yet she does feel as if prayer allowed her to stay sober, eventually to receive a grant for her work and to open up her career. As she will describe the effect of prayer upon her life, "Whether you believe prayers like this affect external affairs doesn't matter. They measure the overhaul in my psyche and character."[35]

What Karr is ultimately noticing, and I believe this is at least part of the reason why her story reflects a certain authenticity in terms of a struggle for faith, is that there is something at work in the nature of prayer itself that

---

32. Karr, *Lit*, 207.
33. Karr, *Lit*, 219.
34. Karr, *Lit*, 255.
35. Karr, *Lit*, 296.

affects a person's entire disposition, and not just a static form of one-way communication such as many imagine prayer to be. This is not a stale version of "ask and receive" that a lot of us imagine prayer to exist as (in relation to an omnipotent deity who simply grants wishes), and that we also realize ends eventually in disappointment for most everyone who sees it that way. Indeed, how many of us approach relationships this way, as something that can give us what we want, rather than going into a relationship in the hopes of becoming more vulnerable to the other we have opened ourselves to?

What I think is important to comprehend here about the nature of prayer in Karr's experience is how the genuine granting of prayer, even if it were to (appear to) occur in a literal manner, is not what we should focus on, or take with us. This is the real eye-opening point. Such experiences of prayer can provoke a deep gratitude within us, to be sure, but it is the way in which gratitude affects us on a very deep level that matters—this is what we should be taking with us as we go forward, not some "amazing" story of the miraculous bound to make just as many turn away from our story as it makes others turn toward it.

We might in fact compare such a position to Paul's comment on knowing someone who travelled to the third heaven, about which he will say "nothing is to be gained by it" (1 Corinthians 12:1). He even chooses not to talk about such things: "But I refrain from it, so that no one may think better of me than what is seen in me or heard from me, even considering the exceptional character of the revelations" (1 Corinthians 1:6–7). Similarly, we find such thoughts present in Saint John of the Cross's recognition that such matters are purely private, and do not help to build up the faith of others, and, if they did build up someone's faith, then that person's faith is really very weak in nature. The faith we should be seeking is such that we do not rely at all upon such miraculous tales.[36] Miracles are great, to be sure, but they aren't the building blocks of Christian faith. As Paul had put it: "For Jews demand signs and Greeks desire wisdom, but we proclaim Christ crucified, a stumbling block to Jews and foolishness to Gentiles, but to those who are the called, both Jews and Greeks, Christ the power of God and the wisdom of God" (1 Corinthians 1:22–24). There is something else that the life of faith is centered upon, and which I am pursuing throughout this book, something more to do with the recognition of our own brokenness, or "smallness" as Karr might put it, "Christ crucified" within us even, rather than with a "successful" source of wisdom or the miraculous.

What Karr begins to comprehend in her own life is that the "acceptance" of one's self as it is, in its failures as much as in its successes, is the big

---

36. John of the Cross, *The Collected Works of St. John of the Cross*.

piece sought after in the prayer puzzle—to accept whatever reality we are in, looking for "practical solutions rather than issuing orders in prayer."[37] Such insight leads her eventually to a different understanding of what it means to acquire faith within one's life, something that is paradoxically achieved, and at times when we might least expect it to come about. In her words, "Whatever you want emotionally, you have to start giving away. Want to find company? Open up to other people."[38] Another way to put it might be to suggest that if you want faith, you should try giving faith to others, or learning to let go of the "strong" faith you once thought essential to the structure of your own faith life, as strange as this may sound.

I believe we might also take some time here to re-examine the nature of obedience in light of these comments, for in many ways this is what Karr was being "taught" at this point in her life: what does it mean to be humble before that which is larger than us, but also to follow it in going beyond yourself? Why is *obedience* such a reviled word today, and with respect to so many authorities, religious or not? What does it mean to refuse obedience as a virtue connected explicitly to faith? And how might we learn a good deal about practicing faith simply *through* obedience?

The fear, of course, is that "blind" obedience will rule the day, and that reason will be thrust out the window. But what if there is so much more to obedience than this? What if practicing obedience was something that helped to shape our faith in more significant ways than we have realized? One could, for example, come to think of obedience as a form of trusting the ground underneath our feet, those persons and traditions that have brought us this far, and which are here for a reason, though it is one that we must yet discern.[39] A good example for many people is to be found in a mentorship in which you trust in and obey someone's advice, and realize at the same time that you didn't know what you were doing beforehand and so are grateful for the advice given. Religious instruction *should* be little different than this in many ways, though, in practice, far fewer people experience it this way.

In Karr's life, prayer teaches her a new sense of obedience, one that looks out beyond herself for the answers she needs. What she finds eventually becomes a practice that causes her to have a "revelation" moment while working at a homeless shelter, as deplorably unpleasant as this experience was for her. At a certain point, Karr felt, at long last, compelled to

---

37. Karr, *Lit*, 316.

38. Karr, *Lit*, 321.

39. See the remarks on obedience in Martin, *The Jesuit Guide to (Almost) Everything*, 266–304.

"surrender," the classic way to understand obedience, but which is altered slightly as it also means, for her, to "yield up what scares you. Yield up what makes you want to scream and cry. Enter into that quiet."[40]

A few moments later, she will "let go" while on her knees before the toilet, opening herself up to a sense of joy that she had never felt in her life before.[41] This is all part of the process of letting go of the shame, fear, and bitterness that she had been storing up and utilizing for so long, the benefit of obedience that we rarely hear people talk about.[42] It was for her a process she later sums up, in the context of having to spend some time in a facility to help her manage her "disease" of alcoholism, as such:

> In the loony bin, I surrendered—not full bore, the way saints do, once and for all, blowing away my ego in perfect service to God—not even close. But watching the world through chicken wire convinced me that my unguided thought process would no doubt swerve me into concrete. Before, I'd feared surrender would sand me down to nothing. Now I've started believing it can bloom me more solidly into myself.[43]

She feels, in a very realistic manner, *saved*, allowing us to begin to see why such terms have such a strong religious resonance, and this is the case despite centuries of the abuse and misuse of terms such as *saved*.

There is no doubt that Karr's understanding of what she has been through at this point is the outcome of a more mature position, but also a very difficult one to arrive at, mainly because to arrive at this particular juncture in one's life means to have "dislocated" oneself from one's former self—the "old self" that Paul had spoken about earlier. What Karr encounters in this precise space is an opening toward other possibilities than she has seen before, something that both releases her from what has bound her, but also adds new dimensions of choice that can be difficult to grasp as well.

> There's an initial uprush of relief at first, then—for me, anyway—a profound dislocation. My old assumptions about how the world works are buried, yet my new ones aren't yet operational. There's been a death of sorts, but without a few days in hell, no resurrection is possible. You don't have to be Christian for the metaphor to make sense, psychologically speaking.[44]

---

40. Karr, *Lit*, 234.
41. Karr, *Lit*, 283.
42. Karr, *Lit*, 303.
43. Karr, *Lit*, 299.
44. Karr, *Lit*, 260.

I think Karr is right to suggest that you don't have to be religious to recognize this process of personal growth, which should also mean that you don't have to discard religious insights either. Indeed, such a freeing of perspectives, if anything, should cause us to re-examine the strengths to be found within a given religious tradition and why they have been so meaningful for people throughout the centuries. What Karr discovers, and here through her utilization of the daily Examen, a common recollection of the day's events popularized among the Jesuits, is that, in her own life, "the spiritual lens—even just the nightly gratitude list and going over each day's actions—is starting to rewrite the story of my life in the present, and I begin to feel like somebody snatched out of the fire, salvaged, saved."[45]

Now, to be clear, she isn't having an experience of the heavens opening up before her very eyes, which some of us mistakenly think will be the only thing to bring us to faith. Her experience is rather so completely mundane as to seem unbelievable when she recounts how much it has helped her to live the life of faith. The presence of God that she begins to discern is rather a subtle but entirely pervasive force moving through her life. She even notes parenthetically how

> Vis-à-vis God speaking to me, I don't mean the voice of Charlton Heston playing Moses booming from on high, but reversals of attitude so contrary to my typical thoughts—so solidly true—as to seem divinely external. And quiet these thoughts are, strong and quiet. View it as some sane self or healthy ego taking charge, if you like.[46]

In other words, "I've stopped figuring so hard and begun to wait, sometimes with increasing hope, to be shown."[47] The stress she places, then, is upon learning obedience to that which is seemingly *beyond* her as much as it now lives *within* her, a strange paradox perhaps, but one that gives the Christian tradition a powerful scope to extend itself into every life that it encounters.

What her behavior likewise exhibits is an admission of what we might call the "smallness," or weakness, of faith, what Newman would've said was something akin to demonstrating the proper relationship between reason and faith.[48] This position of humility that we now find ourselves in is exactly

---

45. Karr, *Lit*, 304.
46. Karr, *Lit*, 276.
47. Karr, *Lit*, 276.
48. See, among other places, the sermons given on the subject in John Henry Newman, *Fifteen Sermons Preached before the University of Oxford Between A.D. 1826 and 1843*.

what makes us human, and what allows us to see the fullness of our humanity as what undergirds the life of faith, not as what rejects it.

Her eventual search for the community of a church, as the religious community that acknowledges the "higher power" we can all surrender to, is a difficult one, but one she is blatantly honest about going through. Her son, Dev, at this point in his life, simply wants "to see if God's there"—a poignant and critically productive way to put it.[49] What she ultimately finds appealing in the Catholic Church, amongst all the other churches she visits but finds herself not swayed by, is the people's "collective surrender," as she puts it.[50] It is in one particular parish that she encounters a very down-to-earth priest named Father Kane, who informs her that "God's after you. Struggle all you want."[51] Through his blunt honesty, she herself comes to realize that there may be something for her within this community, though she does not hesitate to declare how strange she feels when trying to pray with others: "There's something different about praying in company—I can't deny it—once you get over feeling like a poser."[52] She will even eventually become immersed in the *Spiritual Exercises* of Saint Ignatius, trying to find God in all things, as he would put it.

What Karr experiences, I would wager, is a gained sense of perspective, of proper proportions actually, on her own life and struggles, that comes through being part of a community of faith that can assist us in seeing our proper dimensions as they really are, "knowing our place" in this sense. Though this isn't always, historically, what the church has been, it is certainly what the church *should* be: a place to recognize the reality of yourself, in all its brokenness, but then also to feel that you have a place amongst such people striving to live their lives together, in openness and charity toward one another.

Karr still had to sort through her views on the Bible, of course, as well as the reasons why she believed in certain divine interventions in her life—which may or may not have anything to do with God—but these are less significant things in the grander scheme of coming to the life of faith. Hence, she only slowly starts to use "the G-word"—*God*—and this is how things should be for far more people too quick to use God's name in whatever way they think fit.[53] Being slow to invoke God and quick to criticize its wrong usage is in reality the point at which theology properly speaking begins. It

---

49. Karr, *Lit*, 331, de-emphasized from the original.
50. Karr, *Lit*, 335.
51. Karr, *Lit*, 337.
52. Karr, *Lit*, 337.
53. Karr, *Lit*, 349.

is only at this point, after the relationship has begun, that one begins the arduous task of discerning what is a good theological proposition and what is not, and of then going through one's beliefs one by one, often with other persons to accompany one along the way.

One of the larger problems in today's world, I would argue, is that we live in such a fragmented age where so many live under the myth of autonomy, that I am not sure if many people ever really reach this stage of theological reflection. Maybe this is a good thing in some ways, as it forces us to reconsider the question "What is theology?" anew each time. But it could also be a bad thing in that we are often lacking depth in our theological engagements, as it takes so much time to find the starting point, that we are often left far behind on a journey still ahead of us that we should've been taking all along. The value of religious traditions and communities is often significantly downplayed when such resources contain so much that might benefit those who struggle under a heavy burden imposed upon them.

What Karr does at least, and as many of us will do, is to begin to let in the "sliver of possibility" for something miraculous to happen in her life, and so, by her reckoning, "it's not long before the stone rolls away from the tomb."[54] It is also not long, then, before she recognizes the sanctity of the sacraments, such as the Eucharist, for example, something that, again, could only come about after the relationship with God has already begun. This isn't to suggest that her understanding and practice of such religious staples is on par with a traditional reading of them (e.g., as she'll describe both baptism and the Eucharist: "God reaches people by giving them the only kind of gory crap they'll pay attention to"[55]), rather it is to indicate her embrace of faith as an embrace of the ongoing life of faith that has already been happening within the religious and liturgical traditions of the Catholic Church.

What Karr begins to embrace is what I would call the core essentials of faith, that the reality of embodying faith means at times submitting oneself to the messy, complex mysteries of life, even ones that involve other people (as by definition, they will), and being better off for the experience, more fully human in fact. The original translation of "sacrament" is simply "mystery," as I noted above, and I believe that what Karr is reaching out for in her embrace of the Catholic sacramental life is a sense of that mystery in her own life that bolsters her faith and allows it to evolve as it needs to, in the fullness of life. She is willing to claim that she does not understand (have a definition for) all of herself and that this recognition actually entails

---

54. Karr, *Lit*, 350.
55. Karr, *Lit*, 353.

a freedom far beyond what she had earlier sought after, but failed to achieve: a mastery of herself that was as elusive as it was destructive.

The closing lines of her memoir, given after telling the story of re-encountering her mother, but from the perspective of faith, and while immersed in prayer during the most difficult times, comes to us like this:

> Every now and then we enter the presence of the numinous and deduce for an instant how we're formed, in what detail the force that infuses every petal might specifically run through us, wishing only to lure us into our full potential. Usually, the closest we get is when we love, or when some beloved beams back, which can galvanize you like steel and make resilient what had heretofore only been soft flesh. . . . It can start you singing as the lion pads over to you, its jaws hinging open, its hot breath on you. Even unto death.[56]

The power of her words and the life that they offer to her in the face of her own destructive impulses is quite profound, not to mention inspiring. The sense we are given is that her entire life was transformed by the simplest, ordinary willingness to take her own life more seriously than she had ever dreamed she would, and which, when fused with centuries of the spiritual insight she found in the Catholic Church (but also in the newer habits of AA), was more than enough to "save" her in the end.

Karr's story is paradigmatically Catholic in many ways. (Her spiritual director these days, so I have read, is Fr. James Martin, SJ, a very popular Catholic priest in the United States.) Yet her story also reflects the deep need for a higher power and a religious tradition that characterizes a fair number of "seekers" these days. This tension between the "spiritual" but not "religious," as well as the traditional religious identification (i.e., Catholic) maintained within her story is a very modern and very real one. Rather than look at her story as merely a challenge to traditional, religious structures, however, I am tempted to suggest the striking parallel—which she herself nods toward at the end of her book—between the faith she found, even one that has yet to begin its theological journey, and the earliest members of the Christian faith, the martyrs and witnesses who themselves often had no "proper" theological education. There was only the deep resonance of faith with the crucified Jesus that moved them deeply and that caused them to sing "as the lion pads over to you, its hot breath on you. Even unto death."[57]

---

56. Karr, *Lit*, 385–86.
57. Karr, *Lit*, 386.

CHAPTER FOUR

Christian Wiman

A Poetic Meditation on Life, Suffering, Faith, and Jesus Christ

Born in west Texas in 1966, Christian Wiman is no stranger to the realm of faith. A strict Southern Baptist community was the backdrop of his upbringing and also proved to be the catalyst for his abandonment of religion, as the hypocrisy of those around him stunted his spiritual growth. The abusive marriage of his parents that ended in divorce and the horrific scene of his grandfather murdering his grandmother before committing suicide would ensure that Wiman's adolescence would be spent avoiding the realm of theology. He would go on to earn a BA from Washington and Lee University before receiving an honorary doctorate from North Central College for his extensive work in the field of poetry, which includes the publication of The Long Home *(1998),* Ambition and Survival: Becoming a Poet *(2007),* Every Riven Thing *(2010),* Stolen Air *(2012),* The Open Door: One Hundred Poems, One Hundred Years of Poetry Magazine *(2012), and* Once in the West *(2014), and his work as the editor of* Poetry *magazine from 2003 to 2013. Wiman's experience with tragedy surfaced once again in 2005 when he was diagnosed with an incurable form of blood cancer, a subject that forced him to revisit his previous conclusions about the realm of faith and has been the source of many of his most recent poetic endeavors. Alongside his impressive publication list, Wiman has taught at Stanford University, Northwestern University, and Lynchburg College, and is currently a professor of the Practice of Religion and Literature at Yale Divinity school. One of his most recent works,* Joy: 100 Poems *(2017) wrestles with the absence of joy within the sphere of contemporary literature and is a must read by those who feel moved by the analysis of Wiman and* My Bright Abyss *presented below.*

The memoirs of the poet Christian Wiman encapsulate the modern believer's (but also, in some ways, *non*-believer's) quest for God, and how such a journey has much to teach us about the grounds upon which any faith today must be constructed. For Wiman, the life of faith is a constant dialogue between belief and unbelief, a state that cannot ever fully be eradicated. There is, therefore, in his eyes, a dynamic and permanent tension between the idea of an abstract God and another, different face of God, the Jesus whom Wiman claims is a "permanent challenge" to, and even disturbs, our beliefs about this God—something akin to what I would call a translation of how God has previously been defined. Wiman will, perhaps as a reaction to so many centuries of institutional, hierarchical, doctrinal, and creedal impositions upon people of faith, take a determinate look at the fluid experiences that yet contain the possibility of granting faith, even a specifically Christian faith, to an individual believer.

His starting point, however, much as Karr's, is in the yearning for something *beyond* himself, that which is greater than he is and that opens him up to an experience of not being entirely alone in his aloneness. For Wiman, the quest for faith in the midst of also trying to find oneself is one that must take a detour through poetry—that is, through the role of language in our lives and the fundamental problems associated with putting our faith into definable terms. As he would describe this challenge in his life,

> As if it weren't hard enough to articulate one's belief, I seem to have wanted to distill it into a single stanza. Still, that is the way I have usually known my own mind, feeling through the sounds of words to the forms they make, and through the forms they make to the forms of life that are beyond them. And I have always believed in that "beyond," even during the long years when I would not acknowledge God.[1]

What Wiman seems to be taking aim at is the form of life lived beyond its description in words—that which lies wholly beyond words, even behind the words, and which points toward a presence that cannot be brought into language. What he demonstrates for matters of faith is more or less the same mechanism that works for poetry as well: a good poem points toward the person or the experience behind the poem, not just the language

---

1. Wiman, *My Bright Abyss*, 3.

of the poem itself. This is why he will be fascinated throughout the book, as throughout his life, with those poets who seem to point us directly toward "multiple dimensions" of reality present in a single moment. Such dimensions, he goes on to describe, "are not discovering the extraordinary within the ordinary. They are, for the briefest of instants, perceiving something of reality as it truly is . . . ," what we have already seen in Karr's story as the very thing we should be searching for.[2]

For Wiman, these brief, poetic instants that widen us still further to what lies beyond us are what give shape to his reflections on faith in the modern world, which means, for him, also having to nuance and redefine what exactly faith is, or can be, for us still:

> I tell myself that I have no problem believing in God, if "belief" can be defined as some utter interior assent to a life that is both beyond and within this one, and if "assent" can be understood as at once active and unconscious, and if "God" is in some mysterious way both this action and its object, and if after all these qualifications this sentence still makes any effing sense.[3]

To put things this way is to perceive God as what propels the belief *and* as the end goal of it. It is to see belief as encompassing this world *and* also as what lies beyond it. What he aims for is our assent to such a presence, or our bringing ourselves to acknowledge its power within our lives, as both active and unconscious, at work within us when we are not even aware of it, but coming to life when we sense it and finally take hold of it. Wiman realizes, of course, that such configurations of faith will often make little or no sense to other people besides those who experience such a reality directly, and yet he persists in trying to grasp the significance of belief in his own life, which walks the border between the two. This tension will, beautifully, result in his paradoxical reformulations of faith, such as when he brings nonbelief into the realm of belief, abandonment into presence, and doubt into the life of faith—a series of realizations that we have already been building toward with both Augustine and Karr.

On this score, his meditations upon doubt as ultimately a sign that one is closer to something true than one realizes—that one is facing it and taking the time to look at it—is what will allow him to suggest that doubt is actually a process involving humility, insufficiency, and mystery, those things that prepare the soil for the eventual growth of faith, a point Augustine had already confirmed for us in many ways.[4] Moreover, as he is at

2. Wiman, *My Bright Abyss*, 52.
3. Wiman, *My Bright Abyss*, 72.
4. Wiman, *My Bright Abyss*, 76.

pains to stress, faith is something that takes place in the here and now, in the material world we live in and inhabit daily. Therefore, for him, "To have faith is to acknowledge the absolute materiality of existence while acknowledging at the same time the compulsion toward transfiguring order that seems not outside of things but within them, and within you—not an idea imposed on the world, but a vital, answering instinct."[5] Following the writings of the mystic Simone Weil, who was also fervently committed to social and political justice in *this* world, Wiman suggests that we must learn to "inhabit" a new understanding of God in the modern world, one that allows for "limitedness, contingency, suffering, death."[6]

What we witness in all of this theological and poetic speculation is yet the vulnerable person of Wiman, at this midpoint in his life, trying to articulate what it is that he believes, as a modern believer, whatever such a thing is, and if that is even possible, while also undergoing treatment for cancer and wondering if he will be able to sustain his life into an increasingly opaque future. "I have no hope of experiencing you God as I experience the world—directly, immediately—yet I want nothing more . . ."[7] This is a proposition that recognizes his desires for God, though he may only be able at times to say that he is drawn toward "something" beyond himself, and not the church, or Christianity per se (again, much as we have already seen with both Karr and Augustine).[8] What he senses, however, and I think his logic on this count is profoundly accurate, is that it is only by turning away from the intoxications of his self that he will find himself, and others as well—or, as Jesus put it, by losing his life he might save it (Luke 17:33). In practical terms, by shunning religion, institutional churches, and such external embodiments of one's faith, Wiman considers how he might actually find them in the end, though this may sound like a paradoxical formulation to some. For Wiman, however, it is the very logic that offers to save one's life: "Turning inward turned me outward too, to a world made radiant by my ability to believe in it."[9]

In Wiman's memoir, the circulation around language—as what captures his struggle with shared, social, and cultural forms, institutions, and the like—is palpable and central to his analysis (and contrast) of religion and faith, an uneasy pairing. For example, as he recalls a childhood experience

---

5. Wiman, *My Bright Abyss*, 77.
6. Wiman, *My Bright Abyss*, 81.
7. Wiman, *My Bright Abyss*, 13.
8. Wiman, *My Bright Abyss*, 65.
9. Wiman, *My Bright Abyss*, 67.

of something like "the divine," he considers its ability to speak to him beyond language:

> If eternity touched you, if all the trappings of time and self were stripped away and you were all soul, if God "happened" to you—then isn't it possible that the experience could not be translated back into the land of pumpjacks and pickup trucks, the daily round wherein we use words like self and soul, revelation and conversion, as if we know what those words meant?[10]

I believe that what Wiman is talking about is the mysterious and very complex terrain of revelation, of coming to terms with the experience of something that goes entirely beyond words, but which humanity has tried, in part, to put into language—what we have seen both Augustine and Karr struggle with so much within their own stories. It is clear from historical record that revelation, as recorded in both Scripture and tradition (according to Catholic and Orthodox Christians at least), is the documentation of an experience (or of many *experiences*) of God that also struggle to come to terms with the very conditions by which we receive revelation. We cannot forget this valuable fact, then, that those revelations recorded in the religious traditions that we have with us today are a record of so many voices trying to fathom just what has happened to them.

The struggle Wiman feels is very real for him as well: how do we bring such moments of the divine into language, how do we move from the fluid realm of experience into the reified, institutionalized structures of our world? As I have been arguing already, Wiman's conclusion is that we can't really do this with any sort of expectation of justice ever being fully performed, but yet that we must do this as the only way in which to communicate our faith with anyone. Like Karr's suggestion of translation as a way with which to rethink the divine through language, Wiman looks toward the poetic resonances with language that faith also contains:

> There is an analogue with poetry here: you can't spend your whole life questioning whether language can represent reality. At some point you have to believe that the inadequacies of the words you use will be transcended by the faith with which you use them. You have to believe that poetry has some reach into reality itself, or you have to go silent.[11]

This is where poetry, like religion, shares its profound truth with us about our humanity: we cannot describe the divine, and yet we must make an

---

10. Wiman, *My Bright Abyss*, 6.
11. Wiman, *My Bright Abyss*, 141.

attempt to do so. We pray to be rid of God as the famous Christian mystic Meister Eckhart once did, and only then does God return to us.[12] We are lost, and only by recognizing our being lost are we subsequently found. We are sinners, and yet only by confessing our sins can we ultimately be saved, especially when we are saved from ourselves.

Wiman recognizes, of course, that we do not need organized religion in order engage these processes and their truths. For his part, he sits on the fence between Christianity, in all its historical fullness and sadness (the ritual and tradition side), *and* his own experiences of God, just as he sits between language *and* the "thing itself" beyond language that he is desperately searching for. What he declares as his goal thereby becomes a "poetics of belief" that mirrors much of what organized religion is, has been, or even could or should be: "We need a poetics of belief, a language capacious enough to include a mystery that, ultimately, defeats it, and sufficiently intimate and inclusive to serve not only as individual expression but as communal need."[13] In accord with this observation, he too begins to speculate on how this "poetics of belief" is perhaps already, artistically happening outside the walls of the traditional church *as* institution, though he does so *in relation to* a sense of religious community—making his proximity to the church a tension-filled one that yet orients his outlook on faith.

Wiman makes clear throughout his mediations on his life and belief that his definition of faith rests upon the (poetic) experience of faith, one that recognizes its own uncomfortability with institutional forms and remains, in his words, "fluid" and "restless." As he describes this state of things himself, "every single expression of faith is provisional—because life carries us always forward to a place where the faith we'd fought so hard to articulate to ourselves must now be reformulated, and because faith in God is, finally, faith in change."[14] Such expressions are what will allow him to conclude that there is "no right way" that appears to us like a shining light, telling us how to live our lives once and for all—and rather than this being a disturbing turn of events, it is actually the best way to embrace the vitality of life before us.[15] We may spend many long hours discovering theological insights and arguing for particular metaphysical positions, but what Wiman is after—and this is the proposition of *what matters* that we have to take most seriously as people of faith trying to discern what faith is in the first place—is "the depth and

---

12. Eckhart, *The Complete Mystical Works of Meister Eckhart.*
13. Wiman, *My Bright Abyss*, 124.
14. Wiman, *My Bright Abyss*, 26.
15. Wiman, *My Bright Abyss*, 29.

integrity and essential innocence of the communion between two people."[16] This is everything to him, and what causes his poetic formulations ultimately to resonate deeply with the Christian stories of God's presence permeating any gathering of persons, in communion, in the name of Jesus.

In Wiman's more abstract depiction: "the soul is the verb that makes an exchange between the self and reality—or the self and other selves—possible. It is the soul that turns perception into communication, and communication—even if it's just between one man and the storm of atoms around him—into communion."[17] His critique of religious understandings of belief, and even of doctrine or the contents of faith, is central to his rearticulation of the human person's relationship to faith. What I want to highlight in this is the way in which doctrine itself is actually—or at least *should* be—that which articulates our struggles to wrestle with a God that cannot be named. It is a record of this experience of the divine, one that is itself often highly mysterious and unnameable, though this is rarely how doctrine has been understood. We should not forget, however, and in ways that might actually open us up to religious tradition, that this sense of mystery is part of how we are to comprehend the very existence of doctrine, an all-too-human attempt to deal with the mysteries and complexities of both God and humanity.

From the start of his memoir, Wiman identifies how faith has been grossly underdeveloped in many people's minds, even being misunderstood so as to narrow a person's openness to the otherness before them, something he fights to prevent so that believers might become much more open to the mysteries of life that lay before us: "If faith requires you to foreclose on an inspiration, surely it is not faith."[18] Wiman, in this fashion, sees the absence of God as being at the heart of belief. There is a gap or distance within God's own life, perhaps another, insightful way of understanding the nature and existence of the Trinity. Jesus is important to Wiman in a way that wasn't there for Augustine because he radically challenges our ideas of God *with* and *through* the person of Jesus. As he further develops the thought, such an inspiration of a challenging Jesus is a dynamic force within one's life, not something that simply articulates a normative vision of the divine:

> any notion of God that is static is—since it asserts singular knowledge of God and seeks to limit his being to that knowledge—blasphemous. "God's truth is life," as Patrick Kavanagh says, "even the grotesque shapes of its foulest fire." One part of that truth, for

---

16. Wiman, *My Bright Abyss*, 26.
17. Wiman, *My Bright Abyss*, 93.
18. Wiman, *My Bright Abyss*, 60.

even the most devout among us, is the void of godlessness—and sometimes, mysteriously, the joy of that void.[19]

Though such a "void of godlessness" may sound like the opposite of a believer's desires, we find it located here as a fundamental resource for the growth of the life of faith. Wiman will return to this experience of the "void of God" or of God's absence, or of feeling abandoned by God at some point in our lives, as a great source of spiritual inspiration and insofar as it forms one part of the necessary steps to be taken in developing one's life of faith. Christian revelation, he will go on to state, "like creation, arises not merely out of nothingness but *by means of it* . . ."[20] It arises from out of this void itself, not as a stranger to it.

Creation, in biblical accounts at least, is a complex affair, at times resembling a process of working with the substance that is already given (the Genesis narratives would do well to testify to this reality), and at times a bringing something to be that was never there before—a creation *ex nihilo* (brought up biblically in the deuterocanonical book of 2 Maccabees). Perhaps taking both notions in combination with each other is the way to proceed in terms of our determining the location of the human being who stands in relation to God as if God established every facet of our being (since we are made in the image of God, or *imago dei*), but who also stands in many ways apart from God, alone and isolated in the world. Rather than view such a configuration as little more than a failing to account for the fullness of the human being, perhaps there is a way to preserve this paradoxical existence, even one analogous to various conceptualizations of the Trinity. For some, in fact, there is a hollow center in God's *own* being, a *perichorisis* (meaning "to make room for"), that dictates how God relates to God's own self, but also, that gives space for God to relate to God's own self, to enact a distance if need be (and as the incarnation and death of Jesus would seem to indicate).[21] This would certainly speak directly to the significance of relationship in the life of faith as it is manifest within God's own self as well.

What we need to take note of explicitly in this too is the reality that even God has to step *outside of* God's self. This is another way of saying that even God (in the story of Jesus' death on the cross in particular) needs to get outside of God's own self in order to gain a necessary perspective in some ways—in order to make that act of translation that pushes beyond the given definition. When Jesus prays that he doesn't want to go to his death, but then prays for God's will and not his own to be done, we are in

19. Wiman, *My Bright Abyss*, 61.
20. Wiman, *My Bright Abyss*, 136.
21. Moltmann, *The Trinity and the Kingdom*.

a very unusual circumstance where God is stepping outside of God's own will in some measure, but also, significantly but also highly paradoxically, back into it at the same time. In putting things thus, I am stressing the importance of viewing faith as relationship, since to do what God does, to follow God in this activity, we must step outside of ourselves in order to relate to others and not to become isolated in such a way that we do not fundamentally relate to one another.

In the notion of the Trinity, God relates even to God's own self, which, I believe, means that even God has to step outside of God's own self in order to relate to God's own self—a powerful image of how we sometimes have to embrace our own differences (see ourselves from another point of view) in order to learn how to better relate to our own selves as well. In other words, it is only by losing our conceptions of God, as God loses a conceptualization of even God's own self, that we are able to gain something of God (and ourselves too) back once again. This, in a very direct sense, is what the "death of God" seems to indicate to us.[22] Jesus' death on the cross (God's division from God's own self) opens up for us a path to the profane that rules out the "false sacred," or a "false transcendence," in order to wake us up from our complacency with so many false "sacralities" within the world—a point that speaks to Augustine's varied tensions concerning God as much as it speaks to our own.

I would compare such reflections on the emptiness or void within God's own self with those made centuries ago by Saint John of the Cross, who speaks of an experience of the absence of God as that which actually purifies us of our false conceptions of God, that purges us too of the need for a "spiritual sweetness," which can be a false lure for those weak in faith (a critique we will see taken up later by Saint Teresa of Ávila). I think this disclosure is what Wiman has in mind when he suggests, quite radically to some ears, that "Sometimes God calls a person to unbelief in order that faith may take new forms."[23] Such sentiments are perhaps mirrored too by the way in which Teresa of Calcutta ("Mother Teresa") went through a long struggle in the latter portion of her life to feel the presence of God at all. She indeed seems only to have felt the absence of God as a long and sustained experience somehow also *of* God.

This may be terribly hard to grasp for the average "believer," but the truth of its applicability should awaken us to something much deeper. Are there not many "believers" who believe in wrong or even terrible things? Is it not easily conceivable that many should lose such horrific "beliefs" in

---

22. Caputo and Vattimo, *After the Death of God*.
23. Wiman, *My Bright Abyss*, 61.

order to arrive at a deeper truth of the way things are, even if such a "failing" appears as socially awkward, religiously weak, or culturally isolationist? Why should such a loss of wrong beliefs be something we fear, as we might fear the absence of God—that which, in the end, may have been what our faith needed most in some ways?

The difficulty of admitting such things is that many of us have a completely wrongheaded notion of faith to begin with: that faith is in need of clear definition and defending against the many modern obstacles that seem to impede it from without, and therefore that faith should be kept at a remove from the necessary act of translation that opens us up to transformative encounter in the first place. This context, Wiman reminds us, is a false representation of the world we live in and the faith that we should be developing within us. In his words,

> So long as faith is something that "withstands" the assaults of reason, experience, secularization, or even simply the slow erosion of certainty within my own heart and mind; so long as that verb accurately describes the dynamic between my belief and all that seems to threaten it, then faith is an illusion in me, a dream that weakness clings to, rather than the truest form of fruition of strength.[24]

Faith, in his estimation, should be the first to embrace the erosion of one's certainty as a pivotal point for change. Faith should work completely *with* reason in all its fullness, but not with reason *alone* (as Newman had suggested earlier in the nineteenth century). Faith should embrace our experiences, though also critically engage them in order to arrive at a proper understanding of what they are saying to us. Faith should look to the cultural "loss" of God, and any resultant secularization, as an opportunity to move deeper into the real nature of faith and not necessarily as something to fear. It is therefore important to remember, according to Wiman and as born from his own experiences of vulnerability, that such a form of "strength" will actually appear to us—internally even, to ourselves—as a form of weakness or poverty, precisely because it seems to "give way" at certain points to reason, secularization, our experiences, the loss of certainty, and the like. But, in reality, this is not actually the case, not if we are actually engaging the spiritual reality of a dynamic faith.

Hence, in order to refocus our vision upon this world in order to move through it and toward the transcendent, whatever this may be, Wiman demonstrates how God is part of *this* life and not merely the "beyond," as

---

24. Wiman, *My Bright Abyss*, 107.

generations have envisioned it.[25] This is what will cause Wiman to challenge certain people's dependence upon some idea of the afterlife as well.[26] His is a focus upon the immanent world around him, though the transcendent is perhaps grasped as well in it, but only *through* the immanent domain and *through* its failure to capture all of reality. In other words, this world is *not* all there is, he will conclude, but you have to go through this life in order to see things from this viewpoint.[27] What he is able to see then is "God straining through matter to make me see, and to grant me the grace of simple praise."[28] Another way to describe this shift in perspective is to suggest that "The meanings that God calls us to in our lives are never abstract."[29]

Such meaning is actually quite concrete, more so than we might ever suspect. This is the reason why, as well, we are not to think of our faith as something we simply "believe in," as an object that may or may not exist, for example. We must reside in our faith, as we reside in each other, and in God, striving to reach out toward something beyond us that cannot be named, but which will be named eventually, and, once on the other side of this act of naming, we will own it in a completely different way: "To *imagine* it—this peace, this unity, this life beyond the one we're in—not necessarily to 'believe' in it. To have faith in the meaning and final fruition of this impulse in us, but not to anxiously attempt to fill out that faith with content."[30]

But what exactly would a faith *without* content look like? Is it a series of empty churches and vacant schools? Is it the feared end of religion as we know it, and as so many people of faith in the modern world have suspected was lurking on the edges of society the whole time? Is it an embrace of a relativist nihilism that is often feared by devout religious persons and theologians alike? To be sure, I don't think that this is what Wiman envisions, though I do think we have to try to understanding the passage through unbelief to belief he is wanting to make. As he summarizes the journey, "Only when doctrine itself is understood to be provisional does doctrine begin to take on a more than provisional significance. Truth inheres not in doctrine itself, but in the spirit with which it is engaged, for the spirit of God is always seeking and creating new forms."[31]

---

25. Wiman, *My Bright Abyss*, 8.
26. Wiman, *My Bright Abyss*, 105.
27. Wiman, *My Bright Abyss*, 10.
28. Wiman, *My Bright Abyss*, 156.
29. Wiman, *My Bright Abyss*, 93.
30. Wiman, *My Bright Abyss*, 104.
31. Wiman, *My Bright Abyss*, 111.

This is a great difficulty to comprehend for many of us today, because we tend to perceive doctrine as itself the truth that we must adhere to in order for certainty to take hold of us, and as that which cannot be provisional in any sense. Doctrine offers to define clearly what seems to be only ambiguous, though it also threatens at times to remove the mystery at the heart of faith (and relationship) that seeks to be cultivated. Barring the accompanying act of translation that lets definition remain, but also shows it its proper place, doctrine functions as a static tomb rather than as it was intended: a dynamic partner in an ongoing dance with translation. Wiman's claim is that faith must allow itself to oscillate between definition (as doctrine or identity) and the ceaseless acts of translation that slide alongside it so that meaning might be brought into the life of the individual who engages in the transformations such a dialectic entails.

What we frequently misunderstand, then, is not only the nature of the relationship between scriptural narratives and doctrine—which is *nothing but* provisional—but also the way in which we are to relate *to* doctrine, which is *anything but* a provisional relationship. What Wiman is noting in his reflections is that, despite the provisional nature of doctrine, there is something steadfast and pure that can arise from it, just as with a relationship between lovers who met under completely contingent circumstances. Only when you realize how provisional and precarious your love or relationship is, he suggests, can you really cherish it for what it can be for you. I think that this understanding is how we are to conceive of the precarious relationships that enter into union with each other, and become a source of strength, a foundation, for the members who enter into it. Love, in lived reality, is something precarious and fragile, capable of being destroyed by a word; yet it is also the most precious treasure, and one that can yield the greatest strength humankind knows. This is in many ways what marriage strives to be, a covenant between two persons who know the absolute fragility of their bond, yet enter into it so that they might gain a deeper understanding and appreciation of love as it permeates their lives.

The logic of these meditations resonates throughout many of Wiman's (re)conceptualizations of faith. For example, he will also suggest that "You must let go of all conception of what eternity *is*, which means letting go of who *you* are, in order to feel the truth of eternity and its meaning in your life—and in your death."[32] Likewise, he will follow Meister Eckhart in praying to God to be free of God—at least of his particular conceptualizations of God, which will only allow him to bring a truer presence of God closer in the end, though he may not be able to describe such a transformative

---

32. Wiman, *My Bright Abyss*, 167.

encounter himself.³³ Holding a specific religious proposition or doctrinal belief is not the major point he is trying to underscore through such examples. His point, again and again, seems to be one concerning the way in which we use such beliefs within our life, in how we treat others and in the general orientation we have to our world.

This logic of faith is what will eventually also bring him to consider the apparent absence of God as a way toward finding his presence. This too is why the death of Jesus is so central to Christianity. This is the same process we undergo as the brokenness and failure of our identities. The intensity of a felt absence can lead to a felt presence. Going through something difficult can sometimes lead us to a new strength, and to help others who are going through the same things.

Though it may sound like an increasingly paradoxical way of comprehending the divine, this is the manner through which God has always been perceived, a mixture of hiddenness and revelation that we struggle to make sense of even as it presents itself directly to us. Wiman will initially hint toward such an understanding through his acknowledgment that "I never truly felt the pain of unbelief until I began to believe..."³⁴ Such belief allowed him to perceive unbelief anew and to realize the general experience of belief itself. He eventually comes likewise to experience what he describes "as an assent to a faith that had long been latent within me..."³⁵ This was an only *apparent* absence of faith that became a form of presence *through* him much later, that which had once been preparing itself within him to receive, at a much later point, a confirmation of the faith after which he had been seeking. He subsequently reframes the notion of atonement, a notion which is sometimes repugnant to many today. In his eyes, rather than being a process of having to make up for our sins, atonement could be something rather like going through this process of absence and brokenness in order to lead us out of it.

In his description of the divine, we are able to locate a profound narrative of absence and presence that resonates very deeply with the Christian story, specifically the death of Jesus on the cross. Wiman will put it thus: "the void of God and the love of God come together in the mystery of the cross."³⁶ But what he is intent on further discerning are the dual presences of "a mercy and mystery that are greater than we are, when the void of God and the love of God, incomprehensible pain and the peace that passeth understanding,

---

33. Wiman, *My Bright Abyss*, 136.
34. Wiman, *My Bright Abyss*, 12.
35. Wiman, *My Bright Abyss*, 22.
36. Wiman, *My Bright Abyss*, 68.

come together in a simply human act."[37] This is an act bound up in the love of Jesus that God gives to us on the cross, one that fully admits there are yet moments of complete spiritual dryness and absence in the midst of—rather than apart from—a dynamic life of faith. Instead of denouncing such a state as a futile endeavor, or as something we should forsake for that which offers a more "substantial" presence, Wiman considers how this state is how things should and will forever be, as otherwise our faith would be a static, unyielding illusion not fit for relationship with either God or others. Communion is here experienced when the brokenness of the community is opened and exposed to all. And to walk into the concomitant feelings of absence, vulnerability, and loss is to live a life of spiritual poverty.

For Wiman, there is no more dynamic impression of God than the figure of Christ, the thorn in the side of our depictions of God that will not relent in confronting us with the hard realities we often wish to ignore. Christ is the humanity that upends our representations of God, much as Augustine had often imagined them. This clash between preconceived ideas of God and the reality of Christ's ugly death on the cross becomes, in turn, the beacon that guides the believer toward a more grounded and realistic depiction of a God who yet lives, as well as how faith takes shape in the modern world.

> Modern spiritual consciousness is predicated upon the fact that God is gone, and spiritual experience, for many of us, amounts mostly to an essential, deeply felt and necessary, but ultimately inchoate and transitory feeling of oneness or unity with existence. It is mystical and valuable, but distant. Christ, though, is a shard of glass in your gut. Christ is God crying *I am here*, and here not only in what exalts and completes and uplifts you, but here in what appalls, offends, and degrades you, here in what activates and exacerbates all that you would call not-God. To walk through the fog of God toward the clarity of Christ is difficult because of how unlovely, how "ungodly" that clarity often turns out to be.[38]

The Christ that he confronts in the midst of his own spiritual journey criticizes or at least realigns a good many of his representations of God, and this is as things should be. Christ's death, you might say, is an experience of God that continues to render our most cherished notions of God invalid and beyond practical use. Christ is not vague, in the way that some theologians or priests speak of God. Christ is specific to our lives in a meaningful way

---

37. Wiman, *My Bright Abyss*, 69.
38. Wiman, *My Bright Abyss*, 121.

that we still struggle to comprehend: "If God is love, Christ is love for this one person, this one place, this one time-bound and time-ravaged self."[39] Christ is the particularity of God in the particularity of history and, forever after, in the particularity of our lives.

Wiman's sense of this imposing and very real Christ comes, in a very direct way, from his own experience of suffering, which eroded his abstractions about the divine and placed a solid notion of a suffering deity before him as a genuine possibility of faith—further described by him as a "mystical sense of God-in-nature obliterated by nature wrecking havoc with my body."[40] It is a truism to state that we often find the message of Christianity resonates more deeply with those who have hit some sort of rock bottom in their lives. Such a hitting of the bottom—the cancerous infection that was "wrecking havoc" with Wiman's body—is what will attract him to the German theologian Jürgen Moltmann's thought as presented in *The Crucified God*, a powerful political theology that points directly toward the suffering of Christ as the only way forward for any relevant theology born after Auschwitz.[41]

> I don't know what it means to say that Christ "died for my sins" (who wants that? who invented that perverse calculus?), but I do understand—or intuit, rather—the notion of God not above or beyond or immune to human suffering, but in the very midst of it, intimately with us in our sorrow, our sense of abandonment, our hellish astonishment at finding ourselves utterly alone, utterly helpless.[42]

Such suggestions indicate why Wiman is able to find significant Moltmann's claim that if Christians really understand what Christ is about, they would want to flee from Christ, because the person of Jesus is simply asking too much of them. We relish our alienation and our sin—as Augustine and Karr both well knew—and we do not want to give it up so easily. Despite this reluctance and resistance, however, God comes into our lives in order, not to take away our alienation, but—in a way that echoes Paul's division of all social divisions and identities, as noted earlier—to alienate our alienation, to go through it with us and to expose its futility from *within*.[43] Suddenly, with Christ, and *in* his suffering, we see that our own suffering and alienation are

39. Wiman, *My Bright Abyss*, 121.
40. Wiman, *My Bright Abyss*, 123.
41. Moltmann, *The Crucified God*. See Wiman, *My Bright Abyss*, 133.
42. Wiman, *My Bright Abyss*, 134.
43. See Wiman's lengthy quote from Moltmann's *The Crucified God* in Wiman, *My Bright Abyss*, 135.

not as unique as we might have once thought, and that there are so many others who suffer as we do, who suffer much worse in fact. Our elevation of our unique suffering as such becomes exposed as a lie that we tell ourselves and that truly has no stake in light of the suffering that has gone before us, what we comprehend when we look through the eyes of others and cease projecting our own suffering upon them.

Wiman will declare himself a Christian because he identifies with the dying moments of Jesus on the cross, as he cries out in abandonment "My God, my God, why have you abandoned me?"[44] As Wiman describes it, "I am a Christian because I understand that moment of Christ's passion to have meaning in my own life, and what it means is that the absolutely solitary and singular nature of extreme human pain is an illusion."[45] In other words, there is always someone else who shares it with us: Jesus Christ, but also, those following this Christ who take up his calling and demonstrate empathy, solidarity, and compassion for those who suffer—who in fact suffer with others, and even *through* their suffering. "Human love *can* reach right into death, then, but not if it is *merely* human love."[46] There is something *beyond* our love that goes *with* our love and that lends it a depth we could never give it alone, by ourselves. It is a force implicated and caught up within the nature of relationship itself and that cannot be extracted as an autonomous element and utilized for a single individual alone.

This faith, as I would call it, is one that refocuses us completely on the suffering (and marginality) of God, but also on the contingency of God and of our encounter with God. In the incarnation, which is what will forever subject God to human conditions, Wiman considers, "There's no release from reality, no 'outside' or 'beyond' from which some transforming touch might come. But what a relief it can be to befriend contingency, to meet God right here in the havoc of chance, to feeling enduring love like a stroke of pure luck."[47] This contingency is not a bad thing at all, but the very coordinates along which faith develops. As Wiman will immediately call to mind in this context, as with Christ's contingency in taking flesh, faith changes over time, as it takes different forms and evolves with the person who carries it. "For many people, God is simply a gauze applied to the wound of not knowing, when in fact that wound has bled into every part of the world, is bleeding now in a way that is life if we acknowledge it, death

---

44. Wiman, *My Bright Abyss*, 155.
45. Wiman, *My Bright Abyss*, 155.
46. Wiman, *My Bright Abyss*, 155.
47. Wiman, *My Bright Abyss*, 17.

if we don't. Christ is contingency. Christ's life is *right now*."[48] This is the living God that Jesus himself spoke of, and that continues to permeate the Christian sense of the divine. Jesus did not die so long ago—he continues, in the Spirit, in himself, in God the Father, to die again and again, but also to fill the world with his presence. As Wiman will phrase it, "Christ comes alive in the communion between people."[49]

In this sense as well, Christ is reborn in every age anew, born to new contexts and persons and capable of spreading an ever-refined message of hope and love. "A deeper truth, though, one that scripture suggests when it speak of the eternal Word being made specific flesh, is that there is no permutation of humanity in which Christ is not present."[50] Wiman focuses on the very human nature of Jesus, who walked besides people as a person, in the flesh, in order to get them to see the "deeper truth" they had been missing, one that was immanent to their daily lives. One of these truths is revealed in the precarious humanity of Jesus, or, as Wiman puts it, "Christ is contingency."[51]

> Contingency. Meaning subject to change, not absolute. Meaning uncertain, as reality, right down to the molecular level, is uncertain. As all of human life is uncertain. I suppose that to think of God in these terms might seem for some people deeply troubling (not to mention heretical), but I find it a comfort. It is akin to the notion of God entering and understanding—or understanding that there could be no understanding . . . —human suffering.[52]

This is the nature of the ongoing conversion (transformation) of us all—a *metanoia* or transformative encounter that defines the Christian life of a dynamic and vitalizing faith. To perceive such encounters as vital aspects of what moves beyond oneself, yet moving inside oneself as well, is to see faith as "a motion of the soul toward God."[53] Or, as he will later put it, "Faith is faith *in* change."[54]

Not only does such an emphasis on contingency cause us to rethink the nature of faith; it also prompts a radical rethinking of the figure of God. If Christ is the contingency within God, we must reconsider how

---

48. Wiman, *My Bright Abyss*, 20.
49. Wiman, *My Bright Abyss*, 20.
50. Wiman, *My Bright Abyss*, 11.
51. Wiman, *My Bright Abyss*, 16, de-emphasized from the original.
52. Wiman, *My Bright Abyss*, 17.
53. Wiman, *My Bright Abyss*, 139.
54. Wiman, *My Bright Abyss*, 104.

God moves beyond the dichotomy of the contingent and the necessary. Seeing Jesus Christ as the person with two natures, both human and divine, living as the Messiah given to humanity, is itself a difficult thing to comprehend, but especially so as Wiman inverts how we normally think of these terms in relation to God. Typically, God or Jesus is seen as a necessary being, and, of course, humanity is contingent. How we perceive Jesus, and consequently God, in relation to this tension is a vital characterization that can actually inform us about how we receive necessity and contingency in our own lives as well.

Yet Wiman's stress is placed on the way in which the person of Christ can be said to be the contingency of God, the moment where God enters into human time and is, as such, subject to the same shifting sands as humanity. To see it this way is in a very direct sense the opposite of Augustine's formulations of God's being absolute and immutable. The divergence here is radical, though both Augustine and Wiman are at pains to stress how human love ends in the love of God, or it is misdirected, and that humility in our lack of understanding is to be stressed perhaps above all else. In Wiman's words, "Human love has an end, which is God, who makes it endless."[55] And this seems to be enough of an "answer" to the problematic nature of God's existence, something about which we cannot know much of anything. But this relationship we are to develop with the divine, he also emphasizes, is where we find a foundation more secure than proving the existence, qualities, or attributes of God. As he will continue this line of thought, "You cannot work on the structure of your life if the ground of your being is unsure."[56]

Parallel to Augustine's stress upon living a life full of humility in order to actually comprehend the working of the divine in one's life, Wiman emphasizes the significance of innocence and wonder in maintaining faith and cultivating wisdom.[57] As he explains its scope and measure,

> The frustration we feel when trying to explain or justify God, whether to ourselves or to others, is a symptom of knowledge untethered from innocence, of words in which no silence lives, of belief occurring wholly on a human plane. Innocence returns us to the first call of God, to any moment in our lives when we were rendered mute with awe, fear, wonder. Absent this, there is

---

55. Wiman, *My Bright Abyss*, 29.
56. Wiman, *My Bright Abyss*, 98.
57. Wiman, *My Bright Abyss*, 63–64.

no sense in arguing for God in order to convince others, for we ourselves are not convinced.[58]

Within this suggestion, he is able to redefine religion entirely, though not to jettison its meaning for humanity on the whole: "Religion is what you *do* with these moments of over-mastery in your life, these rare times in which you are utterly innocent."[59] Religion is our reaction and our gratitude to learning to see beyond our feeble attempts to gain control over a reality that we cannot control, including our own lives even. Yet, to be sure, this sense of innocence is not merely a "childlike" position to be in, one of absolute resignation to whatever forces assail or overtake us. Faith is a dynamic force that returns us to ourselves even as it seems to evolve past whatever we had thought we were: "whatever faith you emerge with at the end of your life is going to be not simply affected by that life but intimately dependent upon it for faith in God is, in the deepest sense, faith in life—which means that even the staunchest life of faith is a life of great change."[60]

To change is to have faith, one that is not stagnant, but alive and lived in expectation of the future always yet to come to us. To experience such a faith *as* change is, ultimately, to find a place from which to accept one's vulnerability to change, to receive it openly and to learn to center oneself upon the process itself, what might be described as a process of learning how to love—the cornerstone of the Christian faith, and that which Wiman is after above all else. That is, we might begin to see love redefined as an openness and a receptivity or form of hospitality that allows us to welcome the other before us in whatever place we find them, even when they do not measure up to what we had taken them to be. This is the very meaning and significance of what I am calling translation, the directional movement that opens us up to love. "What might it mean to be drawn into meanings that, in some profound and necessary sense, shatter us? This is what it means to love."[61] To love like this is to ponder, along with both Wiman and Augustine, what we love when we love our God, and how we love when we love those whom we love (i.e., not as a practice of being in love with love itself, but of loving an actual object, or person before us). It also means being open to the ways in which we are called into question by those we love, challenged, but also provoked to personal growth through the "shattering" experiences of love that open us up still further.

58. Wiman, *My Bright Abyss*, 71.
59. Wiman, *My Bright Abyss*, 70.
60. Wiman, *My Bright Abyss*, 7.
61. Wiman, *My Bright Abyss*, 50.

Wiman's is a strange theology for the modern (non)believer, but one rife with implications for the rethinking of faith. His is a call to take more seriously than we perhaps ever have the necessity for rethinking the role of contingency in our lives and in God's, and from this place to rethink the very words we utter in trying to speak about God.

> [I]f you find that you cannot believe in God, then do not worry yourself with it. No one can say what names or forms God might take, nor gauge the intensity of unbelief we may need to wake up our souls. My love is still true, my children, still with you, still straining through your ambitions and your disappointments, your frenzies and forgetfulness, through all the glints and gulfs of implacable matter—to reach you, to help you, to heal you.[62]

This is the place where contingency and love meet up and shake hands, becoming friends in a lifelong quest to demonstrate the reality of faith as a very concrete communion between persons. What we encounter as well in this formulation of things is that what we thought theology was going to be is most likely going to be challenged once again, reformulated and given back to us in an almost unrecognizable form.

> The purpose of theology—the purpose of any thinking about God—is to make the silences clearer and starker to us, to make the unmeaning—by which I mean those aspects of the divine that will not be reduced to human meanings—more irreducible and more terrible, and thus ultimately more wonderful. This is why art is so often better at theology than theology is.[63]

Even theology, in this estimation, can be shattered by an experience of Christ that undoes our dependence upon certain representations of God. Though this might appear as a refusal to accept the insights that theology has gained throughout the centuries, it is rather a "new beginning" for theology and not its end.[64] It is what allows us to return to theology's long history and its traditions anew after we had thought them to be irrelevant to a secular culture. What Wiman envisions is a theology more capable of handling the paradoxes and difficulties that come its way, one more just in its relations with all persons throughout time.

> The single most damaging and distorting thing that religion has done to faith involves overlooking, undervaluing, and even outright suppressing this interior, ulterior kind of consciousness.

---

62. Wiman, *My Bright Abyss*, 161.
63. Wiman, *My Bright Abyss*, 130.
64. Wiman, *My Bright Abyss*, 132.

> So much Western theology has been constructed on a fundamental disfigurement of the mind and reality. In neglecting the voices of women, who are more attuned to the immanent nature of divinity, who feel that eruption in their very bodies, theology has silenced a powerful—perhaps the most powerful—side of God.[65]

By placing stress upon the much neglected role of women in theological discourse (and though many other marginalized groups could, and should, also be named here), Wiman reminds us that the contingency of Christ opens us up to other contingent presences in our world, especially ones so contingent that we have often repressed or neglected to hear their messages almost entirely. The time, however, has come to rectify such imbalanced relationships and to proceed in such a way as to welcome the other in love, no matter who the other is or how foreign to us they may seem, and with a steadfast commitment to take seriously that which "shatters" us through its love.

---

65. Wiman, *My Bright Abyss*, 153.

CHAPTER FIVE

Leo Tolstoy

*Finding Faith Amidst the
Tensions of the World*

Leo Tolstoy was born on September 9, 1828, in the Tula province of Russia, just south of Moscow. His family's aristocratic status ensured that Tolstoy would receive the finest education that money could buy, including Western European tutors and a spell at the University of Kazan. However, an unhealthy partying habit led to his failing out of the university to pursue a life of drinking and gambling in Moscow, which would plunge young Leo into debt. The need for structure and stability in his life was evident to those around him and his family eventually convinced Tolstoy to join the military just prior to the outbreak of the Crimean War in 1855. His status as a nobleman provided ample leisure time in the absence of military campaigns and this period of Tolstoy's life would launch his writing career through the publication of an autobiography, Childhood (1852), and an account of his military service, Cossacks (1862). As Russia entered a new era that included a shift towards industrialization in the aftermath of the freeing of the serfs, Tolstoy would continue to describe his surroundings in vivid fictional detail through the publication of such works as War and Peace (1865), Anna Karenina (1877), The Death of Ivan Ilyich (1886), and The Resurrection (1899). In his later years, Tolstoy's struggles with depression and his perceived meaninglessness of life led to a transition period away from fiction and towards a style of writing that was deeply self-reflective and involved a return to religion. The brilliant Russian novelist would die in 1910 after a lengthy pilgrimage severely weakened his health, though his writings would go on to become some of the most renowned and well recognized in history.

Raised in the traditions and rituals of the Russian Orthodox Church, Leo Tolstoy, the great Russian novelist of the late nineteenth and early twentieth centuries, sought a balance in his life of faith that he could not achieve early on in his life, only later recognizing that he was perpetually caught in a tension between the traditions of the church he was brought up in and his own personal experiences of faith—a dynamic tension that underlies every person's quest for spiritual and religious fulfillment. Nonetheless, in the midst of the articulation of his journey, we find a refreshingly honest presentation of how his faith went through a number of very realistic trials, all somewhat characteristic of the modern era in which we live, and, for this reason, capable of resonating with a contemporary audience in ways that may also surprise us.

Take, for example, his initial summation of how he found himself in his adolescence, rejecting the teachings of the church and becoming more honest with himself about where he stood concerning his personal beliefs:

> The decline of my faith occurred in the way in which it has always happened, and still happens, among those from our kind of background. It seems to me that in the majority of instances it happens like this: people live as everyone lives, but on the basis of principles that not only have nothing in common with religious doctrines but are, on the whole, contrary to them; religious doctrine plays no part in life, or in relations between people, neither are we confronted with it in our personal lives.[1]

We lose faith, he seems to suggest, because we live our lives according to values that are not simply foreign to religious doctrine, but are actually "contrary" to them. There is a tension that we somehow refuse to acknowledge and that slowly eats away at our religious beliefs, though it is one that we barely know how to recognize, let alone alter.

What he began to become aware of within this state of affairs was that such a possibility for losing faith becomes the reality for many "believers" when they are not forced by society, or anyone for that matter, to confront the problematic contradictions between their beliefs and their actions. Such contradictions, as we have already seen, often arise in the simplest form: we know that we are broken, but we insist on presenting ourselves as entirely whole, as successful, or as being without blame or fault. For the most part, the problem with such contradictions becomes heightened because one cannot tell, for example, what really differentiates persons who believe from those who do not. In fact, it seemed to Tolstoy that those who professed an

---

1. Tolstoy, *A Confession*, 19.

orthodox faith were actually more likely than not to be opposed to living a life according to the teachings of that faith. In his sharp words,

> Now, just as then, it is impossible to judge from a person's life, or behaviour, whether or not he is a believer. If there is a difference between those who openly profess Orthodoxy and those who deny it, then it is not to the advantage of the former. Nowadays, as before, the public declaration and confession of Orthodoxy is usually encountered among the dull-witted, cruel and immoral people who tend to consider themselves very important.[2]

Sparing no critique of those who claimed to hold an orthodox position in terms of their professed beliefs, he looked beyond surface appearances and toward the sincerity of the life lived by the individual who professes the belief. This move is the first indication of his search for an authenticity of faith, an authenticity *in* one's faith, that will guide him to form a self-critical faith that will sustain him long after the contradictions that often eliminate faith from one's life are addressed. This quest also led him to recognize the common dilemmas that the modern believer faces, and continues to face today, as well as to look squarely at how one might more adequately deal with them.

We should recall, of course, that the church has long been filled with a tension between heresy and orthodoxy. Often presented as a contrast that appears to pit "true" against "false" believers, this distinction, however, is not always what we take it to be, as Tolstoy reminds us. Heretics, we would do well to note, are not simply those who doubt or test a particular teaching; they are those who actively seek to destroy the faith, whereas the orthodox are merely those who continue to struggle with their beliefs, even when they appear to deviate from them. Though I am not convinced that this highly dualistic framework is always entirely helpful in our day and age, we might still see how, from Tolstoy's perspective, a genuine "heretic" puts faith entirely in themselves; the "orthodox" person knows that faith is larger than themselves. Faith actually puts the self in a proper, much smaller perspective. This is the act of "becoming small" that Karr had earlier referred to.

What Tolstoy focuses our attention toward is the slow, almost unrecognizable death of belief at the hands of our overreliance upon either our knowledge or our experiences, which would be something like a "heretical" belief:

> Thus today, just as in earlier times, religious teaching, which is accepted on trust and sustained by external pressure, gradually weakens under the influence of knowledge and experiences of

2. Tolstoy, *A Confession*, 20.

life that stands in opposition to the religious doctrines; a person can go on living for a long time imagining that the body of religious instruction imparted to him when he was a child is still there, whereas it has in fact disappeared without leaving a trace.[3]

And what does this mean? In short, it means that, for many of us, we have already lost our faith, but have failed to recognize that fact. It also means that we might find ourselves giving lip service to faith, attending to religious rituals and gestures, all the while not really believing, but giving precedence to either our knowledge alone, or our experiences, and refusing to endow our faith with a sensibility that extends far beyond these two realms of our faculties. Eventually, as Tolstoy will conclude, the meaninglessness of one's religious gestures will catch up to the person for whom faith has silently died, and will soon thereafter be discarded altogether. In his estimation, either a person has realized how empty these gestures have become to them, and so they are discarded, or they profess the faith, but are caught up in trying to attain some worldly aim that runs contrary to the stated beliefs of religious teaching, an effort that brands them as "the most fundamental nonbelievers" (again, "heretics") according to Tolstoy, despite whatever else they might claim to be.[4]

What place is there among these personal circumstances for genuine belief? What shape would or could faith take in a person's life should they confront such contradictions? At this point in Tolstoy's youth, his only truly lasting belief was that he could somehow achieve perfection within himself, and this in order to gain power, to be "more famous, more important, wealthier."[5] Perhaps these are typical goals for a person to seek after, but, for Tolstoy, they were at one point the most important things he could want, and he was eager to achieve perfection in whatever form he was best able to utilize. What he recognized as well was that the virtues he cultivated in order to attain this level of perfection were contrary to religious teaching, and yet, in a very literal sense, he did not care: "Ambition, lust for power, self-interest, lechery, pride, anger, revenge, were all respected qualities. As I yielded to these passions I became like my elders and I felt that they were pleased with me."[6] And so he wrote and wrote, winning success and fame and fortune, in order to cultivate what he would later describe as ultimately vices. There was simply no room in his life for

---

3. Tolstoy, *A Confession*, 20.
4. Tolstoy, *A Confession*, 21.
5. Tolstoy, *A Confession*, 21.
6. Tolstoy, *A Confession*, 22.

a practice of the virtues, which appeared to be absent from his horizon as the vices were all that received his attention.[7]

For his part, Tolstoy noticed that living life according to this quest for perfection was what had also led him to tolerate a certain life of moral ambiguity, one embodied by many of his colleagues and friends: "[T]here were many among us who were unconcerned as to who was right and who wrong, but who simply achieved their own selfish ends by means of this activity of ours. All this forced me to doubt the truth of the faith."[8] This "faith," as he ironically labels it, was, as Karr had put it, a "warped communion," an evil masquerading as a virtue. It was also something that felt hollow to him, and yet he felt almost powerless to stop it from dominating his life, so strong was the pull toward the praise he received from his peers for his striving toward a perfection he seemed so close to achieving.

Yet, despite his successes, he began to see the limitations of this "writer"s religion" and its "priests": "But strange to say, even though the utter falsehood of this creed was something I came quickly to understand and to reject, I did not discard the rank these people bestowed on me: that of artist, poet and teacher."[9] In a sense, he began to encounter the real obstacle preventing him from changing course: he knew there was a moral uncertainty that dominated his life, and that gave him no life of his own, but he felt powerless to stop its force because this would actually cost him the social prestige that others had given him. In other words, when the sacrifice required too much of him, he was unwilling, seemingly unable even, to let go of what little privilege he had gained. In a very genuine manner, any talk of personal sacrifice—a practice so central to the story of Christianity—was denied to him, for his quest for perfection was unwilling to give up anything that it had deemed its own. The idea of losing his life in order to truly gain it was not an option he was willing to contemplate; he was focused only on obtaining and keeping what pleased him most in the eyes of others.

---

7. What he did not seek to cultivate, and I would suspect a good many "people of faith" caught up in living contradictory lives likewise care little about, are the things contained in centuries of writing and contemplation on the nature of virtues. These include how to go about fighting one's temptations, what living a moral life might look like, and how one is to go about making choices that matter, that build up the self and leave us, not with a temporary sense of elation regarding our self-worth, but a deep and lasting sense of who we are and what our purpose in life is. The life and history of the church is almost overflowing with the writings of many people who have pondered these questions over a span of centuries, and yet we often neglect such writings almost entirely as we are swept up in the tyranny of our present circumstances.

8. Tolstoy, *A Confession*, 23.

9. Tolstoy, *A Confession*, 24.

Tolstoy could not himself tell good from evil, he makes clear, and yet he wrote tirelessly in order to proclaim to others the vagueness of his own clouded perceptions. He was, in his words, a follower of their creed: "everything that exists is rational and all that exists evolves. And it evolves through enlightenment. Enlightenment is measured through the distribution of books and journals. We are paid and respected for writing these books and papers, so we must be the most important and useful people."[10] Karr had spoken of being trapped in the "myth" of autonomy. Tolstoy echoes this claim, reiterating certain mantras of the Enlightenment, and further encapsulating himself within a fortress of reason alone, from which he was frequently unable to escape. He would at times find glimpses beyond what captivated and held him, in ways that would foreshadow his later return to faith under different premises, but they were fleeting and ephemeral: "Only occasionally, led more by instinct than reason, I rebelled against the superstition so prevalent in our age by which people shield themselves from their failure to understand life."[11]

"More by instinct than reason," he says, and though he still needs to elaborate upon what exactly this means to him, he begins to enact a profound shift in his comprehension of the role of reason with regard to living the life of faith. This is what eventually gives him an alternative perspective on faith that causes him to reexamine his previous relationship to the myth of his autonomy. In his words, "It is now clear to me that there was no difference between our behaviour and that of people in a madhouse; but at the time I only dimly suspected this, and, like all madmen, I thought everyone was mad except myself."[12] Where he had ended up was nowhere other than trapped within his own head, within the confines of "reason alone," and he was almost fully unable to escape from its snares. What we will see later in the development of his faith life is therefore a radical contrast between trying to live a life of faith in an authentic manner and the ways of the world that seek to praise vice and to elevate the seemingly worst qualities of being-human to the highest ranks.

Tolstoy encountered such a contrast sharply at one point in his life, in fact, while visiting France. Upon viewing an execution enacted as the public spectacle of beheading a man in the midst of a Paris square, he was moved to think with his "whole being" and not just with his reason, to think moreover that nothing could justify this violence done to this man, criminal though he was. Though his mind was capable of justifying the death of

---

10. Tolstoy, *A Confession*, 24.
11. Tolstoy, *A Confession*, 26.
12. Tolstoy, *A Confession*, 25.

this man, whose "criminal" intentions we do not need even to know, his body was moved by the man's body, its vulnerability and its subjection to a barbaric cruelty that silenced his life entirely—a realization that Augustine's experience of his mother's death foreshadows only slightly. For Tolstoy, he was awakened to more of the fullness of his humanity through this experience, which brought about a profound realization for him that we are all much more than our capacity to reason. This realization was followed by his reflections upon the death of his own brother, who died young enough not to understand much of his life, or even why he was dying.

What Tolstoy was discovering through such extreme experiences was that the fullness of the human person opened him up to the "instincts of his soul" and how such a faculty could be that upon which he could base his moral judgments.[13] His quest for perfection, however, which was now "sublimated" into the desire to attain what was best for his family, as he would understand it, continued to dominate his life precisely because it had masked itself as a "nobler" cause than his previously self-centered goals for self-perfection.[14] The desire at the core of both, nonetheless, was the same, and undealt with. Yet despite the reality that he began to sense that he would achieve literary fame as great as many of the greatest authors (a claim which history suggests he was correct in assuming), he had no answer to the question of *why* such fame would matter, to him or to anyone else. As a result of such conflicting thoughts, he would continue to seek out the "best" for himself and his family, though it was not at all clear why he should do this, or what its result would truly be.

What began to haunt him in no small measure was the "truth" he grasped intuitively, that "life is meaningless."[15] In the absence of something larger than himself that would unite his world and give it meaning for him, he found himself staring over the edge of an abyss of despair. Fate, it seemed, had brought him little consolation in terms of his reason for existing: "This spiritual condition presented itself to me in the following manner: my life is some kind of stupid and evil joke that someone is playing on me."[16] Though this may sound ludicrous to some, especially when one thinks about the lasting significance that he had upon the field of literature, for Tolstoy it was a reality that could not be evaded. There was seemingly nothing he could tell himself that would change his patterns of thought or perspective on himself.

13. Tolstoy, *A Confession*, 26.
14. Tolstoy, *A Confession*, 28.
15. Tolstoy, *A Confession*, 30.
16. Tolstoy, *A Confession*, 31.

In short, due to such thoughts, he entered a deep existential despair that would not be placated by living an epicurean lifestyle bent on avoiding the pain and realities of life. As he frames this problematic situation that continued to dominate him:

> The delusion of the joys of life that had formerly stifled my fear of the dragon no longer deceived me. No matter how many times I am told: you cannot understand the meaning of life, do not think about it but live, I cannot do so because I have already done it for too long. Now I cannot help seeing day and night chasing me and leading me to my death. This is all I can see because it is the only truth. All the rest is a lie.[17]

He was simply unable to ignore what became a worsening situation, and the habits of his mind continued to win out over the simple consolations that had once prevented him from seeing the deeper truth of his existence. Using Karr's language, it would appear that Tolstoy was unable to "self-hypnotize," unable to find a way to trick his mind into other patterns of thought, and thus to avoid the crushing (and ultimately false) dichotomy of truth and lies beneath which he was brutalizing himself.

In a search for solutions, he contemplated a wide variety of possible answers, including scientific responses to existence: that he was an evolved, complex part of an infinite universe. But this answer, for him, did not entail any inherent meaning, a point that perhaps reminds us of how science addresses questions of "how?" but does not necessarily touch the deeper questions of "why?" The philosophical answers Tolstoy posed to himself involved paying attention to a spiritual dimension that could be cultivated in life, in one's ideals, the arts, through literary expression, etc., but this too did not seem enough to him. There was perhaps still too great a sense of artifice to each expression. His continuous probing for answers pointed him toward a reality that slowly became more complex, though the answers yet remained the same: "I do not know."[18] Meaning, as such, continued to elude him. In his own words, "[W]hat is the meaning given to my life? It has none. Or: what will come of my life? Nothing. Or: why does everything there is exist, and why do I exist? Because it does."[19] His readings of those who appeared to contain great wisdom, such as Socrates, Schopenhauer, Solomon, and Buddha, all seemed only to confirm his suspicions that these answers were indeed the correct ones. All was vanity and a chasing after the wind, as

---

17. Tolstoy, *A Confession*, 32.
18. Tolstoy, *A Confession*, 38.
19. Tolstoy, *A Confession*, 39.

Solomon had put it in the biblical book of Ecclesiastes. There was little hope for more reassurance than this.

Tolstoy began to take note, in addition to these insights, of how people would escape the situation in life in which he found himself, mainly through recourse to either ignorance, a so-called Epicureanism, strength and energy in order to end the ordeal (i.e., suicide) or, finally, the weakness of knowing that death is preferable, having no reason not to enact their own departure from this world, but being simply too weak to make this movement happen. Again, however, he realized that none of these options would be a suitable destination.

In the end, the "answer" would come to him, and it would be one that resonates deeply with what we have been following thus far in this book. It was only in the relationships around him, in getting outside of his limited and self-absorbed viewpoint and seeing that there were others beyond him who moved and thought and dwelt beyond the confines of his limited world that he would find any consolation. "It seems so strange to me now, so utterly incomprehensible, that in my reasoning of life I could have overlooked the life of humanity that surrounded me on all sides and that I could have been so ridiculously mistaken as to think that my life ... was the true, normal life, while the lives of millions was not worthy of attention."[20] In this discovery that removed such perplexing difficulties, Tolstoy began to learn another way of living life, one outside of his stratified existence amongst the privileged classes of Russian society, and made available to him through his living among the "working classes" whose embrace of religious belonging was much deeper than his own—a first indication to us that the downward movement toward that which seems beneath us, a conscious choice for "poverty," may contain something deeply instructive for the cultivation of the spiritual life on the whole.

There was an irony in his turning, almost paradoxically, to those who were themselves unable to give an articulate description of their beliefs, but, be that as it may, it was in such people that he found relief for his mental and emotional anguish. In his words,

> I sensed anyway that if I wanted to live and to understand the meaning of life I must not seek it among those who have lost it and wish to kill themselves, but among the millions of people living and dead who have created life, and who carry the weight of our lives together with their own. And I looked around at the enormous masses of simple, uneducated people

---

20. Tolstoy, *A Confession*, 49.

without wealth, who have lived and who still live, and I saw something quite different.[21]

What one notices about such "masses," of course, is that they do not fit into his fourfold scheme of labeling all the peoples of the world. These masses, so often criticized by the great thinkers of Western society for their inability to stand above the crowd (e.g., Nietzsche's critique of the "herd" mentality), suffered with an endurance that is rarely understood, were not simply irrational creatures or beasts, were opposed to suicide on the whole and were certainly some of the strongest people on the planet. Tolstoy's characterizations of them, he soon came to feel, had been misplaced, and his newfound respect and admiration for what they endured began to illuminate another path in life that would offer him something beyond the confines of his extremely narrow worldview. There was something else that motivated this mass of humanity, and it was this faith that spoke clearest and most significantly to him:

> Rational knowledge, as presented by the learned and wise, negates the meaning of life, yet the vast masses—humanity as a whole—recognize that this meaning lies in irrational knowledge. And this irrational knowledge is faith, the very thing I could not help rejecting. This God, one in three, the creation in six days, the devils and angels and all the rest that I could not accept without going mad.[22]

Accordingly, he began to feel that he should reject his use of reason in order to find faith, even though it had been reason alone that seemed like the only solid foundation of his world. To be clear on this, I don't think that his world suddenly became entirely "irrational," and I don't think we should be swayed by the strength of his rhetoric to believe that he renounced the use of reason altogether. The evidence in fact points to its continued usage in his life in multiple and necessary ways.

I believe that what he was trying to express was that making a choice for faith was something that removed him from his confinement to reason *alone*. The fullness of his humanity, what constituted the "soul" that guided him, was much more than his reason by itself, powerful though such a faculty may be. It was faith that, in his eyes, "affords the possibility of living," and that was something he had to personally encounter seemingly beyond his mental abilities.[23] I do not think he simply decided to live contrary to reason.

---

21. Tolstoy, *A Confession*, 50.
22. Tolstoy, *A Confession*, 50.
23. Tolstoy, *A Confession*, 53.

I think rather that he discovered how "Faith is the force of life," and to get to this comprehension, he would have to step outside of the mental traps he had been setting for himself.[24] Hence, his efforts to reject faith based simply on the claims of his reason became repugnant to him, as they sought to negate the only means he actually had to living his life to the fullest. Taking stock of the faith of the "masses" began to alter his perception of reality, and allowed him to reassess what he saw before his eyes.

Around this time, he also turned his eye to investigate those among his class who professed to be Orthodox believers, Christians indeed, but he found that, though they claimed to believe in God, they lived their lives as a form of deception. In his estimation, "if they had possessed a meaning that annihilated the fear of deprivation, suffering and death, they would not have been afraid of these things. But these believers of our class lived, just as I did, in excess, striving to maintain and increase it and fearing deprivation, suffering and death."[25] As a counterpoint to this blatant self-deception that seeks no critical platform from which to view itself, and hence, I would submit, denies a fundamental part of the Christian faith as well, he found himself drifting toward the poor, uneducated classes and the strength of their lives of faith, which, though they included things deemed superstitious by the "enlightened" class, yet seamlessly wove such beliefs into the very fabric of their lives. Such a turn allowed him to conclude in fact that "The whole way of life of the believers of my own circle stood in contradiction to their faith, whereas the whole way of life of the believers from the working population reaffirmed the meaning their faith gave to life."[26]

Tolstoy's personal revolution in faith hinged upon the ordinary, uneducated persons of faith whose lives were not to be despised, but were to be regarded as even more worthy than those of the socially privileged he had been accustomed to living among. If his revelation strikes us as more akin to Jesus' own fundamental observations about those around him and their simple lives of faith, I do not think it is a coincidence. I prefer to think that this is how difficult it is to make such a transition in a world so based on evaluative criteria so divergent from the proclamation of God's concerns (for the poor, the marginalized, etc.). And yet, despite the difficulty of seeing this reality, and the reality of our shying away from such persons who often embody what is considered to be the "worst" aspects of culture and society, Tolstoy began to reach out to the faith that he found there, altering his own path likewise: "And I started to look more closely at the life and faith of these

---

24. Tolstoy, *A Confession*, 54.
25. Tolstoy, *A Confession*, 57.
26. Tolstoy, *A Confession*, 58.

people, and the further I looked the more convinced I became that theirs was the true faith, that their faith was essential to them, and that it alone provides a sense of the meaning and possibility of life."[27]

In this reversal of values that was indeed nothing short of revolutionary for his personal existence, he found a peace that passes our common understanding of things, much as Wiman has already noted for us. As Tolstoy describes the experience, "Contrary to us, who the more intelligent we are the less we understand the meaning of life and see some kind of malicious joke in the fact that we suffer and die, these people live, suffer and approach death peacefully and, more often than not, joyfully."[28] What they seemed to find to their benefit, he had once feared. Letting go of such fears and learning to walk toward the suffering became—or at least held the possibility of becoming—a paradoxical strength through one's weakness, the very thing that Paul's words call each Christian toward, but which so many find too difficult to take up for themselves. Suffering paradoxically held the possibility of giving life meaning in a way that had evaded Tolstoy when all he had previously sought was to avoid suffering.

> I looked at the lives of the multitudes who have lived in the past and who live today. And of those who understood the meaning of life I saw not two, or three, or ten, but hundreds, thousands and millions. And all of them, endlessly varied in their customs, minds, educations and positions, and in complete contrast to my ignorance, knew the meaning of life and death, enduring suffering and hardship, lived and died and saw this not as vanity but good.[29]

Another way to describe this transformation would be to say that, just as he had to step outside the confines of his rational worldview (his act of *translation*, as I have been discussing it so far), so too did he have to step outside of the social confines that bound him. He had to leave his comfort zone (or *definition* of himself and his life) in order to penetrate the wisdom of those who find meaning within their suffering and hardship. This realization actually prompted him to reevaluate the real cause of his being unable to find meaning, for it would seem that it was not simply reason that had prevented him from seeing the truth, but rather his social condition: "I had strayed not so much because my ideas had been incorrect as because I had lived foolishly."[30]

27. Tolstoy, *A Confession*, 58.
28. Tolstoy, *A Confession*, 59.
29. Tolstoy, *A Confession*, 59.
30. Tolstoy, *A Confession*, 60.

The place he reached, therefore, was one of ease, but not the kind of ease that is socially recognized as the "easy life." Rather, his understanding was transformed through the relationships he fostered to those on the margins of society, but who were content to live there and to endure there as best they could, with a faith that somehow yet sustained them. Within such relationships, Tolstoy was able to find a connection to his own "roots" that secured him to a faith he had been unable to access before, but which he now found flourishing all around him:

> And I came to love these people. The further I penetrated into the lives of those living and dead about whom I had read and heard, the more I loved them and the easier it became for me to live. I lived like this for about two years and a great change took place within me, for which I had been preparing for a long time and the roots of which had always been in me.[31]

In a sense, Tolstoy was becoming one of the "least" among all people in order to realize the true heights and depths of his own humanity. Rather than shy away from those on the margins of all "good" society, he found that it was his own humanity that was given back to him the further he moved away from the traps and contradictions that had confined him amongst the "upper" classes.

The logic of this transformation is laid bare through a simple analogy between mathematics and the moral world, though it is a logic that many of us do not want to observe as active within ourselves:

> The truth has always been the truth, just as $2 \times 2 = 4$, but I had not admitted it, because in acknowledging that $2 \times 2 = 4$ I would have had to admit that I was a bad man. And it was more important and necessary for me to feel that I was good than to admit that $2 \times 2 = 4$. I came to love good people and to loathe myself, and I acknowledged the truth. And then it all became clear to me.[32]

The "uneducated" masses, he calculates, do the will of their master without complaining, while those who believe themselves to be the masters, "eat the master's food without doing what he asks of us" and then "we think it over and decide that either the master is stupid, or that he does not exist and that we are the only intelligent ones."[33] The truth he came to realize, however, was that such a calculation was not only baseless but a self-absorbed assessment. We are the ones quick to dismiss the role of the master because it is

31. Tolstoy, *A Confession*, 59.
32. Tolstoy, *A Confession*, 60.
33. Tolstoy, *A Confession*, 62.

to our benefit to do so. This is how we strive to secure our autonomy as our only power. It is we who end up in a sovereign position by denying the will of whomever we perceive to be the master, shunning any lessons that obedience might bring us. Rather than be left contented to ourselves, however, we are in a worse position than when we heeded the master's call: "The only thing is, we feel that we are no good for anything and that we must somehow escape from ourselves."[34] In the midst of his moments of despair, Tolstoy yet recognized a "tormenting feeling" that he later characterized as "a quest for God" that had been in him all along—the "roots" that secured him when all else seemed to fail.[35] "I say that this quest for God was not a debate but an emotion because it did not arise from my stream of thoughts—it was in fact quite contrary to them—but from my heart. It was a feeling of fear, abandonment, loneliness, amid all that was strange to me, and a sense of hope that someone would help me."[36]

What this sentiment demonstrates to us, I believe, is the only path that one can take toward finding what one is looking for: a stepping outside the self (or translation) that can only be characterized as a search for relationship, the very thing that will allow us to find something larger than ourselves (whether God or the person before us), but also that which will continue to define faith as itself a form of relationship. Unless the person of faith is willing to search for a relationship outside of themselves, no true friendship or belief will arise.

We might consider that this is what comes to define the task of *prayer* as a reaching out beyond the self to something other than ourselves, even though it is something we know not of. "Despite the fact that I was utterly convinced of the impossibility of proving the existence of God . . . I nevertheless searched for God in the hope that I might find Him, and reverting to an old habit of prayer, I prayed to Him whom I sought but could not find."[37] We certainly could not say at this point in his life that Tolstoy is fully aware of the God to whom he is reaching out. Though he recognized that a conceptualization of God is not God, he yet strove to find a God whom he did not have a completely formed picture of, much as Karr, Augustine, and Wiman have all also affirmed as the only way to go about finding God in one's life.[38] Despite this necessary vagueness, then, there was enough of "God" there in his own desire for God that spoke to him and moved him deeply. "I remembered

---

34. Tolstoy, *A Confession*, 62.
35. Tolstoy, *A Confession*, 63.
36. Tolstoy, *A Confession*, 63.
37. Tolstoy, *A Confession*, 63.
38. Tolstoy, *A Confession*, 65.

that I only lived during those times when I believed in God. Then, as now, I said to myself: I have only to believe in God in order to live. I have only to disbelieve in Him, or to forget Him, in order to die."[39]

It is with such a realization that he opens himself up toward a presence that he cannot mistake as that which allows him to push past his own capabilities and toward something other than himself that is yet within himself, the very life that pulsates within him: "What then is it you are seeking? a voice exclaimed inside me. There He is! He, without whom it is impossible to live. To know God and to live are one and the same thing. God is life."[40] Recalling Augustine's "restlessness" that finds no rest except in God, Tolstoy's emphasis upon his desire for God as leading him toward God is paramount above all else, and became that which granted him the possibility of finding rest from his tormented existence: "'Live in search of God and there will be no life without God!' And more powerfully than ever before everything within and around me came to light, and the light has not deserted me since."[41] Rather than suggest, however, that such a realization was without precedent, he finds that his truest "roots" are revealed: "And, strangely, the life force that returned to me was not a new one but the same old one that had attracted me during the early period of my life. I returned to all those things that had been part of my childhood and youth. I returned to a belief in that will that had given birth to me and which asked something of me."[42] And, as he continues, "In other words, I returned to a belief in God, in moral perfection, and to that tradition which had given life a meaning. Only the difference now was that whereas before I had accepted all this unconsciously, I now knew that I could not live without it."[43]

For Tolstoy, this newfound faith, which was also a return to the childlike simplicity of faith (though not a "child's faith," to be sure), was also a conscious rejection of the social class in which he had been living. In addition, this shift opened him up to a critique of ecclesiastical structures, which were keener on labeling others as heretics and maintaining their own power than on embracing the truth that he found moving amongst the poorest and most uneducated of the masses of believers.

To see such conflict and to be open to its critique is a tension that has not gone away since Tolstoy's time, and it most likely will never go away—as we will see again in Dorothy Day's story. Theology, or the church, or the

---

39. Tolstoy, *A Confession*, 65.
40. Tolstoy, *A Confession*, 65.
41. Tolstoy, *A Confession*, 65.
42. Tolstoy, *A Confession*, 65.
43. Tolstoy, *A Confession*, 65–66.

general mass of believers who inhabit the world, will always run the risk of misunderstanding the nature of the task as followers of a complex God who cannot be defined as neatly or simply as we would like. It is for this reason that those who work the hardest to secure their foundations—their definition or identity—may often be those who are, in turn, actually destroying the real roots of faith (and this certainly includes theologians). Tolstoy himself is taken aback at points by the way in which the church, and even theology, had turned away from this source of spiritual growth located in one's advancement toward poverty: "And assuming that truth lies in union by love, I was struck by the fact that theology was destroying the thing it should be advancing."[44] Indeed, it is often those who proclaim allegiance to a particular theological viewpoint who are, in reality, actively working against the faith that should be advanced, in Tolstoy's language. In this refusal of what actually matters, we should be struck once again by the realization that, even for those who are immersed in a particular church, theology, or worldview, the path of self-critique becomes available to us once again only when we realize that we are never fully settled on the path that God puts us on.

What Tolstoy witnessed in the church were a good many things repugnant to him, not least of which was the violence it had justified and condoned throughout the centuries. In short, "As I turned my attention to all that is done by people who profess Christianity, I was horrified."[45] A good deal of discernment would be needed to sift through this mess and maze of incongruent theologies and structures. As he quizzically pondered to himself at the end of his "confession," "But where did falsehood come from, and where did the truth come from? Both had been passed down by what is called the Church. But falsehood and truth are contained in tradition, in the so-called holy tradition and in the Scriptures."[46] Quite reasonably, he concludes that "I have no doubt that there is truth in the teachings, but I also have no doubt that there is falsehood in them too, and that I must discover what is true and what is false and separate one from the other. This is what I have set out to do."[47] This quest, we might add, was that which was to be left for another day, as at last he had found the path he was looking for, and was contented to walk along.

What is admirable in Tolstoy's account is that he is willing, much like Ignatius of Loyola as we will soon see, to investigate and learn from other

---

44. Tolstoy, *A Confession*, 74.
45. Tolstoy, *A Confession*, 76.
46. Tolstoy, *A Confession*, 77.
47. Tolstoy, *A Confession*, 78.

theological minds once he has himself undergone the journey of finding the faith that he had been longing for. His journey, having reached the plateau upon which he might rest in his faith, becomes one of a willing submission to the voices of others within the faith who are more experienced than he is with the ways in which faith might further develop. Though the tension between (religious) tradition and his own personal experience will never fade entirely from the horizon, he is content at this point of finding what he had long searched for, to listen to how others had cultivated their faith in light of long centuries of questing for the divine within the most ordinary of our world. His thought also opens a deeper pathway toward an embracing of the poverty of faith that we would do well to be attentive to as we continue to inspect the lives of faith of those who are drawn to similar paths.

CHAPTER SIX

Rachel Held Evans and Dani Shapiro

Finding a Way Forward for Critical Faith Today

Rachel Held Evans was born in Birmingham Alabama on June 8, 1981 but spent a majority of her adolescence in Dayton, Tennessee, where her father was an administrator at Bryan College. After graduating with a BA in English, she spent time writing for local newspapers throughout Tennessee before settling down to start her own blog. With her familial background lying firmly within the bounds of nondenominational evangelicalism, Evans spent a large portion of her thinking and writing traversing the borders between conventional orthodoxy and the unknown consequences of stepping outside of a literalist framework. Although her work was controversial within her own faith background, her ability to balance her traditional framework with the intent of remaining within the spectrum of evangelicalism led to a much-needed breath of fresh air within one of America's most insular communities. Questioning gender roles, the absolute authority of the Bible, and the rigidity of the evangelical umbrella are just the surface of what Evans's line of inquiry included, and her witty but sharp writing style gave her the tools to truly subvert normativity within her sphere. Among Evans's recent publications are Faith Unraveled (2010), A Year of Biblical Womanhood (2012), and Searching for Sunday (2015). Tragically, Evans died suddenly in 2019 after experiencing an allergic reaction to medication.

  Dani Shapiro was born in New York in 1962 to Orthodox Jewish parents who raised her within the tradition, a facet of her life that would become one of the building blocks of her writing style. In terms of memoirs, she has authored Slow Motion: A True Story

(1998), Devotion: A Memoir *(2010)*, Still Writing: The Perils and Pleasures of a Creative Life *(2013)*, *and most recently* Hourglass: Time, Memory, Marriage *(2017)*. *Additionally, she has published five novels, including the bestsellers* Black & White *and* Family History. *Her work has appeared in* The New Yorker, The New York Times Book Review, The New York Times, The Los Angeles Times, O (The Oprah Magazine), *and has been broadcast on NPR's "This American Life." Additionally, Shapiro has taught writing classes at Columbia, NYU, The New School, and Wesleyan University. When she is not writing at her Connecticut home, she is often found at various speaking engagements, an active part of her memoir process.*

Tolstoy's wrestling with the peoples and traditions that comprised what he saw of Russian Orthodoxy around him reminds us of how important religious traditions can be in the face of the struggle to narrate our lives, which are never wholly autonomous. Our stories are actually encircled by the stories of others, a fact that can be as difficult to deal with when we feel oppressed by their weight, as it can also be comforting when we feel alone and misunderstood. In this chapter, I want to take a look at a set of contrasting authors whom I feel provide an accurate snapshot of both what is reasonable for a genuine faith to hold as true in the modern world—that is, what is reasonable for faith today—and insofar as they also point a way forward for living an authentic, though often very messy and realistic, life of faith in relation to the communities and traditions of faith in which they were brought up. I want to illuminate these relationships at this juncture in the present study too because the central dynamics of a contrast between tradition and experience have been a bit more fully exposed by Tolstoy's account.

By looking at Rachel Held Evans's memoir *Evolving in Monkeytown* alongside Dani Shapiro's *Devotion*, I hope to show how they unfold their relationships to community in very different ways, though there is a shared trait in their willingness to translate their lives into new idioms, forging new paths and traditions along the way. The main point of contrast in what follows, however, is not that one author's perspective is more valid than the other; rather, I want to emphasize how they merely differ in their starting and ending points as they undertake their spiritual journeys, something that will give us a unique vantage point from which to view the significance of how one never really "completes" such a journey at all, no matter where they begin or where they end.

The first author I want to take up is Rachel Held Evans and her memoir *Evolving in Monkeytown*, which considers the survival of an evolving faith in the midst of a Christian evangelical, fundamentalist American context. It is her struggle to come to terms with a faith lived beyond the confines of what she experienced growing up in the church that strikes me as both critically self-aware and wholly in line with the desires of so many of the authors covered in this book. Echoing a good deal of what Wiman, for one, puts forth as his acceptance of a life of faith lived within the flux of change, Evans takes the time to consider how "If there's one thing I know for sure, it's that faith can survive just about anything, so long as it's able to evolve."[1] Within such an understanding of faith, her journey of self-exploration can only come across to us as a further deepening of a self-critical movement toward the heart of faith and its ability to move beyond whatever we had thought it to be—beyond then any static definition.

Being a self-described "model" Christian at a young age in a fundamentalist evangelical church, for Evans, was about imitating a certain puritanical mind-set that has indeed come to dominate many people's conceptions of what it means to be religious in America. This was for her something that seemed to make being a Christian almost fully dependent upon her moral behavior, which included the apparent virtue of not doubting what you were taught to believe about the life of faith to be lived as a secure source of one's identity. The profound moral rectitude and certainty of belief that resulted in forming such a view of herself were ultimately, however, debilitating, though, previously, they had appeared as bedrocks of security in the face of her unending fears.

> I was a fundamentalist because my security and self-worth and sense of purpose in life were all wrapped up in getting God right—in believing the right things about him, saying the right things about him, and convincing others to embrace the right things about him too. Good Christians, I believed, don't succumb to the shifting sands of culture. Good Christians, I used to think, don't change their minds.[2]

Though this was an essential misreading of what faith would become to her as an evolving perspective on life, God, and the world, she was mired early on within such snares because her quest for a fixed, strong identity had been so successful in keeping her deep, underlying insecurities at bay. We can see this, perhaps better than anywhere else, in the way in which she clung to her beliefs—that is, in the desire with which she held her faith, and which

---

1. Evans, *Evolving in Monkeytown*, 17.
2. Evans, *Evolving in Monkeytown*, 17.

actually says a lot more about the nature of our beliefs than a good many "believers" would like to admit: "I was a fundamentalist not because of the beliefs I held but because of how I held them: with a death grip. It would take God himself to finally pry some of them out of my hand."[3]

As but one example of how this impacted the structure and performance of her faith in general, she held to an interpretation of the Bible that refused to admit that one's perspective on it could change over time, and her outlook on her personal faith suffered a good deal as a result. What she came to realize eventually, however, was that "In truth, the Bible represents a cacophony of voices. It is a text teeming with conflict and contrast, brimming with paradox, held together by creative tension."[4] This complexity within the scriptural narrative—as much as it was also present in her personal life—was a possibility that had eluded her for so long because such a recognition would deny the very foundation of what a strong identity or sense of definition (whether personal or communal) is about. In truth, to be sure, our readings of Scripture *are* shaped by all of the various cultural factors that make up our lives and this is not a bad thing at all, as she discovers; it is rather the foundation from which we begin to see our lives and ourselves within a given scriptural account of the life of faith. As she will describe this discovery as it began to reveal to her the ways in which she had unjustly denounced others for things that she herself was guilty of, "we criticized relativists for picking and choosing truth, while our own biblical approach required some selectivity of its own."[5] By seeing the depth of her own hypocrisy as such, she is able to open up her worldview beyond its narrow confines, and to allow herself to wonder "if perhaps there is no such thing as one, single biblical worldview, if perhaps there are as many worldviews out there as there are people."[6]

As I have noted already, this capacity to reach beyond one's identity and community—the very things that define our world—and to translate oneself into other worldviews and within relationships with other persons we had once deemed foreign or strange to us is essential for forming a lasting sense of faith, one that evolves or changes as we evolve and change too. Such a process does not mean that we forsake identity or definition altogether; rather, we are able to hold such things differently, and to make use of them so that we might relate to others and establish a more authentic faith in our lives.

3. Evans, *Evolving in Monkeytown*, 17–18.
4. Evans, *Evolving in Monkeytown*, 189.
5. Evans, *Evolving in Monkeytown*, 80.
6. Evans, *Evolving in Monkeytown*, 68.

As she eventually began to open her mind toward other, "alternative" possibilities, she began too to grasp the complexity of faith and its development over time, something that does not overturn its relevance, but rather deepens the sense of it within a person's life: "[T]he real story of Christianity is a lot less streamlined. The real story involves centuries of upheaval, challenge, and change."[7] As her realization came to demonstrate, the Christian faithful cannot simply skip over history and pretend as if our perception of Jesus did not change over time, or were not changed by both time and the traditions we have come to call the church, much as Newman had reminded us earlier.

Coming to this realization helped Evans to understand her own complexity and how she herself was implicated by the structures that we typically identify ourselves with so that we don't have to face the complexity that exists in our world:

> We would all like to believe that had we lived in the days of the early church or the Protestant Reformation, we would have chosen the side of truth, but in nearly every case, this would have required a deep questioning of the fundamental teachings of the time. It would have required a willingness to change. We must be wary of imitating the Pharisees, who bragged that had *they* lived during the time of the prophets, they would have protected the innocent, but who then plotted against Jesus and persecuted the disciples.[8]

How are we to know which side of history we are on, unless we first learn to critically examine the context in which we live and our longing to identify with it? We must remember always that those on the "wrong side" of history typically have believed they were on the "right side," working for the good of humanity, when it was the opposite that actually came about as a result of their efforts. We would do well to recall too, in fact, that it was at times multitudes of "good Christians" in Germany and elsewhere, prior to and throughout the Second World War, who did such horrible things to others, or who simply refused to stand up and protest what was going on around them.

Evans, through such revelations, becomes a self-avowed "evolutionist" in terms not only of her scientific views, but regarding faith as well—a faith, as Wiman had also alerted us, that must evolve if it is to stay around, and to stay relevant. For Evans, this meant letting go of her fears: "It means being okay with being wrong, okay with not having all the answers, okay with

---

7. Evans, *Evolving in Monkeytown*, 18.
8. Evans, *Evolving in Monkeytown*, 20–21.

never being finished."⁹ Such a sentiment would be, in many ways, the complete opposite of how she was taught to embrace the faith of her childhood, a faith that came with a sense of certainty that appealed to her child's longing for a solution to every problem or question. But, as she would find out later, such a construction of things was often the result of having to make that perilous journey from childhood to adulthood in terms of faith too, for they are very different worlds, though this is a journey that we often do not make. She senses this difficulty and the potential for misunderstandings when she states that "It is perhaps an unfair thing to ask of a child, but few who decide to follow Jesus know from the beginning what they're getting themselves into."[10] For Evans, Christianity, or at least the version she grew up with, was a necessary cultural element to life, and one that she felt very much at home in throughout her youth, though, in hindsight, she was not always the most kind and generous of "model" Christians.

In her adult life, she was able to locate something of the missteps she took in relation to her fears and insecurities: "Growing up, my greatest fear was that I would find God out, that I would accidentally stumble upon some terrible, unspeakable thing that proved he wasn't as great and good as grown-ups made him out to be."[11] And, of course, there are the unsettling questions that plagued her for quite some time, for example, "What if I'm wrong?"[12]—a sentiment that accompanied her secret feelings of really being a fraud deep down inside.

In many ways, it is interesting and important to note how these sentiments of a fear of being wrong about one's chosen faith (something mistakenly built upon a foundation of reason alone) could be maintained for any religious person, in whatever traditional religious upbringing, not just Christianity. When such an inquiry is presented to us in the modern world, it is typically a significant sign of how we are dealing with a much larger problematic than just "Is this one particular religion the true one?," a question that is actually not very helpful in getting to the heart of the problem.

Evans's failure to identify the complexity of her faith early on in her life is why we see her relationship to her faith eventually become detached from the particularities of that faith—at least initially in her life, and though she would return to the particularities of their traditions in a completely different way later on, much as Tolstoy had experienced. As she describes such nostalgic longings for the faith she was raised with, "Sometimes I long

9. Evans, *Evolving in Monkeytown*, 23.
10. Evans, *Evolving in Monkeytown*, 27.
11. Evans, *Evolving in Monkeytown*, 35.
12. Evans, *Evolving in Monkeytown*, 35.

for the days when I was so certain, when faith was as sure a thing as thunder after a lightning flash or the scent of almond cherry at night. Things have changed a lot since then, but not necessarily for the worst."[13] The temptation to see things in "black and white"[14] had diminished, and the complexity of her own life had opened up to her more fully. This is why, I would suggest, she was ultimately able to go back to the Christian narrative and reexamine its constituent parts, asking deeper and better questions concerning the content of what is present within it.

She came to this place perhaps most directly when she realized how the critical insights that she had honed while engaging in Christian apologetics—the effort to defend the faith, often through rational arguments alone, and in almost hyper-critical vigilance against perceived secular, nonbelieving persons—ironically served her now in other ways: "You might say that the apologetics movement had created a monster. I'd gotten so good at critiquing all the fallacies of opposing worldviews, at searching for truth through objective analysis, that it was only a matter of time before I turned the same skeptical eye upon my own faith."[15] Here we have the same impetus for self-critique we have seen already active in so many other lives of faith, even if in this case generated from the "other side" of faith, one initially not open to difference and complexity. This is a desire to defend the faith turned on itself and pushing her to generate a self-reflexive view of her own life.

Such a self-reflexive understanding through questioning was brought about, for Evans, through witnessing the video of the death of a woman at the hands of the oppressive Taliban regime in the recent history of Afghanistan. She realized through her contemplation of this horrific act the absurdity of condemning someone like this woman to hell, which is what her fundamentalist beliefs had taught her, simply because the woman had not received the gospel message in the way that Evans had believed a person should for the sake of their salvation. In her words, "the idea that this woman passed from agony to agony, from torture to torture, from a lifetime of pain and sadness to an eternity of pain and sadness, all because she had less information about the gospel than I did, seemed cruel, even sadistic."[16] This was not the God she wanted to believe in. "If salvation is available only to Christians, then the gospel isn't good news at all. For most of the human race, it is terrible news."[17]

13. Evans, *Evolving in Monkeytown*, 43.
14. Evans, *Evolving in Monkeytown*, 85.
15. Evans, *Evolving in Monkeytown*, 79.
16. Evans, *Evolving in Monkeytown*, 91.
17. Evans, *Evolving in Monkeytown*, 92–93.

What Evans was critically discerning at this point in her life was a very different idea of salvation than she had been raised with, but also of what we might consider to be the kingdom of God, our images of heaven and hell, and even the community we call the church, as the body of Christ. Are such things to be understood as ideals we aspire toward, or as practical realities that we strive to achieve, but know we never will? Are they exclusive communities of the "elect," or are they open to all? Far too often throughout history these terms have been used in a political sense, as means of exclusion and as a way to enact boundaries (static definitions) between persons, groups, societies, and nations. What Evans is pushing us toward, however, is another way to think about these terms, one that hinges upon the inclusion of those who are capable of admitting the brokenness of their identities, even and especially when such identities are communally understood. This is the heart of what I have been calling the act of translation. Later, in fact, she will realize: "Perhaps being a Christian isn't about experiencing the kingdom of heaven someday but about experiencing the kingdom of heaven every day."[18]

This sentiment echoes so many of the authors we are looking at and their desire to move away from talk about the afterlife and to look toward the construction of meaning within the lives and suffering that take place entirely in *this* world. To shift one's perception as such can bring about a completely new way of envisioning how one orients oneself *in* this world. Very directly, for Evans, this realization was what precipitated her "crisis" of faith that was really a significant moment in the evolution of her life of faith: "What makes a faith crisis so scary is that once you allow yourself to ask one or two questions, more inevitably follow. Before you know it, everything looks suspicious. Doubts I'd been shoving to the back of my mind for years came rushing forward in an avalanche of questions . . ."[19] Regarding the existence of God, for example, she indicates: "First I doubted that he is good; then I doubted that he is real. It seemed the teleological argument in support of his existence was a lot less effective when I was unsure of his benevolence. I never realized how important hope is to belief."[20]

Hope is the foundation from which, for many, belief springs. It is also, from another viewpoint, that which develops out of faith, the hope in what is "unseen" and yet believed in. In many ways, hope is to be comprehended not simply as a naïve wishing in that which one cannot see with their own eyes —akin to magic for many—but a fundamental state of being, a dwelling in that which one believes, but also insofar as what one believes leads

18. Evans, *Evolving in Monkeytown*, 173.
19. Evans, *Evolving in Monkeytown*, 95–96.
20. Evans, *Evolving in Monkeytown*, 96–97.

to a transformative capacity to love. The relationship, since Paul, has been one of interwoven virtue: faith, hope, and love, coexisting together (as in 1 Corinthians 13).

Evans was, as she went through this profound transformation, in her own words, becoming a skeptic, and this was, to her mind at the time, a terrible thing. It was later, however, once she began to understand and seize it for what it was, a potentially new path toward a radically more secure foundation for her faith. At this early point, though, and perhaps even scarier to her, was the fact that she began to realize that Jesus himself was a lousy apologist and that he asked more questions than he gave answers. He seemed to almost delight in not being direct and in telling stories rather than giving moral pronouncements (a point that lends a fair amount of credence to the focus I am taking on the autobiographical stories theology needs to pursue as well). Such reexaminations of the particularities of the Christian story are what allowed her to feel "secure" in a certain "insecure" space of identity, one that seeks more to embody the faith than to understand it: "Being a Christian, it seemed, isn't about agreeing to a certain way; it is about embodying a certain way. It is about living as an Incarnation of God."[21]

Essentially, to frame things in the language I have been using, she was beginning to refuse the abstractions that her fundamentalist theology had forced her to conjure in order to justify her position as certain or justified over others. The rejection of such abstractions, in turn, opened her up to the particular lives of the people she found before her. In her words, "I needed to know that God does not make disposable people."[22] Everyone's life counts, not just those who are part of a select religious group. A certain form of inclusion therefore began to set in her mind as a genuine theological possibility. Such movements and realizations are also, I would add, an intellectually honest way of doing theology:

> To be wrong about God is the condition of humanity, for better or for worse. Sometimes it lures us into questioning God; sometimes it summons us to give him another chance. After I'd thought for so many years that good Christians are always ready with an answer, it was a question that eventually drew me back to belief.[23]

Or, in other words, "In the end, it would be doubt that saved my faith."[24]

---

21. Evans, *Evolving in Monkeytown*, 108.
22. Evans, *Evolving in Monkeytown*, 117.
23. Evans, *Evolving in Monkeytown*, 119.
24. Evans, *Evolving in Monkeytown*, 119.

An eventual experience in India, while living there and working with certain marginalized persons for a time, would also open her up to an inclusive sense of religious belonging, as well as the nature of how theology is, or should be, done. As she recalls, and in ways that will echo Henri Nouwen's relearning of theological discourse from those with significant mental and physical forms of poverty, as well as Tolstoy's revelation that faith dwelt among the "masses" more profoundly than among the educated classes, "an illiterate widow taught me more about faith than any theologian ever could . . ."[25] This realization, of course, is not to generalize that every person in an impoverished situation has profound insights to offer the rest of humanity (which may of course be true in some contexts, less so in others), though it does indicate a general truth overall: that those in situations of poverty often do have a better grasp of how the humility experienced in poverty is an essential ingredient in growing the life of faith.

What Evans unveils through her experiences of learning about God's grace through other, non-literate, non-Western persons are her limitations, and her desire to become intimate with them, much as Nouwen will himself express, but also to push past these limitations in order to reach out in relationship to others. To go through such an experience is the nature of understanding our "sinful" side, as well as the necessity of confession for the growth of faith. Her desire, as such, was to remove the obstacles that prevented her from grasping the depths of faith.

This insight will draw us back to comprehending why poverty is such a big deal in terms of getting to know one's life of faith. In Evans's words, "I'm afraid that just as wealth and privilege can be a stumbling block on the path to the gospel, theological expertise and piety can also get in the way of the kingdom."[26] It is not only wealth and privilege that can prevent the words of God from sinking into our minds and actions, but also those who claim to have a coherent (entirely *defined*) theological vision, to have rationally justified the "answer" to themselves, or to live a pious life of moral rectitude that can also prevent us from finding a more authentic form of an evolving faith. As she would describe her revelation, "In India, I learned that among Hindus, the goal of reincarnation is to be reborn into nobler circumstances. And in India, I learned that in the kingdom of God, the goal is to be reborn into humbler ones."[27] This is a statement that takes very seriously the Christian claims of poverty and weakness in a way that challenges not only those within Christianity who would ignore its claims upon them, but also

25. Evans, *Evolving in Monkeytown*, 144.
26. Evans, *Evolving in Monkeytown*, 154.
27. Evans, *Evolving in Monkeytown*, 156.

those of other faiths that perpetuate discrimination against those living in conditions of poverty, whatever they may be.

What Evans was after was, in her words, a true experience of liberation,[28] one which included being free to ask questions, something that many Christians want to experience, but often feel that they are denied the privilege of undertaking—another, illuminating expression of a liberation theology.[29] Instead of searching for such a pouring out of the self, most Christians, as well as many religious and non-religious people, shield themselves from the hard truths that would cause us to have to change our way of living by engaging that which appears to be wholly foreign to us. As Evans struggled with this insight, but also valiantly considered the cost she was willing to undergo, "Every good Christian knows that the best way to insulate yourself from criticism or input is to say that God wants whatever you want."[30] To express as much in one's life is, of course, the path of little to no personal or spiritual growth.

Real theology, she suggests, is something perhaps very different from how it has been practiced in the past. It is more an understanding of theology as a form of relationship, for "I believe absolute truth is embodied in the person of Jesus Christ, which means it is relational, because everyone experiences Jesus a little differently."[31] There is a willingness in this suggestion that listening and relating to one another is what Jesus had in mind when he spoke to those who brought their problems to him, and that this was what mattered most—perhaps even a good deal more than naming or thoroughly defining the God we wish to follow with our lives. "How lovely and how terrible that absolute truth exists in something that cannot really be named."[32] Evans's conclusion is essentially a reflection on the real dialectic of faith in a person's life, that doubt can provide a foundation for faith in ways that we often miss or misperceive. In her words,

> Doubt is a difficult animal to master because it requires that we learn the difference between doubting God and doubting what we believe about God. The former has the potential to destroy faith; the latter has the power to enrich and refine it. The former is a vice; the latter a virtue.[33]

28. Evans, *Evolving in Monkeytown*, 174.
29. Evans, *Evolving in Monkeytown*, 204.
30. Evans, *Evolving in Monkeytown*, 148.
31. Evans, *Evolving in Monkeytown*, 221.
32. Evans, *Evolving in Monkeytown*, 210.
33. Evans, *Evolving in Monkeytown*, 219.

> I sometimes wonder if I might have spent fewer nights in angry, resentful prayer if only I'd known that my little systems—my theology, my presuppositions, my beliefs, even my fundamentals—were but broken lights of a holy, transcendent God. I wish I had known to question them, not him.[34]

> What my generation is learning the hard way is that faith is not about defending conquered ground but about discovering new territory. Faith isn't about being right, or settling down, or refusing to change. Faith is a journey, and every generation contributes its own sketches to the map.[35]

As Augustine embodied in his *Confessions*, and in the act of "confessing" itself, Evans puts an explicit stress upon the necessity of asking and "living in" the questions before one can experience "the answer, some distant day."[36] To suggest this method for pursuing faith is likewise to confirm the necessity of confession itself within the life of faith that she, among others, wishes to see vibrantly alive within her.

> If there's one thing I know for sure, it's that serious doubt—the kind that leads to despair—begins not when we start asking God questions but when, out of fear, we stop. In our darkest hours of confusion and in our most glorious moments of clarity, we remain but curious and dependent little children, tugging frantically at God's outstretched hands and pleading with every question and every prayer and every tantrum we can muster.[37]

I will take leave of Evans's story at this point, but only insofar as we will be able to see how her story converges with, even as it differs from, the next life story I want to examine in depth. Though the memoir of Dani Shapiro might seem to be heading down a different path altogether than Evans, I rather feel that the reflections of the one flow into the other, and vice versa. Evans's openness to an inclusive faith prompts, to my mind, the inclusive and searching desires of Shapiro, who enters our story from a completely different perspective—and yet one that resonates deeply with Evans's own life story in many ways.

* * *

---

34. Evans, *Evolving in Monkeytown*, 220.
35. Evans, *Evolving in Monkeytown*, 220.
36. Evans, *Evolving in Monkeytown*, 224.
37. Evans, *Evolving in Monkeytown*, 226–27.

In Shapiro's memoir *Devotion*, a book about struggle and loss as well as the fears of potential loss, we find a longing for religious tradition and grounding in a way that Evans's tale lacked. For Evans, the journey was about coming from the thickness of the Christian fundamentalist tradition to the inclusive experience of longing to see beyond what her religious upbringing had shown her. For Shapiro, the journey is admittedly set in the opposite direction, and so charted to move from vague experiences of the divine to a religious tradition that offers to "root" her in one place. The journey Shapiro takes is, of course, equally valid to Evans's; the route, however, is very different.

Struggling to face her Jewish roots, and so struggling to comprehend the relevance of "ritual so distant from our daily lives that we might as well have been kneeling at a Buddhist temple, or a Catholic church, or wherever people kneel the world over,"[38] Shapiro tried to embrace the complexity of faith in a modern world and to make a movement toward organized religious practices. This does not mean, though, that her efforts would be easily met by simply attending a given religious tradition's services. She recognizes that she has too much baggage that could not be easily shed for this to be the case. In her words, "I was instantly lost in the place I always found myself during the rare times I summoned up the nerve to reach back and grasp for a bit of the tradition I grew up with."[39] In essence, she found herself lost amidst so many religious traditions and practices that did not seem like "home," while searching for something she did not know how to describe, let alone find—though she was certain, at least, that she needed to find *something* to assist her along this path: "I had reached the middle of my life and knew less than I ever had before. . . . From the outside, things looked pretty good. But deep inside myself, I had begun to quietly fall apart."[40]

Her experiences of parenting and the dire sickness of her young son brought her very close to the reality of the precariousness of life, its vulnerability and fragility, though such experiences also brought her down lower than she might have anticipated. As a result, afterwards, she says, "I hadn't figured out how to live with my heightened awareness of exactly how fragile it all is. . . . I was trying to control the universe—and it's hard work to try to control the universe."[41] This is a slightly sarcastic way of putting things, of course. We cannot control the universe, to be sure. But we often try to do just that as an attempt to deal with the fragility and chaos of our own

38. Shapiro, *Devotion*, 6.
39. Shapiro, *Devotion*, 7.
40. Shapiro, *Devotion*, 9.
41. Shapiro, *Devotion*, 14.

lives. This was exactly what had motivated Tolstoy earlier to provide every comfort he could manage for his family in a quest for perfection that had also been attempted to stave off his own fears.

Shapiro began, through her exposure to her own vulnerability, to see the difference, in kind, between "those with an awareness of life's inherent fragility and randomness, and those who believed they were exempt."[42] Finding herself within the former lot based on her experiences of parenting and life in general, she yet aimed herself toward a third option, which involves recognizing the fragility of life and yet dares to hold "this paradox lightly in one's own hands."[43] This is certainly not an easy thing to do, especially when so much threatens us from without and our anxieties rear up again and again, including the fear of losing what we love most. In many ways, this attempt would characterize a good deal of the anxiety that threatened to overwhelm her at several points throughout her recounting of her struggles to locate a spirituality *and* religious tradition suitable to her.

In many ways, Shapiro represents a category that is very popular these days, that of being "spiritual but not religious." Those who fit in this category may believe that there is something out there for them, but words fail to describe it. They may feel they have a very personal spirituality but do not want to identify with any religious tradition, which may seem too rule-based or imposing. In a way, the phrase "spiritual but not religious" expresses a breakdown in religious terminology and definition. We do not know what to do with a lot of those terms like *atheism, agnosticism, theism, deism, pantheism,* etc., that humanity has traditionally used to define its belief systems. Being "spiritual but not religious" is consequently in some ways a reaction against too many people who are religious but not spiritual. It is also a gesture towards the act of translation that must accompany every act of definition. Perhaps one of the best ways for theists to understand their own lives of faith, following Wiman in some ways, is to look for the atheist within, and vice versa, thus revealing how the terms, or identities, we use are themselves more permeable (or translatable) than we may like to think.

Shapiro's struggle with her religious identity, much like Evans's, mirrors her struggle with the fragility of her own life and her attempt to find security in ways that are not really possible. In this transition between identities there is an attempt to locate the basis of one's own spirituality independent of any institutional structure, a potentially scary, but also ultimately liberating definition of what a conversion could be in many ways.

---

42. Shapiro, *Devotion*, 139.

43. Shapiro, *Devotion*, 139.

In the midst of this fluctuation between a spirituality devoid of religious structure and the hypocritical feelings of being a part of a religious institution devoid of spiritual depth, her mind began to wonder, "Was there no pattern, no wisdom, no plan?"[44] She was racing to grasp something solid that would indicate where the meaning in life was to be found. As such, she declares, much like Karr had experienced, that "I needed to place my faith in *something*."[45] Using the language of lovers, we might be able to detect here a sentiment that resonates with the experience of when we feel as though we need to find *someone* to be in love with, which is really a quest too to find ourselves and who we are. For many persons, we think that if we find the right person we will be "complete," though we miss the point that this quest actually speaks more directly to our deep-seated insecurities, and our ability to project our desires onto others, than it does to the reality of the person we are trying to form a relationship with. What Shapiro discovers when she looks deep enough, then, much like Sentilles discovered earlier, is that "I was lonely for myself."[46] In this confusing nexus of trying to find something outside herself to ground her in her life while also trying to find *herself* and the meaning in her life, she searched for a significant way to link the two quests through religious ritual and the life of prayer, which is really what prayer is all about, making the linkage between the world of patterns and plans and the small selves that we actually are. If faith is a relationship, prayer is an attempt to relate.

What we witness throughout her memoir is subsequently her quest for the spiritual *and* religious life, that which frames her recovery of "something" resembling faith. As she describes the situation, "I had arrived—in the words of Thomas Merton—at an abyss of irrationality, confusion, pointlessness, and apparent chaos. This, Merton believed, was the only point at which faith was possible. But most days, I felt the chaos without the faith."[47] Where does faith begin? To start with, it is not that which happens when a person finally gets their life entirely sorted out. It commences, as she notes, in the abyss and insecurities of life, though this is precisely the state that most of us avoid encountering directly. Instead of facing such a place of emptiness, and thereby of feeling small and vulnerable, we often feel rather that once we figure things out, and make a reasonable gesture toward getting life "in order," then we can enter into the deeper search for faith. But what if that narrative has things backwards?

44. Shapiro, *Devotion*, 10.
45. Shapiro, *Devotion*, 10.
46. Shapiro, *Devotion*, 123.
47. Shapiro, *Devotion*, 160.

Shapiro, much like Karr, had once found Alcoholics Anonymous to be a "sanctuary" during times of crisis, the "higher power" that gave her some consolation.[48] AA had helped her to see something different about how the divine might potentially work in our world. As she would phrase such a transformative period in her life:

> As much as I had tried to leave God out of it, once in a while, as I looked around any given dingy church basement, it would occur to me that perhaps this *was* God. Not the terrifying gray-bearded figure of my youth. Not the heavenly father from the Lord's Prayer. But right here, in the eloquence rising out of despair, the laughter out of darkness. The nodding heads, the clasping hands. The kindness extended to strangers. The sense—each and every time—of *Me too, I've been there too*. Never before had I listened so carefully or learned so much.[49]

It can be a profound moment of connection to see someone else's brokenness or to break down and have someone see your self in a way we might normally avoid revealing. In these experiences of finding God amongst those who were struggling and marginalized within society, the addicts whose stories many would take to be beneath the "saintliness" we so often search for in spiritual terms, she opened herself up to something beyond herself through the relationships around her (again, as a vital act of translation), and she also struggled to get hold of the varieties and uncertainties of faith that circulated around her.

She reflects at one point how most of the people she talks to about God are "disenchanted," realizing that the most they can say about God is that "I can't believe in a God who would . . ."—leaving us to fill in the blank with so many false conceptions of God and divine activity in our world.[50] She eventually came to provide, among other things, a crushing blow to those who believe that "God doesn't give us more than we can handle" and who see everything "happening for a reason"—the typical answers to theodicy that involve God reigning sovereign over every human action.[51] Shapiro's response to this is simply, "I was certain that there was no reason. No reason at all. There was only this: luck, timing, consequences."[52] Some people like to respond to situations of suffering with a convenient answer that things happen for a reason because it makes them feel comfortable

---

48. Shapiro, *Devotion*, 89.
49. Shapiro, *Devotion*, 92.
50. Shapiro, *Devotion*, 98, de-emphasized from the original.
51. Shapiro, *Devotion*, 108.
52. Shapiro, *Devotion*, 111.

or powerful, or secure in a situation that is deeply marred by insecurity. In Wiman's terms, such moments of suffering are a large dose of contingency, but perhaps also a contingency that could be capable of including God's presence from time to time, *within* the suffering that we undergo. Meaning, Shapiro affirms, is something we can create, even in moments of despair, as difficult as this may sound.[53] We create meaning in our lives through relationships, for example, by going out and doing things with other people. Faith and other relationships may be contingent—we may meet the love of our life in the grocery store, or at a music festival, or even online, among other places—but this does not mean such relationships are devoid of meaning. Contingent events that are absolutely fragile are actually the only way to relate to something that may eventually turn out to be certain and secure in a completely different sense.

What Shapiro highlights for any reexamination of faith is the general problem of theodicy, of why suffering and evil exist in a world that is said to be governed by a "good" God. What she is also doing, however, is opening up our understanding of such a God who appears to control everything to a place beyond where many of us have ceased to evolve in our understanding of who this deity might be beyond that image. So, rather than see God as judgmental and violent, capricious and unjust, Shapiro began to see in her life the possibility for another side to the divine, one wherein God goes through suffering *with* humanity, though often unnamed (even by Shapiro at times, much as with Sentilles earlier), but who is mysteriously present nonetheless.

To begin to see God differently, however, she had to contemplate and reconceive the presence of religious rituals in her life. When contemplating her Jewish background, for example, Shapiro admits that

> I never knew *why* we did what we did—It was simply the way it was. I had fled this at the earliest opportunity, but replaced it with nothing. I wasn't exactly a nonbeliever. Nor was I a believer. Where did that leave me? Anxious, fearful, lonely, resentful, depressed—troubled by a powerful and, some would say, deeply irreverent sense of futility.[54]

The ritual hadn't stuck to her, but "fleeing" it hadn't worked either—a common paradox that many people find themselves in today and which they cheapen the complexity of by reducing themselves to a simplistic label of "atheist" or "agnostic" or "Christian" and so forth in order not to have to face the difficulty

---

53. Shapiro, *Devotion*, 111.
54. Shapiro, *Devotion*, 11.

of where they actually find themselves: in a place that is nearly impossible to describe or define and which shouldn't be too hastily identified.

To those who follow Jesus as God, at least, such a conundrum of identity should pose no particular grief, for the earliest "Christians" in fact were simply Jews who had had their image of God radically challenged, leaving them wondering if they were something "new" in terms of religious identity or whether they remained Jews (a question that the early followers of Jesus were perhaps far too quick to sort out). For Shapiro, however, as for so many people who grow up in whatever religious tradition claims them (including Christians), her youthful reactions to religious structure had propelled her to a space where her inability to identify her own roots had brought about a crisis of identity: "I had spent so much of my life adhering to a strict set of rules, and then rebelling against them. I had no idea who I really was—but wanted to find out."[55] And so she began to contemplate what it might be like to reexamine things from an adult perspective, and to rediscover some things she had missed the first time around. As she will describe this journey she finds herself on: "What if—instead of fleeing—I were to continue to quiver in the darkness? It wasn't so much that I was in search of answers. In fact, I was wary of the whole idea of answers. I wanted to climb all the way inside the questions and see what was there."[56] As we will see a good many times in the authors here under examination, each one searching for a more mature perspective on the life of faith, she describes how "As a child, I had been taught not to question. But as Paul Tillich once wrote, doubt isn't the opposite of faith; it's an element of faith. If only I could hold close to that idea."[57]

It is indeed all too true that many people are raised with the understanding that doubt is the opposite of faith—much as Evans and Wiman had already indicated. As Shapiro too will discover, doubt is part of the life of faith, much as it is part of any relationship we find ourselves in. We should neither wish to remove this dynamic nor alter its function within the life of faith. What we must consider, rather, is how exactly we might be more discriminant in our determination of what doubts come from what experiences, and what certainties arrive from what destinations.

In many ways, what Shapiro clamors for, I would suggest, is little more than a desire to mature into an adult life of faith, to make the movement from childish desires to a mature place of sitting in the insecurity and in what we cannot ever fully know in this life. Growing up spiritually calls us to embrace those difficult moments in life when we realize as never before

---

55. Shapiro, *Devotion*, 89.
56. Shapiro, *Devotion*, 12.
57. Shapiro, *Devotion*, 131.

the depth and responsibility of becoming mature, something, sadly, a lot of people never arrive at, spiritually speaking.

For her part, Shapiro sought to mature her faith through active learning and practice. Spiritual books, yoga practices, trying to confront her Judaic roots—these all appeared as paths toward the recovery of tradition and the divinity she was after. But each also began to feel strangely empty to her. I would suggest that this is the case perhaps because it was her desire itself that remained problematic, much as was the case for Evans earlier, who only later came to realize that how she held her faith was what mattered most, not the contents of the faith itself. Shapiro is seemingly aware of this fundamental dynamic of desire, though she seems to struggle more than Evans in letting it go—a very common experience within the search for faith to be sure. As she tells herself at one point: "Release your stories, and suddenly there is more room to breathe, to feel, to experience the world."[58] But she also stutters at times on the precipice of learning how to actually go about letting go in terms of the religious traditions that often appear to ground us the most.

Her desire was to be "in one place," "rooted," which was for her also "To believe in God."[59] She was, she admits, looking also for a "structure, a system, a way to live my life."[60] And yet her inability to "settle" on one particular religious tradition often caused her to feel like she was missing something, that she was something of a religious fraud. "I wondered out loud whether this desire of mine for a little bit of this, a little bit of that, was spiritual and intellectual laziness. The smorgasbord approach to deeper meaning."[61] To actually try and live the complexity of multiple choices and multiple traditions in harmony with one another, she comes to realize, "required even greater effort and clarity."[62]

She therefore pondered, as I think a good many of us searching for faith and relationship do, what good religious rituals had brought her father, who seemed so sincere in his Judaic faith: "Did he enact this ritual because it gave him some small measure of comfort? Or simply because it was habit? Did he think God was listening? And if God was listening now, where had he disappeared to during all the trouble?"[63] What she was at least certain of is that "The ritual seemed to enliven him; it gave him a sense of

---

58. Shapiro, *Devotion*, 17.
59. Shapiro, *Devotion*, 84.
60. Shapiro, *Devotion*, 91.
61. Shapiro, *Devotion*, 84.
62. Shapiro, *Devotion*, 86.
63. Shapiro, *Devotion*, 21.

his purpose and place."[64] Yet this "enlivening" had not been *her* experience, and so she continuously wondered how she could make it meaningful for herself. She neither saw nor found any of the "vulnerability to what is" that she noticed in her yoga meditations as also present within such traditional religious practices, and she wondered what her father saw in his own, very traditional morning prayers.[65]

As an example of this struggle, prayer became, for Shapiro, a rather mystifying and confusing experience, though, I would wager, she perhaps misses out on the ways in which her framing of these questions actually has its own long history—including saints and mystics of many different faiths, including Meister Eckhart and Teresa of Ávila from the Christian tradition—who asked the same questions over and again. In many ways, religious traditions are just that, a history of people asking and trying to answer these questions. We might recall the statement, for example, of Meister Eckhart's that so deeply moved Wiman wherein he simply prays to God to let him let go of God. "Was this a prayer? Who was it directed to? Was I petitioning some almighty being? The God of my childhood asserted himself: judging, withholding, all-knowing. In turn, the phrases themselves became supplication, bargaining, appeasement."[66] Such a deity is akin to imagining having a lover where all one ever does is to ask them to do things for them, rather than engage them in a dynamic, and more realistic relationship. The static, one-directional God that Wiman had criticized here potentially springs once again back to life, though Shapiro is intent on not following such a deity. "The God of my childhood was a man with a white beard in the sky who judged and found us wanting, who meted out punishment and responded only to heavy-duty petitioning and praise."[67] What is missed through such musings is that prayer is actually a highly complex phenomenon, multidimensional and capable of sustaining a relationship that goes far beyond what a good many people could ever fathom it to be. Thinking you can simply find prayer is like sitting in your bedroom thinking, "I'm going to fall in love with someone" without actually leaving your room to find that special someone. Prayer, in its essence, is something we cultivate like a relationship, not something one simply engages whenever they need something.

In many ways, what Shapiro envisioned was the God that she would have to let go of if she was to develop a different, and perhaps more

---

64. Shapiro, *Devotion*, 21.
65. Shapiro, *Devotion*, 24.
66. Shapiro, *Devotion*, 37.
67. Shapiro, *Devotion*, 90.

accurate vision and desire for God—the very thing that the authors I deal with in this book push us toward: the dislocation (Karr), de-realization (Nouwen), shattering (Wiman), and even violent (Teresa) experiences of the divine that challenge our desire for "roots" as much as they offer them to us in other ways.

In Shapiro's own words, interfused with a prayer, she strived to find her grounding in her own desire for the divine:

> But really, what did it mean to fervently, wholeheartedly name a desire? *May you feel protected and safe.* To speak out of a deep yearning—to set that yearning loose in the world? *May you feel contented and pleased.* Could a wish be a less fraught word for a prayer? *May your physical body support you with strength.* Maybe it wasn't about who, if anyone, was on the other end, listening. Maybe faith had to do with holding up one end of the dialogue. *May your life unfold smoothly, with ease.*[68]

Could prayer be just a desire? Yes, it can. Some of us wait to "give" in a relationship until we are certain that the other person is giving too. The Danish theologian Søren Kierkegaard said, however, that the most genuine relationship of love takes place when the other person is dead, precisely because they can't love you back and give you anything—something that should give us considerable pause for thought.[69] Shapiro made the "leap of faith" in her life—what occurs when you desire God before finding God, as we have seen already—but she struggled too to determine what exactly this meant to her, in her life at the present moment.

In response to the question a friend posed, "So what exactly *do* you believe, then?," she mused on how "I wanted to tell her that *exactly* and *believe* don't belong in the same sentence."[70] She was after a *presence*, but this does not begin to capture what it was that had changed within her. "I no longer felt that I had to embrace it all—nor did I feel that I had to run away. I could take the bits and pieces that made sense to me, and incorporate them into the larger patchwork of our lives."[71] Prayer "certainly didn't hurt," she adds, though what her prayer was directed toward she was not always entirely clear about.[72]

> Let me be perfectly clear: meditation was not helping me feel better. It was hard, scary, and sometimes felt silly. What was I doing? I had deadlines to meet. Students to teach. Food shopping

---

68. Shapiro, *Devotion*, 38–39.
69. Kierkegaard, *Works of Love*, 349.
70. Shapiro, *Devotion*, 205.
71. Shapiro, *Devotion*, 206.
72. Shapiro, *Devotion*, 44.

> to do. But it was helping me to make out the vaguest beginning of an outline. I was starting to see what was there.[73]

This realization stems, at least in part, from the acknowledgement that faith and our religious practices keep changing, evolving and translating themselves anew over time.[74] It also underscores the movement of growing faith we have already seen on display, of desiring God before one actually finds God. What we at last see in her narrative is that Shapiro, contrary to her youthful longing to escape from religion and spirituality, desires to walk toward the sacred spaces in her life, as complicated as these spaces may be to locate. She wants to face the complexity as well as the mystery and to mature within such a place. In fact, the complexity of her own desires and the complexity of the sacred within our world may be ultimately impossible to discern with any degree of certainty, though such an encounter draws her toward the sacred nonetheless.[75]

In the end, she concludes that "I felt like *myself*, here in this house of worship. My past, my present—my *samskaras*, my contradictions—I could bring it all with me and just simply belong."[76] This is not a process of what we typically conceive as a conversion, but rather a going back to where she was and exploring it more deeply. Pope Francis has said that the first task of the pope is to convert the papacy, and in this suggestion, I would reason, he understands that a person has to go back to the place where they already are, where they are from, and yet to see it anew, as both Shapiro and Evans prompt us to do. By doing just this, the nature of the sacred, or the holy, is thereby redefined as the coming together of these contradictions, the allowance of paradox, but also of paradoxes that are not kept separate—they are rather pulled together into one place, into one person, who yet manages to hold them all together simultaneously.

Though Evans continued to struggle with her Christian roots and Shapiro to point toward an ability to dwell outside of any clearly defined religious tradition, both illuminate the essential act of translation that takes us beyond any singular definition of faith. To point to this activity is no doubt an affirmation of the complexity of the human person, one who finds themselves quite realistically at times on the border between different traditions and relationships. In the eyes of both authors, it is their desire to walk toward the complexity, rather than to simplify it with the imposition of an easy identity or dualistic way of thinking that marks their stories as ones devoted to the quest for spiritual truth, in whatever form it might take in our world.

73. Shapiro, *Devotion*, 76.
74. Shapiro, *Devotion*, 222.
75. Shapiro, *Devotion*, 225.
76. Shapiro, *Devotion*, 228.

CHAPTER SEVEN

Guibert of Nogent and Ignatius of Loyola

Errors, Pitfalls, and Reading Life in Light of Divine Activity in the World

Guibert of Nogent (ca. 1060–1125) was a French monk and abbot who provided the Western world of the Middle Ages with its most famous autobiography since Augustine's Confessions. A troubled childhood, which began with a labor process that almost cost Guibert and his mother their lives, ended in his dedication to the monastic life by his parents. Aside from the theological education provided within his abbey context, Guibert also devoted himself to a study of the Greco-Roman classics, which influenced the semi-epic exposition present within his works. Among his most famous writings are his histories of the Crusades, compiled in Dei Gesta per Francos (1108), his memoir, Monodies (1115), and his attack on inauthentic shrines meant to deceive the faithful found in On the Relics of the Saints (c. 1120). Although he would not gain much notoriety within his own lifetime, his insight into the realm of twelfth century monasticism would become invaluable to future generations.

There is perhaps no bigger name in the history of Christian spirituality than Ignatius of Loyola. Born on October 23, 1491 in the small village of Loyola in the Basque region, Ignatius grew up under the privileged tutelage of an uncle who was a royal treasurer. This upbringing provided him with an avenue for entering military service under the Duke of Najera, with an elevated title and a leadership role. After nearly fifteen years of military campaigns in which he managed to go unscathed, Ignatius suffered a career-ending injury at the battle of Pamplona in 1521, after he was hit in the legs by a cannonball. While Ignatius recovered from *a plethora of surgeries aimed at restoring his ability to walk, he also underwent a spiritual transformation. A moment of conversion in the medical tent, following his reading of a biography of Jesus, saw Ignatius devote himself to the religious life. Not tied to any specific order, Ignatius dedicated himself to voluntary poverty, strict asceticism, and a schedule of constant prayer, which led to the development of his famous* Spiritual Exercises *and an affinity for leading everyday believers into a closer communion with Christ. Disavowing his noble status while retaining the leadership skills acquired during his military service, Ignatius would go on to found the Jesuit order, whose missional work would establish universities and seminaries throughout the world.*

Augustine was willing to ask questions of God and of himself, and to let such questions resonate throughout his entire being, often without a direct or discernible answer being given. In fact, the lack of an answer for Augustine, as for Wiman and Shapiro, was not a problematic thing at all. Rather, the young Augustine was more than willing to let the echo of an answerless question permeate his entire life, and by letting it linger within, to let it also transform him. Yet, despite the sincerity of Augustine's approach and the significance of his autobiographical *Confessions* in the construction of the Western subject, why did it take until the twelfth century for another Christian autobiography to appear on a scale of anything like the *Confessions*? And why, when it did appear, was its sense of the self vastly different from Augustine's? Time and the changing of contexts certainly played its role, but what led to such a near-complete reconfiguration of the Christian subject, one completely dependent upon being able to locate the actions of God within the world in a way that Augustine's vision did not see?[1]

When contemplating the autobiographical narratives that arise within medieval and late medieval spiritualities, we are right, I think, to be cautious in accepting them at face value, as we will see illustrated soon, and

---

1. I think that we could speculate a good deal here on the way in which Augustine's form of Christianity, still relatively untainted with Roman politics, was able to freely speak about uncertainty in a way that later theologians would be unable to do. Politically speaking Christianity would become implicated in hierarchical political arrangements that would make it terribly difficult for Christians to appear to waver on anything per se. Belief in the king's power became equal to belief in God's power, and such conjunctions united to force, you might say, ordinary Christians to accept many things in their world, like feudal society, as the status quo given by God to humanity. This will incline the average Christian, starting with Augustine, to question their faith less and to merely accept what happens in their world as some sign of divine activity.

with newfound critical force, in the *Life* of Teresa. The *Monodies* of Guibert of Nogent (1115), which I want to take up in a moment, certainly bears a resemblance to Augustine's most famous work, but it is its divergence from the *Confessions* that interests me the most, and which might shed some light on ways in which the genre of the autobiographical might be misleading for some as well as informative. The work echoes a good deal of what we have read thus far, to be sure, but it also signals a new tone that draws some sharp contrasts with what I have been developing thus far. I think that seeing these differences might enable us, however, to grasp something of the significance of what it means to develop a self-reflexive (i.e., self-critical) faith.

As Guibert begins his autobiographical narrative, one that will start by focusing on mundane events from his childhood before progressing to become essentially a history of occurrences that may or may not have anything to do with God, he states:

> I confess to your greatness, God, my departures from you, caused by countless errors, and the frequent returns you inspired, from my inner wretchedness back to you. I confess the evils of my childhood and youth, still raging within me even as an adult, as well as my inveterate zeal for wickedness, untiring despite my spent and listless flesh.[2]

His opening is a seemingly typical confession of his sins, one that is also characteristic of medieval acts of contrition. He will initially speculate on the depths to which such a confession might take him, as when he contemplates: "A fugitive or deserter from what is pious, when I run back to piety—does piety lose its essence? When it is buried under layers of sin, will we find piety something strange?"[3] And he will even place such meditations next to an explicit awareness of self-understanding which lies at the heart of all such autobiographical writings:

> Therefore, God of goodness, when I once again was coming to recognize you after my inner drunkenness, if at times I did not succeed, I was never entirely without self-knowledge. For how could I catch a glimmer of understanding of you, if I were blind to my own self? If, as Jeremiah says, I am clearly a man who sees my own poverty, I should then determine what fulfills this want of mine and seeks it out. But on the other hand, if I do not know what good is, how could I know evil, much less condemn it? If I do not know beauty, I never shrink from ugliness. I seek knowledge of you, I cannot lack knowledge of myself: therefore,

2. Guibert of Nogent, *Monodies*, 3.
3. Guibert of Nogent, *Monodies*, 4.

to dispel, through confessions such as these, the darkness of my reason by constant inquiry into your light is a most worthwhile and salutary exercise. Then will my reason, illuminated by an unfailing light, never again be unknown to itself.[4]

Theologically, we can, I think, only applaud such a configuration of self-understanding in relation to sin and confession. This is very much in accord with the best of those working within the genre. The track he will first try to ascend along therefore involves recognizing the great mercies that God has shown him throughout his life, at first seeming to be somewhat ordinary, but eventually progressing to supernatural and miraculous occurrences: "And so I must first confess to you the benefits you granted me, so that your servants, God, who read this will fully realize the cruelty of my ingratitude."[5] He accordingly thanks God for his mother, and for her virtue, while also recounting the circumstances surrounding his birth. Through all of this, he shares, "I do confess that I was given to you as a special gift, and yet I do not deny that often I have, knowing it was sacrilegious, taken myself away from you."[6] And further, he contemplates, "When I look at myself, when I consider my troubles, I nearly give up in despair—but then, almost despite myself, I understand that born into my wretched soul is the certainty of finding respite with you."[7] It is within such a context of trying to discern his sinful ways, and to gain something from this inherently critical discourse of self-discovery before God, that he likewise relates stories of his education, and of his teachers especially.

Admitting his own lack of knowledge in certain subjects, while also speaking of the harsh measures which his tutor imposed on him, Guibert acknowledges to the reader: "I am telling this, my God, not to brand such a good friend with a mark of disgrace, but to make every reader understand that I do not want them to take everything I say for certain, nor to envelop anyone else within my nebulous reasoning."[8] And so, once again, we might be able to make out the appearance of a self-critical mind that is searching for a way to recognize how readers might be inclined to distrust his account of things—at least this is what the genre calls for, and Guibert himself seems to acknowledge as much. What becomes problematic in his personal disclosures, however, is that his recognition of critical mechanisms does not make the journey (or *translation*) from the internal to the external world:

4. Guibert of Nogent, *Monodies*, 4–5.
5. Guibert of Nogent, *Monodies*, 5.
6. Guibert of Nogent, *Monodies*, 11.
7. Guibert of Nogent, *Monodies*, 11.
8. Guibert of Nogent, *Monodies*, 16.

they remain entirely internal, as a self-imposed barrier that prevents him from actually receiving the external world in any critical fashion whatsoever, from the stories he hears from others—and which can only appear to us as rumors or complete fabrications—dreams that others have about him, which he thoroughly believes, and the like. Though in many ways, his faults are no greater than many of his fellow monks or countrymen at the time, we must be able to exercise our critique in such a way as to explain some of the terribly unjust and violent practices that also characterized the age and context in which he lived and practiced his life of faith. In essence, my argument will be that his quest for definition, and so for a clear religious identity, far outstripped his willingness to let change affect the construction of his faith, with lasting and often very damaging consequences.

In the midst of ecclesial controversies that were harbored within the Catholic Church at that time, Guibert focused his efforts toward the "state of religion and conversions."[9] In many ways this meant trying to emphasize the roles of poverty and the sincerity of faith that he saw as exemplary in the lives of others, most notably his own mother. This also meant that he would become most attentive to those lives that were not lived in morally exemplary ways, such as when he recounts the stories of the knight who received some gold he should not have sought and therefore instantly went mad when he touched it,[10] the devout faithful who wore "hair shirts" to provoke their faith,[11] and women who "abandoned marriages to prominent men" and their children in order to flock to the convent (including his own mother).[12] Each of these examples of faith becomes more than simply questionable among Guibert's narration of events; they become, in fact, suspect as an irresponsible theological worldview, one closed in upon itself, that must be explored in greater depth so that we might understand better what motivated it.

At one point, for example, he narrates the apparent near rape of his mother in her own bed by the devil—a truly fantastic tale that brings a good many psychological diagnoses to mind.[13] His relationship to his mother, moreover, is very complicated and even quite sad to modern ears. In essence, his mother abandoned him at a young age in order to seek out a "holy" life of prayer for herself, leaving him to struggle with her choice, and then later to actually try to emulate her piety, while simultaneously trying to

---

9. Guibert of Nogent, *Monodies*, 21.
10. Guibert of Nogent, *Monodies*, 27.
11. Guibert of Nogent, *Monodies*, 28.
12. Guibert of Nogent, *Monodies*, 30.
13. Guibert of Nogent, *Monodies*, 36.

be near her in the monastery where she was living. As he tells of her conversion and departure:

> She began in fact to believe—or rather she heard it from others—that she was utterly wicked and cruel. She had barred from her soul, and sent away without any support, a child such as this, so deserving of affection—at least that is what people said, for not only our relatives, but also people outside the family adored me. And you, good God, holy God, in your sweetness, your charity, you had miraculously hardened her heart, surely the most pious heart in the world, lest it be pious to its own detriment. Any softening would have caused her soul harm, if she had shown any care for the things of this world and put me before her own salvation, neglected God instead of me. But her love was strong as death, because the more closely her love bound her to you, the less troubled she seemed to feel at having cast off what she had once loved.[14]

She joins a monastery and devotes her life to prayer, living the "simple life" that the other nuns advocated for the development of her faith. Rather than simply dismissing her these many years later, however, for the suffering that he had undergone by her neglect, Guibert tried to justify his mother's actions, though, again, in a very non-critical fashion. Her actions, he simply concludes, must have been purely motivated, as she chose an externally condoned and elevated religious and social position within the church.

Guibert's initial reaction to his mother's abandonment, so he tells us rather candidly, though with a distance from the events as if he has completely overcome them, was in his youth to rebel against the church and his schooling: "I began to abuse my own authority," as he puts it.[15] He slept a lot and engaged in "wanton behavior," until he saw some monks sitting around and was deeply moved by their piety, and the desire he found within him to imitate them and join their ranks. "For as soon as I put on your habit, at your summons, the cloud over my heart seemed to move away, and everything to which I had long been blind during my aimless wanderings now began to take hold of my heart."[16] It is relatively easy to see the trajectory that Guibert placed himself upon at this point, for it was one that aligned itself with Augustine's path toward his own salvation in many ways (though there will be some tremendous differences between them that we must account for as well). His use of Augustine, in reality, seems to be one of uncritical acceptance

---

14. Guibert of Nogent, *Monodies*, 41.
15. Guibert of Nogent, *Monodies*, 43.
16. Guibert of Nogent, *Monodies*, 45.

of the latter's autobiographical form of describing the inner life without his being able to appropriate such an internal examination for himself, leaving his only critical comments reserved for the observation of "divine acts" in the external world alone. It is as if he were merely trying to adopt Augustine's style of making personal historical confession without actually having to go to the depths that Augustine himself went to. Everything, for Guibert, you might say, is surface-oriented—there is little to no depth to what he says concerning faith in a certain sense. That is, he is not able to exercise critical judgment on external circumstances, and his tale, as well as his life of faith, will be severely hampered by this inability.

Despite this, or maybe as an illustration of this dynamic, he claims that the devil gives him nightmares that inspire fear in him far beyond what others experience at night.[17] He also, on occasion, sees demons standing near him, that nearly drive him to madness.[18] Likewise, and in what probably was a very unhealthy practice, he was finally, due to his taking up of a religious vocation, much closer to his mother, and able to confess all of his sins and temptations to her directly. Like a "good son," though perhaps confiding a bit more to his mother than is advisable, he recounts, "When she warned me to correct my ways, with a sincere desire I promised to do so immediately."[19] Even his mother's dreams speak cautionary tales to him about his own life—and so he listens to her retelling of them most willingly.[20]

One way to describe Guibert's understanding of his world is to say that divine activity appeared to permeate everything in the medieval world—and, for some today, of course, it still does. The problem with divine materiality in the Middle Ages in general, according to Caroline Walker Bynum, was not one of getting objects (or dreams) to talk, but how to make them stop talking—a very different circumstance than we find ourselves in today.[21] Yet this was in many ways the norm at that time. Even the eminent theologian Saint Anselm of Canterbury, if Guibert's narrative is accurate on this score, engaged in such understandings of the world around him.[22] This is another way of saying that, for the average clergyman of the time, the external world and the happenings that come our way were not to be questioned or criticized—they were merely signs of God's involvement in the world. This is not only the opposite position of every major writer we are

---

17. Guibert of Nogent, *Monodies*, 46.
18. Guibert of Nogent, *Monodies*, 47.
19. Guibert of Nogent, *Monodies*, 49.
20. Guibert of Nogent, *Monodies*, 52.
21. Bynum, *Christian Materiality*.
22. Guibert of Nogent, *Monodies*, 55.

looking at—and consequently, a form of "bad theology," you might say—but it is also the exhibition of a complete lack of critical understanding, of the world around us, but also of ourselves.

My point is not to completely disparage a medieval worldview, but to point out rather how the dynamics that Guibert elucidated where not simply problematic for his time, but for ours as well. His inability to move beyond the carefully constructed identities of his world and to translate his experiences into other persons, events, and identities ultimately typifies a good many religious persons in our world today who are also convinced that God's will can be easily discerned through external activity alone.

From Guibert's perspective, the divine and the mysterious were everywhere active, even *over*active, from his belief in the practice of witchcraft which was utilized to prevent his father's "having legitimate intercourse with my mother,"[23] to noting the devil's antics in making his mother's adopted infant cry all night long,[24] a monk's going crazy after confessing his sins and having to be bound in chains,[25] a man's death by dysentery being blamed on his receiving of two gold coins that were found on his body after his death (and which resulted in his being buried outside of the church grounds),[26] a monk being killed by lightning because he joked about the lightning beforehand,[27] various exorcisms of demons,[28] the tale of a Jewish man consorting with the devil who masturbates as his "sacrifice" to the devil and must even taste his own sperm on the devil's orders,[29] a woman turned into a giant dog by an evil sorcerer,[30] demons who play pranks on people,[31] or cause illnesses and epilepsy,[32] the burning of heretics who were tried by water (they floated like the guilty should!),[33]

---

23. Guibert of Nogent, *Monodies*, 60.
24. Guibert of Nogent, *Monodies*, 62.
25. Guibert of Nogent, *Monodies*, 68.
26. Guibert of Nogent, *Monodies*, 70.
27. Guibert of Nogent, *Monodies*, 73.
28. Guibert of Nogent, *Monodies*, 79.
29. Guibert of Nogent, *Monodies*, 80. Guibert's anti-Semitism is on display not only in this tale, but also in further ones where he even recounts the slaughter of Jews who would not convert in very matter-of-factly tones (97) and as he equates Jews with "heretics" in synonymous terms (98).
30. Guibert of Nogent, *Monodies*, 81.
31. Guibert of Nogent, *Monodies*, 101.
32. Guibert of Nogent, *Monodies*, 103.
33. Guibert of Nogent, *Monodies*, 171.

and the devil's having convinced a man to cut off his own penis and then kill himself, among other fantastic tales.[34]

If God's judgment upon the world does occur in a very literal and direct manner, so that events conspiring all around us are visible signs of God's blessings and punishments, then we are left to conclude that there is little, critical introspection necessary—the very stuff that makes autobiographical-spiritual writings so important for theological reflection. Rather one should spend their time, as Guibert ultimately does, simply chronicling the stories that unfold all around him, adding, as appropriate, various interpretations of divine signs as he sees fit to recall them. I would additionally speculate that this is what a good deal of "Christian" writing today merely repeats, recording things like near death experiences of God's looming judgment or an encounter with angels or demons, or simply presenting uncritical retellings of biblical characters and stories as if that were all that was needed to develop a life lived in faith. In reality, however, and as I have tried to demonstrate through the various stories I am recounting in this study, there is so much internal critical discernment needed in order to develop a life of faith that I fear most Christians have little idea what the Christian life might actually look like when viewed from an interior developmental perspective.

It would be helpful to note in this context how Teresa of Ávila will suggest (and as we will soon see) that she was more afraid of the people who were afraid of the devil than the devil himself, and I believe that such a sentiment would no doubt apply to someone like Guibert, who was more concerned with labeling others as sinners than he was with taking a good, critical look at his own faith and its implicit but highly problematic cosmology. To devote one's life of faith to trying to discern the presence of angels, demons, and the devil is mainly *not* to take the time to cultivate one's life of faith as it can and should be developed. It is, for most rather, a distraction from oneself and a displacement of what really matters onto things that typically do not concern us. Perhaps it would be helpful to recall instead how such supernatural beings are not the focal points of the scriptural narratives on faith, for example, but only an occasional aside and even at times a mainly symbolic determination.

For Guibert, for whom potential external events brought about by God are not to be questioned, even the corpses of believers and nonbelievers, the faithful and the sinners, are worthy of being judged: "the judgments of God are renewed against the corpses of the guilty, whose burial in holy places

---

34. Guibert of Nogent, *Monodies*, 175.

is clearly undeserved."[35] Seeing such judgments, one can perhaps begin to imagine why this would be the case. Everything external and material bears the judgment of God, and so even the bodies of the deceased are capable of taking part in this divinely charged atmosphere. It is not Guibert who judges, he might object, but God, and even the material elements in our world that God inhabits speak of God's judgment: "The bishop thus conducted mass and took up the Eucharist in his hands with these words: 'Let the body and blood of the Lord examine you today.'"[36] In this sense, the material reality becomes infused inseparably with divine action, and not even inert materials or dead bodies are removed from such implications.

For his part, Guibert would most likely say, as he *does* say directly at times, that he himself is *not* judging people; it is God who judges them, and Guibert, among others, simply reports what reality presents to him. Yet it is an interpretation of events that he gives, though one that uncritically cannot, *must* not, acknowledge its existence as an interpretation. This is in many ways how political and religious ideologies function pure and simple, as they provide a framework that cannot acknowledge its own existence as a political or theological framework. Sadly, however, such methods continue to be the mainstay of many religious persons throughout our world even today, including many of the world's fundamentalisms.

So, how do we move away from such stunted understandings of faith that focus only on the external events presumed to be delivered by God and into other, better ways of perceiving authentic movement or translation from an internal to an external critique, another way of describing, once again, how we must use our (internal) experiences to critique the (external) structures before us, but also to use the structures to critique our own (inner) experiences? I want to turn to the autobiographical narrative of Ignatius of Loyola, a former Spanish soldier of great bravery and loyalty, who makes a turn toward the religious life after reading of the lives of the saints and the life of Jesus, in order to provide what I will call a better model of self-understanding that yet struggled with some of the same things that Guibert (or even religious fundamentalists in our day) did. I think, in this sense, that the contrast, but also comparison between Ignatius and Guibert might assist us in comprehending something essential to the construction of the (Christian) self.

* * *

35. Guibert of Nogent, *Monodies*, 77.
36. Guibert of Nogent, *Monodies*, 170.

After a significant wartime injury, endured as Ignatius was fighting as a soldier for a Duke in Spain, he was given a few religious books to read and he found himself deeply moved by the portraits of holiness that he read within their pages. As a consequence, he set off more or less on a quest to leave behind his previous ways and to discover God's will for his life, often encountering strange visions and having to discern for himself what God's will for him was. As he relates, he was perpetually asking himself: "How would it be, if I did this which St Francis did, and this which St Dominic did?"[37] Though such questions might seem to be rather typical of those trying to live the "saintly" life, Ignatius was actually never quite comfortable with the path such questions sent him on. In a way, his relief would only come about much later through the discernment that he wasn't called to be either Francis or Dominic, but *himself*—a major revelation that will motivate his later career and missionary fervor.

There was, however, a willingness on Ignatius's part to seek to "know the difference in kind of spirits that were stirring: the one from the devil, and the other from God."[38] But, at this point in his life, he struggled to know the difference between them. He was visited, so he felt, by a vision of "Our Lady," the virgin Mary, mother of Jesus, and, all at once, his sinfulness was revealed to him, and he left "matters of the flesh" behind him.[39] His zeal has been kindled to follow Jesus and "Our Lady," though his understanding had yet to catch up. His was, as he himself puts it, "a soul that was still blind, though with great desires to serve him as far as its knowledge went."[40] Along with making such an honest assessment of himself, he was willing to acknowledge as well how little he knew about the life of faith that he was zealously undertaking to explore with every resource in his capacity. Again, in his words (recorded at the time by others within the Jesuit order, hence the seemingly odd third person references to himself), he was "not knowing what humility was, or charity, or patience, or discernment in regulating and balancing these virtues. Rather, his whole purpose was to do these great exterior deeds because so the saints had done them for the glory of God, without considering any other more individual circumstances."[41] As an example of his lack of understanding, and as a story that really gets to the heart of what he was struggling to connect with within himself, he meets a Moor, a Muslim from the south of Spain, who talks to him of

---

37. Ignatius of Loyola, *Reminiscences, or Autobiography of Ignatius Loyola*, 15.
38. Ignatius of Loyola, *Reminiscences, or Autobiography of Ignatius Loyola*, 15.
39. Ignatius of Loyola, *Reminiscences, or Autobiography of Ignatius Loyola*, 16.
40. Ignatius of Loyola, *Reminiscences, or Autobiography of Ignatius Loyola*, 18.
41. Ignatius of Loyola, *Reminiscences, or Autobiography of Ignatius Loyola*, 19.

religious matters, and refuses to accept that the virgin Mary remained a virgin after giving birth—a proposition that many today would find equally difficult to accept, for after having given birth, how could the physical hymen remain intact (which was mainly how a woman's virginity in the ancient and medieval world was maintained)?[42]

> And at this there came upon him some impulses creating disturbance in his soul; it seemed to him he had not done his duty. And these caused him anger also against the Moor; it seemed to him he had done wrong in allowing that a Moor should say such things of Our Lady, and he was obliged to stand up for her honour. And thus there were coming upon him desires to go and find the Moor, and stab him for what he'd said.[43]

And so he leaves it to God's "chance," that if his mule goes one way, he'll kill the man, and if another way, he'll let him be—a proposition that would not be entirely unfamiliar to Guibert's way of discerning God's will in our world. The mule, randomly but thankfully, goes the direction that ends up preventing the man's death. What we should take note of in this story, however, is that this tale illustrates not only Ignatius's similarity to Guibert at this point in his life, but also Ignatius's lack of understanding of faith and of God's involvement with matters of our world.

Eventually, Ignatius makes his way to the town of Montserrat and pledges himself to God and the wearing of the "armour of Christ."[44] He also begins to have spiritual visions that he cannot understand, but which, later, he will believe to have been temptations coming from the devil. What is interesting in his own depiction of what he was undergoing at the time was that a world that had once been completely unified within him—his monolithic state of being—becomes more complex and diversified. "Up to this time he had always persisted almost in one identical interior state, with largely unvarying happiness, without having any acquaintance with spiritual things within the self."[45] Soon, he will discover, however, a large fluctuation of internal spiritual states which he was previously unaware of and which cause him to wonder "what new life is this we're beginning now?"[46]

The complexity within himself with which he becomes acquainted is something that becomes reflective of the way in which he will start to see the external world around him, and this is what will make all the difference in

42. Ignatius of Loyola, *Reminiscences, or Autobiography of Ignatius Loyola*, 19.
43. Ignatius of Loyola, *Reminiscences, or Autobiography of Ignatius Loyola*, 19.
44. Ignatius of Loyola, *Reminiscences, or Autobiography of Ignatius Loyola*, 20.
45. Ignatius of Loyola, *Reminiscences, or Autobiography of Ignatius Loyola*, 21.
46. Ignatius of Loyola, *Reminiscences, or Autobiography of Ignatius Loyola*, 22.

the development of his inner spirituality. A translation of his experiences, I would suggest, was opening wide his understanding (definition) of himself. As we might expect, no longer should the Spanish codes of honor in terms of men defending the chastity of virgins dictate his actions as a person of faith. He begins to see that there is more going on beneath people's external appearances, and beneath his own as well.

As an example of such a discovery of a complex inner spiritual life, he relates at one point his struggles with his own excessive scruples and how he sought the counsel of spiritual persons who could assist him with overcoming this obstacle to a more genuine faith. Rather than simply let such scruples appear as a self-evident state of dealing with God's actions in the world and within himself, he is able to let go of such a fervent imposition made upon himself (*by* himself) and to learn that such scruples actually arise from a misplaced desire within oneself and from imposing an impossibly difficult external world of judgment upon one's self. Eventually, with the help of others, he is able to break free of such a hold made upon him and to diversify his view of himself amidst a great deal of growing self-complexity. What Ignatius was discovering was that faith grows in a person's life through such an opening toward that which lies beyond our most basic self-definition, hence as a complex process that interweaves self-discovery and critical introspection alongside the search for something beyond ourselves, what faith embraces in relationship with another (or the divine). Indeed, these two steps are, for Ignatius, inseparable, and cannot be disentangled from one another.

From this standpoint, it is highly intriguing that his own descriptions of his inner state—what we might later call the path of a genuine saint—were vague and even devoid of specific recollections. As he phrases it, "he neither knew how to explain these things, nor could he fully and properly remember those spiritual ideas that God was at those times impressing on his soul."[47] As both Teresa of Ávila and Henri Nouwen will later outline for us, there are periods within one's spiritual growth where one is yet unable to detect any work being done at all, and this seems to be what Ignatius, in some sense, experienced himself. He would eventually drop some of the spiritual practices, such as fasting and letting his nails and hair grow lengthy and unkempt, in order to achieve a certain balance in his life of faith. He became clearer in his understanding of himself and of his faith, though he could not say exactly how this even came about. Yet, despite this, through time, he became wiser and more balanced in his discernment of the spiritual state of his life: "And this left him with the understanding enlightened in so great a way that it

---

47. Ignatius of Loyola, *Reminiscences, or Autobiography of Ignatius Loyola*, 26.

seemed to him as if he were a different person, and he had another mind, different from that which he had before."[48] Ignatius continued to have visions of Christ, as well as the experience of an "unnatural" joy when visiting holy places and tears of consolation at the thought of his own death and subsequent union with God. But he also learned to critically examine all of his experiences in light of Catholic tradition and the church's authority itself, as well as, eventually, his theological education that was still on the horizon. His struggles in the creation of a new religious order, especially against the Spanish Inquisition, taught him many things which he continued to submit to, perhaps through his spending many days in prison awaiting word on whether or not he would have permission to undertake such a calling.

What we ultimately witness throughout his life's story is his desire, not to preach the gospel directly, as the Dominicans did, but to "speak about things of God with certain people in an informal way, such as after a meal with some people who invite us."[49] As I have already hinted toward, he was discerning a path for himself, not in imitation of others who had been called to very specific vocations, like Saints Francis and Dominic, but in sole pursuit of where his own unique talents and gifts met up with the calling he felt God giving uniquely to him.

At one point, he was appropriately challenged by a friar who wondered on what knowledge he would be speaking of God, since he had not any learning—a subtle test of his spiritual discernment since those often claiming to work as motivated by the "spirit" were often eager to challenge the authority of the church as a whole. Would it be from the Spirit, then, the friar wondered? And if so, what kind of a spirit would such claims to know the workings of God rest upon? This question, again a central one at the time in discerning heretical movements within the church which frequently relied upon vague claims of the Holy Spirit in order to subvert institutional authority, was what prompted Ignatius's own desire to learn more about the (Catholic) faith from other, learned persons. That is, he desired to put his life in dialogue with the external structures of faith passed on from generation to generation, though not to blindly incorporate them either. This is precisely what captures the best characteristics involved in the dialectic between identity and translation, as both are necessary parts of a complex process.

For the most part, the Holy Spirit has been invoked at times throughout history to explain that which could not be explained, sometimes referring solely to one's own experience, or at least a legitimation of one's

---

48. Ignatius of Loyola, *Reminiscences, or Autobiography of Ignatius Loyola*, 27, de-emphasized from the original.

49. Ignatius of Loyola, *Reminiscences, or Autobiography of Ignatius Loyola*, 44–45.

experiences which were often said to supersede the church's tradition. If, in fact, a religious, typically charismatic movement arose within the church as a challenge to ecclesial hierarchical power, it was most normally associated with the rise of the Holy Spirit, that divine force which had moved like a mighty wind through the early Christian church (Acts 2). To claim that the Holy Spirit was guiding you was, however, typically a vague and perhaps self-legitimating claim, and one that the church was often quick to contest, especially during politically divisive times throughout its history. Most usually, as during the Spanish Inquisition, the church sought, with force if necessary, to bring one's experiences into conformity with church teaching and doctrine.

Such a background context is what makes Ignatius's story an even more intriguing one. That is, there is much to be gained from seeing how he would consent to becoming a student of the church and to learning about theology from those who taught it, while balancing such insights with his own experiences of God, and his own intuitions about living the spiritual life. The two had to go together in Ignatius's life. He simply could not undergo a one-way form of communication, either entirely from his own experience or solely from an external, institutional structure.

Ignatius thus committed himself to catechetical instruction, a learning from the presentation of the doctrines and teachings of the church. But he also took to helping others "suppress some bad practices, and, with the help of God, some things were put in order."[50] Though such a phrase may seem entirely underwhelming as the culmination of his vocation, there is yet within this simple sentence a quest for balance so strong that the most he can say of his "saintly" efforts is that "some things were put in order"—no miracle-working per se, no skies opening up to reveal mysterious messages from the heavens, just good work that persisted in its efforts to bring order to a world challenged with chaos. I would contend that such a reading of things is in fact more than enough, if entirely embodied and intertwined within one's life, to merit the title of a saint.

One of the things that we might note in this regard too is that the outcome of Ignatius's mission was not to perform miracles or to seek divine intervention in difficult, material situations, but simply to use whatever resources were available to him to "put things in order"—again a terribly underwhelming statement perhaps, but also that which indicates something of the reality of the divine presence in our everyday lives. Should a miracle occur, this is not something one should inherently reject, to be sure, but it is a gratuitous gift of God, and not something that one would necessarily

---

50. Ignatius of Loyola, *Reminiscences, or Autobiography of Ignatius Loyola*, 56.

seek out as a primary means of building their faith and of interacting with their world, as I have already noted. To locate God in the ordinary aspects of everyday life was a revolutionary shift in the discernment of God's presence within the life of faith, and one that enabled people of faith to cease looking for God's actions behind the surface activity of our world (e.g., God sending a hurricane to destroy a "sinful" people) and to look for it in the transformative encounters that cause us to rethink our own story and nature (why the autobiographical genre is so important, both to Ignatius and to theological reflection today).

Others within the church at the time would challenge his ways, and even put him and his companions in prison while they awaited a verdict on the work and theology they were spreading amongst the faithful. But, in the end, the pope himself made a decision in their favor and Ignatius and his companions began to set up the Society of Jesus accordingly. Though the Jesuits, as they came to be called, would be an often-controversial religious order within the Catholic Church, experiencing at times harassment and even suppression, they would also continue to live out Ignatius's calling to find a balance in one's life as a spiritual principle well worth contemplating today, Jesuit or not.

What I want to draw attention to at this point are simply a couple things that I think are noteworthy in this account, and worth carrying with us as we move forward in this study, namely the completely underwhelming tone of balance and believability within Ignatius's spirituality and his willingness to submit his own experiences of God to the formal learning of theology, that is, forming a dialectic between theology, as a structural tradition (*definition*), and experience that developed in his life as a consequence of his willingness to learn about what moves beyond his immediate worldview (*translation*). These are the same tension-filled poles that Shapiro and Evans found themselves caught between, and they are the same ones, I would reason, that most of us feel caught up in as well, trying to identify the life of faith as a precarious balancing act between tradition and its symbols, rituals, and language and our own, often indescribable experiences.

Ignatius's spirituality, however, reveals to us a very practical and everyday sensibility about living the spiritual life in between such tensions. It also refocuses us upon what it might truly mean to serve others. Service to one person, loving one person, *is* our access to the universal. Spiritually, this is to say that we should not be engaged in trying to access the vast realm of all divine wonders and powers, but in directing our attention to the one person who needs us to be present to them, sometimes especially when that one person is our own self (again reaffirming the significance of the *auto/biographical*). Ignatius had tried unsuccessfully to focus on *all* of God at once, to be open to the entire realm of the supernatural, and only later corrected this misguided notion, settling in the end upon simply putting some things in order and dealing with the actual realities and relationships that were before him. His journey was one that had escaped Guibert entirely because it was one that placed a tremendous emphasis upon the relationship between the inner *and* the outer worlds, their exchange and ability to flow one from the other, learning from each other about the fullness and complexity of the spiritual life. It was Ignatius's development of a more complex spiritual life too that helped pave the way for a more modern sensibility about religious structures and traditions, something that we will see advanced equally as far in the life of Teresa of Ávila.

CHAPTER EIGHT

Teresa of Ávila

Living the Saintly Life

Teresa of Ávila was born Teresa Ali Fatim Corella Sanchez de Capeda y Ahumada in Ávila, Castile, in 1515. Long before she would become known for her mystical experiences and her reform of the Carmelite Order, Teresa was a young girl torn between the two choices available to women of high standing at that time, marriage or the convent. A tumultuous relationship between her parents saw the girl favor a life dedicated to God and she entered the Carmelite convent of the Incarnation at Ávila in 1535, where she would spend over twenty years combatting poor health and a convent system that she saw as heavily flawed. In 1562, with the permission of Pope Pius IV, Teresa undertook a project of reevaluating the proper aims of her, and her sisters', religious vocation at the newly built convent of St. Joseph. A life rededicated to poverty, contemplation, manual labor, and the formation of community earned Teresa a reputation that would see her reforms applied to the Carmelite order as a whole by the prior general of Rome in 1567, and would earn her a new assignment of creating reformed convents throughout the Spanish countryside. By the time she died in 1582, Teresa had founded seventeen convents and was setting out to found an eighteenth as her health gave out. In addition to the physical foundations and spiritual reforms that Teresa left behind, we also have a catalogue of her deeds and mystical experiences in the form of her Life of the Mother Teresa of Jesus *(1611),* The Book of the Foundations *(1610),* The Way of Perfection *(1583),* The Interior Castle *(1588), and* Spiritual Relations: Exclamations of the Soul to God *(1588).*

What are we to make of the spiritual autobiography of the sixteenth-century Spanish cloistered nun and mystic, Teresa of Ávila? In what way do these memoirs speak to our contemporary context, and how might her work continue to motivate us spiritually today? The first thing I would suggest is that we might benefit a great deal from the manner in which she writes herself into the Christian Scriptures and tradition, putting her life in dialogue with the richness that such canonical norms offer. In this sense, she consciously and consistently puts her life story in terms that are not her own, in order, precisely, to make them her own. As such, her work is continuously provocative and insightful in ways that I have already been highlighting in discussing the various other authors we have been reading about, and which now receive another confirmation through Teresa's own story. That is, she too will provide an evolving description of prayer, and of faith; demonstrate how the church—as a community of faith formation—functions for the growth of faith, though it often fails to assist us in significant ways as well; conceive of faith as a dynamic activity and practice leading to an experience of the divine rather than simply as thoughts or words about God; and respect the processes of autobiographical confession, done in humility and self-critical awareness, as key steps toward the further deepening of one's faith.

These insights, much as we have seen especially in Karr, Augustine, Wiman, and Tolstoy, are present too in Teresa's account of her life. At the same time, she will point, much as Tolstoy did, toward a deepening of faith that can only come about as one moves from thinking about faith to actually living it. As she describes to us from the outset, "But many . . . make the mistake of supposing that they can come to understand spirituality without themselves being spiritual."[1] When discerning just how she writes herself into the Christian tradition, and beyond the numerous biblical verses she recalls throughout her text, Teresa cites Augustine's *Confessions* as having a significant impact upon the development of her spirituality, and this is easy to see in the outline and execution of her autobiography. As she contextualizes this influence: "I derived great comfort from those saints who have sinned and yet whom the Lord has drawn to himself."[2] This is a motto we would do well to note as we consider what exactly the "saintly" life might be, as it certainly is not living a static, holier-than-thou attitude that seems to transcend the world in which we live. As Tolstoy had already come to realize, and as Teresa herself will stress toward the end of her book, the reality of our having bodies that must be accounted for is something that the person

---

1. Teresa of Ávila, *The Life of Saint Teresa of Ávila by Herself*, 254.
2. Teresa of Ávila, *The Life of Saint Teresa of Ávila by Herself*, 69.

of prayer must take account of, and not try to abstract themselves from, as this might lead to physical harm in the process. Recognition of the embodied nature of faith prevents us from abstracting (falsely "transcending") our world, something that often entails granting the "myth of autonomy" much more weight than it is actually due.

One immediately discernible trait of her self-perception, one that is rather foreign to a good many people today, I would argue, is that she is quick to declare herself "wicked," even *most* wicked "among all the Saints who have turned to God."[3] This is a recurring theme in her confessions, as she makes sure to tell her audience repeatedly about how "wicked" she was in turning away from God, and in choosing her own desires over those that God was calling her to embody. Rather than see this as merely a rhetorical device, or as a sort of false modesty (which, I am willing to concede, it nonetheless may possibly be at times), however, I consider it more productive to see such an expression as related directly to her development of a self-critical apparatus for faith, a truly unique development in her mystical theology that is grounded in the recognition of her "sinfulness," but which ends up promoting a focused and increasingly self-aware spiritual life. We see something very similar in one of her colleagues, Saint John of the Cross's writings (and, in a very different but contemporaneous way, in the early modern critical philosophy of René Descartes).

What was pivotal for Teresa was that the Christian who wished to cultivate a life of prayer and spiritual growth not shy away from taking an extended, and critical, look at themselves, as hard as this might be, and as paradoxical as it might seem to someone wishing to live the "holy life." Her considerations in this regard were such that she placed all believers on a similar path, one that oscillated between achieving real heights and sliding back into real lows: "This self-examination must never be neglected, however; for there is no soul on this path who is such a giant that he does not often need to turn back and be a child at the breast again."[4] In other words, even she was capable of acting like "a child," and was never "beyond" even the simplest corrections in terms of spiritual direction.

> A child that has grown up and whose body has formed does not shrink and become small again. But this may, by the Lord's will, happen to the soul, as I know by my own experience, which is my only means of knowledge. This must be in order to humble us for our own greater good, and to prevent our being careless during this exile of ours. For the higher we climb the

---

3. Teresa of Ávila, *The Life of Saint Teresa of Ávila by Herself*, 21.
4. Teresa of Ávila, *The Life of Saint Teresa of Ávila by Herself*, 94.

more cause we have to be afraid, and the less reason we have to trust in ourselves.[5]

What Teresa is referring to on this score is a permanent state of spiritual oscillation between maturity and infancy, not something that would exactly evoke a sense of permanent spiritual satisfaction. But it is also not a stalemate stuck in either childish fantasies or the stark seriousness of adulthood. Indeed, we would be better served to consider such an experience of one's spiritual life as a form of permanent dissatisfaction, a constant coming up against the fact that we are not as comforted or settled, as secure or resting in a foundation, as we might ultimately like to be. This is why the language of exile, or of diaspora even (akin too to Karr's "dislocation"), might be helpful here, because it is this state of existence, in being permanently not "at home" in this world, that we are able to actually grasp something of what our world, as believers, should be like. As a motif very central to Jewish identity, and as an all-too-real experience for migrants, refugees, and stateless persons, it is no less relevant to the Christian, who tries to make their way in this world without ever fully feeling "at home" in it. Christians are exiles, pilgrims, wanderers, who have no place to rest our heads, as Jesus had put it.[6]

Teresa, on a number of occasions, extends this exilic conceptualization to her own intellect, referring to a "distrust" of one's own self as a sign of proper humility, which in reality evidences an openness to truth when it appears in one's presence. It is this sense of performing a constant search for humility that prompts her to declare that "no one can be relied on except God."[7] But it also allowed her to develop a lifelong program of spiritual awareness of one's temptations in order not to rest comfortably on one's laurels: "We must always be distrustful of ourselves and never grow careless so long as we live."[8] Similarly, and in order to live out such a spirituality, she was willing to ask herself whether everything she has learned and every vision seen in prayer were not simply illusions, moments of self-deception that had crept into her mind.[9] She is even self-aware enough to admit that in her visions of the divine that feel entirely real to her there *must* be some element of the "imaginary" in them—a point that Saint Ignatius, at approximately the same time in history, was to develop as a key

---

5. Teresa of Ávila, *The Life of Saint Teresa of Ávila by Herself*, 109.
6. This theme is emphasized in Hauerwas and Willimon, *Resident Aliens*.
7. Teresa of Ávila, *The Life of Saint Teresa of Ávila by Herself*, 302.
8. Teresa of Ávila, *The Life of Saint Teresa of Ávila by Herself*, 229.
9. Teresa of Ávila, *The Life of Saint Teresa of Ávila by Herself*, 242.

principle of the life of prayer.[10] For the time in which she was writing, and as an unparalleled psychological insight for the age in which she lived, to simply recognize that there would inevitably be an imaginary component in her various visions of God is highly remarkable—and a sign that her critical awareness was unyielding in the face of what appeared to her as direct revelations from "on high."

It was precisely such a directness of revelation, you might say, that allowed her to hold the realm of experience in such high regard, as essentially the only "knowledge" she had or could accrue in this lifetime. Because the nature of such experiences was so diverse and varied, she was eager as well to illustrate how a person could advance either quickly or slowly in their prayer life, depending on the humility, effort, and perseverance that they demonstrated. As she would phrase it, "God considers a soul's advancement and progress, but takes no account of time. One soul may have achieved more in six months than another in twenty years, since, as I have said, the Lord gives at his own pleasure, and to him who is readiest to receive."[11] As laid out in the descriptions of the stages of prayer one encounters later in the book (and which occupies a good deal of the book on the whole), there is a certain receptivity (passivity) that comes to those who allow it, and this could elevate the young well above their elders if the sincerity of heart was demonstrable.

It is within such a framework of understanding the merits and value of prayer that Teresa begins to sketch her own life of faith, how it came to her, her response to it, and the journey that it placed her upon so soon in her life. She will accordingly reread so many moments of being "led astray" from God's presence as not only revelations of her "wickedness," but also as signs of God's grace actively working within her life:

> When I look back at these actions of mine I do not know what my intentions were. But what they clearly revealed, O my Spouse, is the difference between You and myself. My joy at having been the means whereby the multitude of Your mercies has been made known certainly moderates my sorrow for my great sins.[12]

Her understanding of her sinful self might be comparable to something the Danish theologian Søren Kierkegaard once said about the person of faith: in standing before God, one is always in the "wrong."[13] As she herself

10. Teresa of Ávila, *The Life of Saint Teresa of Ávila by Herself*, 309.
11. Teresa of Ávila, *The Life of Saint Teresa of Ávila by Herself*, 298.
12. Teresa of Ávila, *The Life of Saint Teresa of Ávila by Herself*, 34.
13. Kierkegaard, *Either/Or*, Part II, 335–54.

phrased the situation, "I know that all the blame has been mine. I do not think that You left anything undone to make me Yours entirely, even from my youth."[14] How are we to understand this "law" of God's grace that puts us always "in the wrong" before God? In many ways, it has been historically aligned with church teaching so that one feels that if you go against church teaching, you go against God's law and cannot receive God's grace, though this sense perhaps misses a major feature *of* God's grace: the purpose of anything that might be called God's law is intended *to bring us to* God's grace. So being shown one's "wickedness" through the disclosing and confessing of one's sins is intended to allow for an experience of grace, the very thing that Teresa is ultimately after.

In her reflections upon her life and the ways in which she misunderstood the role of faith in her life, she is not afraid to say that she had at times throughout her early life approached prayer and adoration in "simplicity," but that this was still, she believes, "beneficial" to her, perhaps without her even being aware of just how it was made so.[15] Despite holding this belief, she is nonetheless firm in her resolve to be responsible for her own actions, or deviations from God's desire for her. She therefore takes account of how she "not only fell back and became worse" after her conversion to faith, "but seem deliberately to have sought ways of resisting the favours which His Majesty granted me. For I knew that I was obliged to serve Him, and realized that, of myself, I could not pay the least part of the debt I owed Him."[16] Through such actions that frequented her early life, she persisted in turning away—somewhat out of shame, we might add—because the gap between her abilities and God's was so great.

Within this youthful phase of her life, she tried to dress ostentatiously, to draw attention to herself, to read novels about chivalry and knights and to converse with those who encouraged her to throw her cares toward the world's ways. Later in her life, she would note as well how the tension between the "pleasures of the world" and her time "with God" was a struggle she was not soon to overcome.[17] As she narrates, "When I thought that no one need ever know, I risked many things which were both dishonourable and sins against God."[18] This is an observation easily coupled with its partner: "I did not see that I could conceal nothing from Him who sees all things."[19]

---

14. Teresa of Ávila, *The Life of Saint Teresa of Ávila by Herself*, 25.
15. Teresa of Ávila, *The Life of Saint Teresa of Ávila by Herself*, 24.
16. Teresa of Ávila, *The Life of Saint Teresa of Ávila by Herself*, 21.
17. Teresa of Ávila, *The Life of Saint Teresa of Ávila by Herself*, 61.
18. Teresa of Ávila, *The Life of Saint Teresa of Ávila by Herself*, 28.
19. Teresa of Ávila, *The Life of Saint Teresa of Ávila by Herself*, 29.

Her eventual response to the call that God puts to her, her preparation "for the state in which He wished me to serve Him," was to be for her a radical departure from her former understanding of herself—something she would come to characterize as a type of "violence" done to her, and which she began to welcome as exactly what she needed in order to make her faith grow at all. This was very much akin, I would suggest, to Wiman's sense of being "shattered" before the Christ who undoes his images of God, as well as Karr's sense of "dislocation" from reality: "Thus, without my willing it, the Lord compelled me to do violence to myself. Blessed be He for ever!"[20] And in other, similar shades, "He gave me courage to fight myself, and so I carried it through."[21] Her experience of God in a state of rapture, at one point, was such that "It came with greater violence than any other spiritual experience, and left me quite shattered. Resistance requires a great struggle, and is of little use in the end when the Lord wills otherwise, for there is no power that can resist His power."[22] There is in such states the experience of a great detachment from the world, and this, we come to see eventually, is as it should be.[23] Though such depictions sound as if there is a complete loss of self-control as God appears to overpower the individual entirely, it is important to note that this scene takes place as fundamentally a fight "against herself" that she embraced in terms that are similar to the notion of obedience addressed earlier. Hence it is something at once coming from beyond us, "compelling" us, but also from within us (giving us "courage") at the same time.

What is particularly interesting in these passages is the way in which her conversion is not likened to anything that could be said to resemble a "spiritual sweetness"—her phrase—or that which misleads believers young in their faith to rest upon weaker grounds than they should, much as we saw a moment ago in the writings of Saint John of the Cross. As she describes it, "But this nature of ours is so greedy for moments of sweetness that it seeks for them in every way. But soon it becomes very cold. For however much we try to kindle the fire in order to catch this sweetness, we seem merely to be pouring water on it and putting it out."[24] Much like trying to (re)ignite the flame of love in a relationship where it has long since died because the relationship was focused on the wrong source of unity between persons, Teresa recognizes how the spiritual life too can be

20. Teresa of Ávila, *The Life of Saint Teresa of Ávila by Herself*, 31.
21. Teresa of Ávila, *The Life of Saint Teresa of Ávila by Herself*, 33.
22. Teresa of Ávila, *The Life of Saint Teresa of Ávila by Herself*, 137.
23. Teresa of Ávila, *The Life of Saint Teresa of Ávila by Herself*, 138.
24. Teresa of Ávila, *The Life of Saint Teresa of Ávila by Herself*, 105.

deadened through a focusing on the wrong elements that sustain it. Feelings of "sweetness," pleasantness, comfort, and consolation may be found at times in one's spiritual progress, but, more often than not, dryness, emptiness, absence, and affliction are what actually bring an almost at times imperceptible awareness of God to one's senses.

The faith that moves a person to great depths appears to Teresa as a form of violence to herself, one that undoes her, so to speak, and removes her entirely from what she knows of her world. We can hear a parallel process at work in Karr's sense of "dislocation" and general uncomfortability with the spiritual life, as well as Wiman's parallel sense of being "shattered" by the reality (of suffering) through which God accompanies us. Such sentiments, if we can discern what they truly offer, are perhaps too what the theologian Jürgen Moltmann had in mind when he suggested that Christians who really know what is in store for them in following Jesus might reconsider and turn back. Teresa, however, seems to want nothing more than this poverty and this cross, all to be taken up directly through her commitment to Christ. Her decision to follow Jesus, though perhaps not ideally made when she first chose to enter the religious life, becomes one that deepens over time and continues to propel her forward in faith.

Reexamining a common theme we have been discussing concerning one's desire (or fear of) the afterlife, Teresa comments that she joined a religious order and donned her habit "more influenced by servile fear, I believe, than by love."[25] So, already, we witness a critical reflection made upon her former motives and beliefs, which were not simply "pure" because she moved into a religious vocation, but themselves were tainted with other motives not actually inclined to seek the rich soil of the spiritual life. At the same time, rather than renounce her decision to join a religious order she would later seek to reform because she recognized its impurity, she is willing to evolve with her decisions, remaining in the life she is in in order to grow more with what she has been given, namely herself. What she comes to discover is that, following Christ, "there is no place for fear, only for desire."[26] As such, she is able to see how the soul, when placed in such a position, "desires nothing but You".[27]

The subject matter of her quest for the divine, much as we have seen already in the various "confessions" I have been looking at, is both God *and* herself, something that assists her in sifting through the various misguided ("theological") abstractions that do not actually help a person of faith in the

---

25. Teresa of Ávila, *The Life of Saint Teresa of Ávila by Herself*, 32.
26. Teresa of Ávila, *The Life of Saint Teresa of Ávila by Herself*, 63.
27. Teresa of Ávila, *The Life of Saint Teresa of Ávila by Herself*, 114.

formation of their spiritual life. There is not a complete denial of the self in lieu of God, but a steady merger of the desires of the two. As she imparts sage advice to the reader, "There is no need to climb up to Heaven, not to go any farther than to our own selves; to do so troubles the spirit, distracts the soul, and brings but little fruit."[28] The focus is placed clearly upon taking a more encapsulating portrait of her own self, her soul, and the various desires that comprise who she is to both herself and to God, and this as the only way that genuine spiritual progress might come about in one's life (much as Ignatian spirituality also teaches).

Historically, notions of heaven, hell, and the afterlife in general have dominated many discussions of religious thought, though, I would add, this was often a distraction or a political maneuver enacted in order to separate those who were part of a community from those who were deemed outside it. Teresa's insight in this regard—that she became a nun, wrongly, for fear of hell—is quite helpful, as she realizes that trying to speculate on something that we have no real conceptualization of, is not really a worthwhile endeavor, and probably reflects more cultural and political prejudice than an actual spiritual foundation. Rather, taking the time to focus on what does matter and what can be dealt with in one's life is the route preferable to the individual seeking to grow in faith.

As an illustration of this problematic in a contemporary context, we might think of how many people consider themselves ready for a relationship (dating, marriage, etc.), but they can't control their desires in terms of shopping, for example, and this, so the thought goes for the individual unwilling to engage themselves as this level, is a completely separate affair from their love life, when, in reality, they function perhaps on exactly the same level of desire. The question to ask oneself in this sense is: If I can't control my desires for material things, why do I think I can deal with the immaterial, such as with matters involving love and relationships? And if such a thing cannot be dealt with, how could I ever presume to be able to deal with the desire for God?

As Teresa was to discover over the years, being honest with herself—the humility she stresses above all else—was the best method of moving toward the greater depths which the spiritual life could offer. And so, she begins by confessing, much like Karr, that "I did not know how to practise prayer or how to recollect myself."[29] She would subsequently relate as well that she would occasionally experience a certain depth in prayer, but she did not know how it came about, and she certainly did not know how to

---

28. Teresa of Ávila, *The Life of Saint Teresa of Ávila by Herself*, 308.
29. Teresa of Ávila, *The Life of Saint Teresa of Ávila by Herself*, 35.

encounter such an experience again. In essence, she lacked the discipline to engage the greater depths of the spiritual life: "For if the will is left without employment, and love has no present object to occupy it, the soul remains without support or activity, solitude and dryness give great pain, and stray thoughts attack most fiercely."[30] Battling these obstacles became her unique task in the world, and she mustered her strength for the challenge, turning to the story of Jesus for her inspiration: "If a man can reflect on the nature of the world, on his debt to God, on Our Lord's great sufferings, on his own small service in return, and on what He gives to those who love Him, he gets material with which to defend himself against stray thoughts, also against perils and occasions for sin."[31]

Within the context of such thoughts, she began to read spiritual books in order to edify herself further and learn about prayer and about living the spiritual life. Yet this was no instant guarantee that she was on the right path, for temptations, she would find, would be lurking nonetheless in nearly every corner. As she discovers in one particular instance:

> I had a fondness for all religious observances, but I could not bear anything that seemed to make me look small. I delighted in being well thought of, and was particular about all that I did; and all this seemed to me a virtue, though that will not serve me for an excuse, for I knew how to get my own pleasure out of everything, and so my wrong-doing cannot be excused as ignorance.[32]

There is a brutal honesty in this statement, an honesty also born of hindsight, that Teresa is willing to display in her account of how she moved from a complete lack of knowing how to pray to the most ecstatic and rapturous of prayers. What stands out in this account, almost above all else, again, is the way in which honesty, brought about through a genuine quest for humility (as we saw in Augustine and Wiman explicitly already), is what allows her to proceed in the direction in which she wishes to advance. We see such an emphasis on humility in her reflections on those who seek to know more about spiritual matters, for example: "I have discovered by experience that so long as they are virtuous and lead holy lives, it is better that they should have no learning than a little. For then they do not trust themselves—and I am not likely to trust them—but refer to those who are really learned."[33] Such distrust continued to serve her well too, as

---

30. Teresa of Ávila, *The Life of Saint Teresa of Ávila by Herself*, 36.
31. Teresa of Ávila, *The Life of Saint Teresa of Ávila by Herself*, 36.
32. Teresa of Ávila, *The Life of Saint Teresa of Ávila by Herself*, 39.
33. Teresa of Ávila, *The Life of Saint Teresa of Ávila by Herself*, 40.

she subsequently developed a relationship with a priest who was himself embroiled in a scandalous affair with a local woman. Teresa got caught up in her relationship with him, out of loyalty to him because he liked her (in a completely Platonic manner, of course), and which was yet an insidious dynamic that she will later discover and correct.

As the story unfolded, a rumor circulated that this priest was cursed by the aforementioned local woman through the use of a special amulet. Teresa's only comment on this is: "I do not altogether believe this story about the spell."[34] What we must keep in mind, however, is that this rejection of supernatural intervention comes from a woman who will tell us within a hundred pages that she was elevated off the floor while lost in divine ecstasy, and that her fellow sisters tried to pull her back down to the ground! So, we must ask the question: why is she so incredulous toward this magical amulet, and not of her own account of levitation?

Presumably, for starters, she believes what happened to her was real, as she experienced it. This is fair enough to presume, though there is no way we can confirm such a miraculous occurrence. What is interesting, however, is that she herself seeks throughout the book to develop a self-critical mechanism of thought, as we have already seen, based on reason in fact, that we must in some sense assume she does not dismiss when it comes to her own experiences—especially as she evaluates herself quite severely at times. I believe we can only conclude that if she did indeed exaggerate or make up her own bouts of levitating off the floor, that this runs contrary to her own critical examinations of others, and even of herself at times—a contradiction that seems unlikely to have occurred if we take the bulk of her accounts at face value.

What is transparent throughout the book, however, is that Teresa is continually afraid of being abandoned by God, at the same time as she has learned to be suspicious of herself and her desires, even when she believes that she is being humble, but is cautiously wondering if the humility is authentic.[35] This is what will cause her, in numerous places, to criticize other religious persons, as well as the church on the whole—something she does quite freely at times (and as we will see in the story of Dorothy Day later). For example, as she puts it in one context, "The way of true religion is so little used that friars or nuns who begin truly to follow their calling have more to fear from members of their own communities than from all the devils."[36] And

---

34. Teresa of Ávila, *The Life of Saint Teresa of Ávila by Herself*, 41.

35. See, for example, Teresa of Ávila, *The Life of Saint Teresa of Ávila by Herself*, 49–50.

36. Teresa of Ávila, *The Life of Saint Teresa of Ávila by Herself*, 52.

later on, she reiterates this sentiment by declaring, "I do not know why we are surprised that there are so many evils in the Church, when these, who should be the models from whom all derive virtue, so nullify the work wrought on the religious Orders by the spirits of the saints of old."[37] The real problems one encounters in the spiritual life, she seems to be suggesting, come from *within* rather than from *without*—a point many of us working within a given religious community would do well to contemplate from time to time. These sentiments also parallel Ignatius's refusal to read external worldly events as signs of God's judgment upon humanity.

Teresa's constant striving for critical attentiveness to herself, moreover, consistently prompts her to turn her evaluative eye toward her own faith and the persons who comprise it. For example, again, when the mind is focused in prayer on that which is greater than itself, and which is the proper object of its thought, she suggests, "It laughs to itself at times when it sees serious men—men of prayer and religion—paying great attention to points of honour, which it long ago trampled underfoot."[38] These are the "men of prayer and religion" whom she sees as distracting people from living true lives of faith. Accordingly, she will say, "I am sure I am more afraid of these people who are so frightened of the devil than I am of the devil himself. He cannot do me any harm, but they, especially if they are confessors, can be most disturbing."[39] All of these experiences and critical perspectives she evidenced perhaps inevitably led her to the next stage in which she finds herself, isolated and alone: "But when it came to picking myself up I found myself completely alone."[40]

There would be a great spiritual undertaking that she felt called to, and which she was most eager to pick up and carry, but it was one that not even the religious persons around her were able to perceive for what it was. Much as Jesus was misunderstood, maligned, and rejected, so too does Teresa see her faith—and the faith of any Christian really—as one that must stand alone and stand firm in the face of adversity, even and especially when it is an adversity arising from within oneself. Maybe it is for this reason as well that she also advises people of prayer to keep their experiences to themselves, and not necessarily to share with others what they encounter in their relationship with God (a point that reminds us of how her autobiography,

---

37. Teresa of Ávila, *The Life of Saint Teresa of Ávila by Herself*, 52.
38. Teresa of Ávila, *The Life of Saint Teresa of Ávila by Herself*, 150.
39. Teresa of Ávila, *The Life of Saint Teresa of Ávila by Herself*, 183.
40. Teresa of Ávila, *The Life of Saint Teresa of Ávila by Herself*, 60.

with its supernatural detail, was not intended for a general public, but only for the superiors in her religious community).[41]

For her part, what she will concentrate on perceiving in her spiritual development is what she will label a "mystical theology," which was for her "no kind of vision," but a way of living life, an orientation and path along which she walked.[42] It is one in accordance with the "violence" and "shattering" experience of the divine in her life, and one that she will struggle at good length to describe to her readers as what she undergoes in the various states of prayer.

> The soul is then so suspended that is seems entirely outside itself. The will loves; the memory is, I think, almost lost, and the mind, I believe, though it is not lost, does not reason—I mean that it does not work, but stands as if amazed at the many things it understands. For God wills it to realize that it understands nothing at all of what His Majesty places before it.[43]

To clarify things a bit, she does *not* say, however, and as many people might misconstrue things, that we shut ourselves off to reason; rather, God himself "suspends it." As she formulates this condition: "What we must not do is to presume or imagine that we can suspend it ourselves. We must not cease to work with it, or we shall find ourselves stupid and apathetic, and the result will be neither the one thing nor the other."[44] Again, very much affirming the use of (critical) reason in her own theological methods, Teresa seeks in reality to utilize reason in all of its useful facets in order to continue deducing and analyzing her own ascent toward God.

Like the writers we have already seen deploy the same spiritual tactics, fusing humility with a method bent on discerning the exact nature of what she is undergoing, she tries to disentangle a variety of interrelated experiences that occur during prayer: "I cannot understand what *mind* is, or how it differs from *soul* or *spirit*. They all seem one to me, though the soul sometimes leaps out of itself like a burning fire that has become one whole flame and increases with great force."[45] And yet, she admits, even the flame was part of a larger fire that is hard to separate into distinct parcels. The soul, she goes on to conclude, "has such love that it can neither rest nor contain itself; it has soaked the earth all around it and wishes others to

    41. Teresa of Ávila, *The Life of Saint Teresa of Ávila by Herself*, 167. See also Medwick, *Teresa of Ávila*, 176.
    42. Teresa of Ávila, *The Life of Saint Teresa of Ávila by Herself*, 71.
    43. Teresa of Ávila, *The Life of Saint Teresa of Ávila by Herself*, 71.
    44. Teresa of Ávila, *The Life of Saint Teresa of Ávila by Herself*, 85–86.
    45. Teresa of Ávila, *The Life of Saint Teresa of Ávila by Herself*, 122–23.

drink of its love because there is more than enough for itself, and to join it in praising God."[46]

In this context, she will soon link the voluntary suffering of Jesus, as his primary state of existing in the world, with an existence defined as one of deliberate poverty, and this will provide us with a key definition of how faith must develop in light of Christian proclamation. That is, we are only able to encounter the risen Lord, to encounter God in fact, through our embrace of poverty. Succinctly formulated, she notes, "It is most certain that, so long as we at the same time recognize our poverty, the richer we see ourselves to be, the greater will be our progress and the truer our humility."[47] In other words, the more quickly we intentionally embrace forms of poverty that we are called to, the more quickly we ascend in prayer toward God. Such a recognition within oneself is what essentially will also pave the way for a fuller life of prayer in fact.

There is no doubt that in such formulas of the spiritual life poverty and humility are linked, the latter being the inner manifestation of the former and giving light to the "poverty of spirit" of which Matthew's gospel had spoken (Matthew 5:3). By choosing a life of poverty, as it were, one is forced to be humble in the face of the world's (misleading) orientations, and this is why Teresa, for one, chose this life above all the others she was capable of leading, to induce an experience of humility she knew would lead her to where she wanted to go spiritually speaking. We find this understanding of humility as poverty, for example, when we hear her say that, "we shall consider everyone else better than ourselves."[48] We encounter it again when we witness her rebuke of the lifestyles of the "great" persons of society whom she counsels at times, but also takes pity on. On being a "great lady" in society, she resolves, rather bluntly: "God deliver me from this wicked, artificial life. . . . This is slavery, and it is one of the world's greatest lies to call such people masters, when, as I see it, they are slaves in a thousand ways."[49]

A lack of humility, she concludes, much like her role model in writing her life's story, Augustine, is the first obstacle to a deeper life in prayer. Unlike Augustine, however, but in a way that points us toward an evolution of spirituality, the neglect of our bodies in our quest to be "like angels" (or like statues, you might say) is the second.[50] She is even careful to take note of instances where a sort of "false humility" might have overtaken a person.

---

46. Teresa of Ávila, *The Life of Saint Teresa of Ávila by Herself*, 220.
47. Teresa of Ávila, *The Life of Saint Teresa of Ávila by Herself*, 72.
48. Teresa of Ávila, *The Life of Saint Teresa of Ávila by Herself*, 92.
49. Teresa of Ávila, *The Life of Saint Teresa of Ávila by Herself*, 251.
50. Teresa of Ávila, *The Life of Saint Teresa of Ávila by Herself*, 157.

She herself claims to be in need of correction on this count.[51] By bringing the body into the equation of poverty and humility, we can see a form of spirituality developing an increased focus not on an abstract or speculative life of prayer, but on the concrete reality that actually promotes prayer in ways that we often fail to notice. That is, we experience poverty in a bodily way, and this is what causes us to humble ourselves—just as Karr had to physically get on her knees in order to "feel small" and thus begin to feel how there was something out there greater than herself.

Disciplining one's desires requires such bodily measures as Teresa encounters and we should not be ashamed that this is the case for us, though it will be our very first temptation to do just that. Rather, taking account of our bodily being is the very condition of our humanity and one that runs directly into the formation of our spiritual selves. Those who settle for quick comforts and easy consolations in prayer, she cautions,

> will never achieve true poverty of spirit, which lies in not seeking comfort or pleasure in prayer, since it has already given up earthly comforts and pleasures. It must find its consolation in trials, undergone for the sake of Him who lived a life of trials; and these it must endure, remaining calm in times of dryness, though it may grieve at having to suffer them.[52]

Trials, the endurance of suffering, persisting through spiritual dryness—these are the tasks set permanently before the person who wishes to increase and grow in faith. In this, there is not a trace of the desire for spiritual sweetness that we have often sought throughout our lives as the desired "object" of prayer or communion with another.

What Teresa is after is a truer form of the "poverty of spirit" that Jesus once described, and even enacted with his own life, that which was a form of "pouring out" the strength of God into a weaker human vessel (what is known in theological realms as *kenosis*). The very idea of the incarnation readily calls to mind as much, though we rarely see the connection between such an act on God's behalf and our own call to empty ourselves of the "power" that we spend a good deal of our lives trying to accumulate in very worldly terms—a potential distraction and misplacing of what we are actually called to engage within our own orbit of desires (much as Tolstoy had himself discovered in the context of his own experiences). The entrance into a form of weakness, in this sense, and as the Apostle Paul once put it,

---

51. Teresa of Ávila, *The Life of Saint Teresa of Ávila by Herself*, 215.
52. Teresa of Ávila, *The Life of Saint Teresa of Ávila by Herself*, 158.

actually provides us with another sense of strength, though it will not, even *cannot*, appear to the world as such.

What Teresa invites us to see next in the recounting of her life might cause some readers to wonder if she has left the autobiographical thread behind altogether, for she will now take us on an intimate tour of the four stages of prayer that one goes through in the spiritual life. In many ways, however, her focus on prayer is, for her, still an accurate autobiographical account, for it was to the life of prayer that she was wholly devoted.[53]

---

53. The first stage is that of "mental prayer", or of contemplation brought about through our efforts and by placing one's focus on the repentance of sins and the passion of Christ, his cross. The second stage is the "prayer of quiet" and surrender wherein the soul becomes "lost" in God, and where many of the faculties we are normally in control of are beyond our grasp in this supernatural state brought about by God. The third stage is one of the "devotion of union," which is an ecstatic state of being, a stepping outside of oneself that brings about a certain inner peace. The fourth stage, finally, is one of "divine rapture," a completely passive state wherein one essentially leaves one's body, one's faculties cease to operate as one enters into an almost "trance-like" state of existence.

The first stages of prayer are, she relates, the hardest, for the person praying does all the labor and God "gives the increase; whereas in the further stages of prayer the chief thing is joy" (77). The first stage, in essence, is almost completely characterized by the absence of feeling anything at all, "nothing but dryness, dislike, distaste and so little desire to go and draw water that he would give it up altogether if he did not remember that he is pleasing and serving the Lord of the garden" (79). Not only can she consequently understand why so many people have rather hollow experiences within their spiritual life, but also why they stop short of moving on to the second stage. Even for those who persist and endure within this first stage, she cautions, "It will often happen that he cannot so much as raise his arms to the task, or think a single good thought" (79). Here, the effort is all ours and we can "help ourselves" as such, though the lack of comfort and consolation drives many away from seeking more depth (84). "For there must be many who have made a beginning and never succeeded in reaching the end. It is, I believe, mainly due to their not having embraced the Cross from the first, that they are now distressed and think they are making no progress. When their understanding ceases to work it is more than they can bear, though perhaps even then their will is putting on weight and gaining new strength without their knowing it. We must realize that the Lord pays no heed to these things, and that though they seem faults to us they are not so" (82). Again, as paradoxical as it might sound, it is nonetheless within this stage that the feeling of God's absence can actually become a moment of divine activity within the self, and of a deeper faith taking root within oneself. As she clarifies this process, "the soul seems to be in a state of destitution, and to be asking itself: 'Where is Thy God?'" (139). As such, she will go on, "The love of the Lord does not consist in tears or in these consolations and tendernesses which we so much desire and in which we find comfort, but in our serving Him in justice, fortitude, and humility. Anything else seems to me rather an act of receiving than of giving on our part" (81). What we are to search for, and this is the prize that the person of faith longs for, can be described as such: "The security of a soul that applies itself to prayer lies in its ceasing to be anxious for anything or anybody, in its watching itself and pleasing God. This is very important. If I were to tell of the mistakes I have seen people make, through reliance on their own good intentions, I should never be done" (92). So we see, through her description of

In her own life of prayer so central to the formation of any life of faith, Teresa longs for the presence of God, the *parousia*, or the "coming" of Jesus that calls us toward a hope that is seemingly never fulfilled, but which is yet also always fulfilled in another sense. Hope, as such, develops in the expectation of a "coming" presence, the "coming" kingdom of God, or these things that we have been longing for. As with the cultivation of responsibility and integrity in our relationships, there is less mysteriousness within the process than we often imagine there to be (e.g., the mistake on the part of many men in today's world of labeling women as "mysterious" in order to not have to take responsibility for complexity of a relationship). Rather, what we see unfold in this is the reality that we must be responsible

---

this stage of prayer, how "good intentions" in prayer are not enough, for they do not come close to an embrace of the trials and sufferings that Jesus actually places before us. Again, we must *embody* the spiritual principle entirely or its effect is nonexistent. It is only by taking up the cross and persisting in a perpetual form of self-examination that we are led to lead the saintly life of "a continual martyrdom", which she envisions Saints Paul and Mary Magdalen alike must have undergone (149).

Finding our way along this path is of course not the same for everyone, however, though the stress upon trials and suffering, humility and poverty, will remain as guideposts for us all. Yet, she will say, "there are many souls who make more progress by meditating on other subjects than the Holy Passion. For as there are many mansions in heaven, so there are many roads leading to them" (93). There are to be sure innumerable focal points for prayer, each seemingly tailored to the individual trying to pray, and no one method may be best, or most suitable for one's entire life. Faith, as Wiman has already put it, changes throughout time, and we must maintain a certain flexibility to allow for such change. This flexibility was what had been so problematic for Teresa, earlier in her life, when she tried to "wish everyone else to be very spiritual too," and which did not make much allowance for the different paths that those around her were on at the time (91). Yet what works for one person at a given moment in time, may not work for someone else, and this is a point well worth considering again and again (and it is a formative thought we saw in Ignatius's life as well).

Such a realization, however, is not something that causes Teresa to claim that all religions are relative, or that some people should just stay away from spiritual growth altogether. This is indeed not what she is suggesting at all. There can be a genuine direction to God found within the cultivation of this faith, but it is one that takes many shapes and even different paths in order to arrive at its final goal. What we see unfold for us here is a vastly different understanding of the spiritual life than many of us have ever considered it to be. We witness as well how prayer is not a static one-way system of asking and receiving, but a complex process of personal growth and relationship, one undertaken on a variety of levels, and which does not always involve asking for anything. Later, in the second stage of prayer, for example, she will talk about a "satisfaction" obtained in prayer "which does not know whence nor how it came. Often it does not even know what to do or wish or ask for. It seems to find everything at once, and yet not to know what it has found" (100). We merely rest within the presence of God, something that challenges us and provokes us, but which also defines us through the love that it grants us, for "love calls out love", as she reminds us (159), and truly we should know this when it happens to us, and want for nothing more.

for that which we do not understand, often in very practical terms too. We must own it as the Apostle Paul does when he talks about the sin within himself that acts as if it was not even him, and yet he takes on its burden and puts it to death within himself (see Romans 7). He does not blame someone else for its presence within him, but takes responsibility for it so that he might see it to its end.

At the very least, what we witness in the autobiography of Teresa is a fervent call to critically analyze her own actions and to approach the life of prayer as the means of sustaining the life of faith, for prayer is an embodiment of the spiritual life, that which we cannot neglect while claiming that we have a spiritual life in any sense.

CHAPTER NINE

Dorothy Day

*Faith in the Context of Suffering
and Marginalization*

Dorothy Day was born on November 8, 1897 in Brooklyn, New York. Her family moved to San Francisco in 1904 so that her father could pursue his career as a sports journalist. Her time in California was cut short by the San Francisco earthquake of 1906 as her family sought refuge in Chicago, but the charitable outreach that she witnessed in the aftermath of the disaster would be forever engrained in her mind. As a response to this early episode in her life, Dorothy would end up studying journalism at the University of Illinois, a field which she saw as an avenue for exposing the plight of the poor and helping disseminate information about the causes of the working class. Her maneuvering through the radical political scene would see her move back to New York City, become a member of the American Communist Party, actively participate in the women's suffrage movement, and catalogue all of her actions in socialist newspapers when she could keep herself out of jail. This formative period of her writing skills was further enhanced by her interaction with the Bohemian community of writers, artists, and musicians living in New York during the early 1920s, an interaction which would also yield failed relationships and some of the most troubling personal decisions of Dorothy's life.

Such a lifestyle weighed heavily on Dorothy. An eventual turning point would come when she gave birth to her daughter Tamar, an event which Dorothy herself describes as the beginning of her conversion to Catholicism. This conversion would become complete upon Dorothy's introduction to Peter Maurin, a French immigrant heavily influenced by the French Personalist philosophers, who undertook Dorothy's reeducation based on Catholic social doctrine. Together, they would start the Catholic Worker, *which aimed to alleviate the suffering felt among the lower classes and the disillusionment present among the rich by uniting all sides of the social spectrum through works of mercy and hospitality. Her outreach with the movement included the creation of Houses of Hospitality, an attempt to return to self-sustaining agriculture dubbed "the Green Revolution," the publication of* The Catholic Worker *newspaper as an outlet of cataloging hope, and the promotion of round table discussions to help bridge an ever-growing gap between the working class and the scholarly academic class. Although* The Long Loneliness *and* Loaves and Fishes *are considered to be her two most complete works in published form, Marquette University has archived an extensive personal collection of her writing and has made all of her columns published in* The Catholic Worker *publicly available online. Dorothy Day passed away on November 29, 1980, protesting injustice alongside Cesar Chavez and the United Farmworkers movement up until the last days of her life.*

Dorothy Day's autobiography is a fascinating piece of American history that reflects what we might call a more mature faith, one that has seen much of the reality of the world, its suffering, and the poor that comprise the majority of its citizens, and yet she has concluded, at this late point in her life when her life's story was written, that a religious structure, if critically engaged, can be a proper way to balance one's personal experiences of the divine and of the world's ways—one of the essential insights I am seeking to portray in the present study.

As the story of a maturing faith, her narrative also demonstrates a sense of compassion and responsibility that we must learn to take up in our lives. We see in her story therefore not only another take on poverty such as we have been looking at thus far, but an address on poverty delivered in such a way as to demonstrate how taking poverty seriously leads inevitably to new critical insights, involving too an unending quest for social justice in our world. From her perspective, there are no witnesses, no innocent bystanders; you're either involved or you're actively turning away. What Day calls us to pay attention to is how feelings of compassion within us allow us to become the kind of people who know what it means to be responsible, even in contexts where you might not feel like you are the one responsible for correcting the poverty you see around you. This compassionate action, in short, is yet what enables justice to enter our world.

An analogy to this situation, for many of us, occurs when we see ourselves doing the same things we can't stand in our parents. At such a point, we have to make a choice: to blame them for our shortcomings, which, to be fair, we may have learned from them entirely, or to take responsibility for it within ourselves, as our actions and choices, no matter where such desires may have originally come from. Such sentiments typically revolve around a compassionate response to seeing the all-too-human vulnerability of our parents' situation. Day's story, if I can put it this way, is one that is willing to show compassion and solidarity with those who suffer and are oppressed in order to take responsibility for the things in life that need attention and even correction. In this surge toward a compassionate living and being responsible, Day teaches us something valuable about both faith and our humanity very much in line with the trajectory of faith I have been following thus far.

From the outset of her life's story, we see the emphasis Day places upon her honest portrayal of how she came to the Catholic faith, and yet how she still maintains a rigorous critical sense of what a community of the faithful might resemble. She was often, for example, a thorn in the side of bishops and cardinals, but beloved by the people. It may come as a surprise to some that, at the moment, she is being championed for sainthood in the Catholic Church, even though she herself had once famously said, "Don't call me a saint. I don't want to be dismissed so easily." Her meaning here being that, to remain a critical voice within the church, one can't be entirely co-opted or domesticated into the dominant narrative, in this case the narrative of the Catholic Church. She rather aimed to be permanently critical both of religious structures and of herself—something that the veil of sainthood can obscure for many who are tempted to idealize individuals into a static form involving some semblance of "perfection."

What we observe in this endeavor to be a critical voice for both the church and herself, once again, is the close proximity between writing one's life into existence through an autobiographical account and the confession of one's sins. It is the unsparingly critical glance into her own motives that first allows us to sense her willingness to go where so many others are afraid to go. "When one writes the story of his life and the work he has been engaged in, it is a confession too, in a way."[1] And yet, she admits at the same time, "Going to confession is hard—hard when you have sins to confess, hard when you haven't . . ."[2] The task before her is admittedly a difficult one, and yet one that she has to consider as a reality she wants to face. There is a great significance in critically retelling her story, as it is the same focus on

---

1. Day, *The Long Loneliness*, 10.
2. Day, *The Long Loneliness*, 9.

herself that will overlap with the way in which she sees both the world and the coming alive of her own faith in the midst of it: "I have a right to give an account of myself, a reason for the faith that is in me."[3]

Her entire autobiographical effort is structured in relation to God, as we have already seen in a number of authors, and so she pens, "I can write only of myself, what I know of myself, and I pray with St. Augustine, 'Lord, that I may know myself, in order to know Thee.'"[4] To know herself, she has discovered, is to know God, and to know God she must both recognize the mystery that we, as human beings, are to ourselves and also look for God within the practices of a community formed through the traditions of the faithful, in this case, the Catholic Church. Indeed, she is often at pains to stress that the communal aspect of Catholic ritual is what aided her in finding expression for the basic desires that her life found itself seeking, but which she had little way of knowing how to access if not for guidance external to her. Such relationships were central to her life; indeed, she recognizes at the same time how sitting down to write her story while others were hungry and sick around her, and so not taking the time to care for them, made her work of writing "a harrowingly painful job."[5] The revolving doors of her communal life, something Day never shut herself away from, were an indicator of just how important to her were the lives of others, their stories and the ways in which the needs of others impact each of our lives. If anything, the significance of personal biography in the work and life of faith was, for Day, valued above all else.

We see in these foundational gestures of her faith life how Day's impression of faith was already a realistic one that takes in the ability of each of us to look away from our relationship to the divine, but also our dependency upon the structures of our cultural and religious heritages: "I have not always felt the richness of life, its sacredness. I do not see how people can, without a religious faith. Children have a sense of joy in life but that soon wears away. One hears adolescents say, 'I did not ask to be born.' Rebellion has started."[6] There is, in this admission too, a sense that Day wants to mature in her life of faith beyond what her childhood faith had entailed for her. To do this, however, will be an encounter with the complexity of her life, her faith, and her relationships that she will seek repeatedly to account for. As she describes the difference, "We did not search for God when we were children. We took Him

---

3. Day, *The Long Loneliness*, 11.
4. Day, *The Long Loneliness*, 10–11.
5. Day, *The Long Loneliness*, 11.
6. Day, *The Long Loneliness*, 11.

for granted."[7] Some people grow up in a bubble of comfort, and whatever they are taught of God is what they keep. And if that is all they keep, people are right to be critical of religious faith. But what Day eventually wants for herself is to take account of God in a way that makes the movement from childhood to adulthood—a transition that a good many "faithful" believers may only rarely contemplate for themselves.

In order to make this transition, Day will place stress upon tradition, the "democracy of the dead," as she calls it from the outset of her recollections, that causes the decisions of our ancestors to have an impact on the way in which we live our lives.[8] Day had had vague notions of the divine in her life and her past, but they were not channeled through a religious lens and so they remained difficult for her to define or put into words. Living at such a point was where organized religion would ultimately give her a language to use, a language to describe what she could not previously put into words. This was also, of course, something she is only able to see in hindsight, once faith has given her such a language. As she struggles to describe what had happened to her prior to the acquisition of such a vocabulary for faith,

> the sudden realization came over me that I was alone, that the world was vast and that there were evil forces therein. I can remember on the one hand my bliss—it was almost a state of natural contemplation—and then suddenly the black fear that overwhelmed me at being alone, so that I ran all the way home.[9]

Her initial experiences of the divine, in all their vagueness, resulted early on in various attempts to lead a pious and morally correct life, one that she would later critique and explicitly reject. She experienced what she termed as a "real piety," "in the sense of the sweetness of faith," a phrase that she may have drawn from Teresa of Ávila, one of her noted favorite authors. Indeed, as we saw a moment ago, far too many Christians seek the sweetness of faith, comfort and warm feelings, and have almost nothing to do with the reality of finding God in an adult life. Day wants something much deeper in her life, and yet, at this point in her story, she tells us, "I believed, but I did not know in what I believed."[10] All of this led her to the point that "I became disgustingly, proudly pious."[11] But this was, to her, a childish response to what she experienced, and not a properly channeled

---

7. Day, *The Long Loneliness*, 17.
8. Day, *The Long Loneliness*, 17.
9. Day, *The Long Loneliness*, 19.
10. Day, *The Long Loneliness*, 20.
11. Day, *The Long Loneliness*, 20.

perspective on living a life of faith. In many ways, this was simply the state wherein most children dwell, and not something to be disheartened about. It was where she had encountered God in some measure, even if she was unable to fully articulate or describe what such experiences might mean, or transform into, in her adolescence.

Events transpired in her life, however, that pushed her toward another perspective on living in the world, and she found herself very receptive to the humanity she encountered in such moments. For example, she witnessed firsthand as a child the 1906 San Francisco earthquake that killed thousands of people and decimated most of the city. What she saw in its aftermath would in fact continue to have a profound effect on her life. She saw strangers coming together to help one another after the great tragedy of losing their homes and their possessions, people being selfless with their possessions and their time so that others might benefit from their acts of charity. The kindness that humanity could potentially exhibit to one another moved her deeply and made a lasting impression upon her, in many ways marking her vocation at an early age.

After moving to Chicago, Day began to have experiences of organized religion as well, and these provided, she tells us, moments of "enthusiasm" and lofty intentions, providing too another avenue through which to understand the channeling of various spiritual experiences. As she remarks, "The Psalms were an outlet for this enthusiasm of joy or grief . . ."[12]—an early indicator of how she would eventually appropriate the rituals of Catholicism as a way of articulating her own feelings. She also had experiences of home life that provided a good deal of those basic necessities that she would seek to replicate years later in her Catholic Worker houses in a much more explicit fashion: "comfort, security, peace, community."[13] These were the basic necessities of life that she wanted to offer to every human being, regardless of their personal lot in life, and though it would take her some years to more clearly identify that these were indeed the necessities that she had sensed powerfully speaking to her from such early experiences. (These necessities are certainly clearly expressed whenever you visit a Catholic Worker home today.)

What she eventually concluded about this early phase in her life vis-à-vis religious faith was that "All those years I believed. I had faith. The argument of authority, of conscience, of creation—I felt the validity of these."[14] But, despite this feeling, she was unable to cultivate such a "natu-

---

12. Day, *The Long Loneliness*, 29.
13. Day, *The Long Loneliness*, 30.
14. Day, *The Long Loneliness*, 36.

ral" faith further due to her lack of guidance and structure in developing these almost rudimentary beliefs.

As we have noted in the previous authors explored, there enters into Day's list as well the appearance of a critical discernment of her life of faith, one which began to assert itself when she, for example, critiques a letter she wrote to a friend when she was fifteen years old: "this letter was filled with pomp and vanity and piety."[15] Later on, we will also hear her express the sentiment: "I am afraid, too, of not telling the truth, or of distorting the truth. I cannot guarantee that I do not, for I am writing of the past."[16]

After reading Upton Sinclair's *The Jungle*, which recounted the horrors of working in the meat packing industry in Chicago, Day herself walked through such districts in the city and began to feel deeply moved toward helping these people, such as the immigrants who worked in these facilities in order to find a better life for themselves in America. She felt strongly that "from then on my life was to be linked to theirs, their interests were to be mine; I had received a call, a vocation, a direction to my life."[17] This was a connection that ultimately drew her to contemplate her role within the religion of the immigrants, which happened to be Catholicism. At this point, however, her reflections were just as simple in their nature, for, as she shares with the reader, "I felt even at fifteen, that God meant man to be happy, that He meant to provide him with what he needed to maintain life in order to be happy, and that we did not need to have quite so much destitution and misery as I saw all around and read of in the daily press."[18] Her quest for such happiness, she would deduce, would have to be something that included everyone around her, especially the least among society. It would have to be this way, or it would not do at all. The only way to experience the "abundant life," as she would call it, was to embrace those who were neglected by society and to celebrate and rejoice in all aspects of life with them.

> I wanted life and I wanted the abundant life. I wanted it for others too. I did not want just the few ... to be kind to the poor, as the poor. I wanted everyone to be kind. I wanted every home to be open to the lame, the halt and the blind, the way it had been after the San Francisco earthquake. Only then did people really live, really love their brothers. In such love was the abundant life and I did not have the slightest idea how to find it.[19]

15. Day, *The Long Loneliness*, 34.
16. Day, *The Long Loneliness*, 59.
17. Day, *The Long Loneliness*, 38.
18. Day, *The Long Loneliness*, 38.
19. Day, *The Long Loneliness*, 38.

Her first forays into finding a way to provide equality for all people, however, were not far behind, and they were political in nature, revolutionary even. As she had then felt, religion had no place within serious and committed political, revolutionary action, since it was concerned only with "peace and meekness and joy."[20] "Youth, I felt, should not be in a state of peace, but of war."[21] The struggles that the workers of the world were uniting in together were ones that demanded vast, organized action—the "war" that she was more than willing to take part in as the only suitable option available to her to change the order of her world.

If she had any faith in God, which she suggests she did cultivate at the time through a reading of authors such as Tolstoy and Dostoevsky, it was something that served only to alienate her from other Christians around her (not to mention other political activists), and this was, in many ways, the reason she stayed away from the church for so long. "I felt that my faith had nothing in common with that of Christians around me."[22] In a certain sense, this sentiment was probably true for her even after she became a Catholic—something of "the long loneliness" that she saw as inextricable from living a life of faith. What she was critical of, she will later reveal, were Christians not concerned with justice and oppression, but only their own situations in life, and comfort, much as Tolstoy himself had remarked. The decision she made therefore, in her youthful impetuousness, was, again like Tolstoy, straightforward and simple: "In my youthful arrogance, in my feeling that I was one of the strong, I felt then for the first time that religion was something that I must ruthlessly cut out of my life."[23] As she elaborates on this decision:

> I felt at the time that religion would only impede my work. I wanted to have nothing to do with the religion of those whom I saw all about me. I felt that I must turn from it as from a drug. I felt it indeed to be an opiate of the people and not a very attractive one, so I hardened my heart. It was a conscious and deliberate process.[24]

This decision to turn away from religion was one made *so that* she might better embrace the "real" means to social transformation, or that which religion had neglected in its turn toward "another world" presumed by many to be beyond this one. "Where were the saints to try to change the social order,

---

20. Day, *The Long Loneliness*, 41.
21. Day, *The Long Loneliness*, 41.
22. Day, *The Long Loneliness*, 43.
23. Day, *The Long Loneliness*, 43.
24. Day, *The Long Loneliness*, 43.

not just to minister to the slaves but to do away with slavery?"[25] Such sentiments have been the sad truth latent within the history of Christianity, and it was a fact that Day was not intent on ignoring. In this refusal to neglect what really matters in this world, we find not only her critique of the institutional church, but also her vocational calling: "Jesus said 'Blessed are the meek,' but I could not be meek at the thought of injustice. I wanted a Lord who would scourge the money-changers out of the temple, and I wanted to help all those who raised their hand against oppression."[26]

She subsequently moved to New York City and took up a post as a journalist, offering in fact to write about those living in severely impoverished conditions. This was a desire within her that, as we can well guess by this point, was something that would allow the concept of poverty to eventually take root in her budding sense of her own spirituality. She lived for a while on the low wages the workers received and wrote about what it was like to live with so little income. It was during this time as well that she also experienced feelings of what she would come to call "the long loneliness," feelings of isolation that caused her to seek out ways in which to be "free of this burden of loneliness," including her desires to be with the poor.[27] At this time too she began to associate with the International Workers of the World (IWW), certain Marxist and communist thinkers, as well as to study certain anarchist teachings, trying to take seriously Proudhon's statement that "Property is Theft."[28]

Throughout all of these experiences, Day situated herself, as well as those around her striving for liberation, within the ever-present tension between authority and freedom, a political sentiment that might also be analyzed under the headings of (religious) structure and (personal) experience.[29] At times, as Day herself would eventually realize, the tendency to move closer to one pole in favor of the other was a temptation almost too difficult to overcome, and one that was often prompted by the challenges of political action. Both polarities in many ways indicate the extremes between which humanity finds itself struggling in order to identify itself. Yet what Day was to find eventually as true in her life was that, despite her willingness to distance herself from all religious structure so that she might taste a freedom she had never experienced before, she discovered that she had never really known freedom at all: "I had thought all those years that I had

---

25. Day, *The Long Loneliness*, 45.
26. Day, *The Long Loneliness*, 46.
27. Day, *The Long Loneliness*, 51.
28. Day, *The Long Loneliness*, 55.
29. Day, *The Long Loneliness*, 56.

freedom, but now I felt that I had never known real freedom nor even had knowledge of what freedom meant."[30] What she began to discover was that "real freedom" was not to be found apart from one side of the tensions, but rather in being able to critically dwell in either side at any given moment, that is, to ask questions of justice and truth to both the structures that surround us and our own experiences as well. This insight, for her, would become the source of "real freedom", just as we could indicate certain experiences as truly authentic experiences while others as not. The same, in fact, could be said of structures and traditions alike. What Day alerts us to are the criteria by which we can judge both structures and experiences, authorities and a true sense of freedom, and those criteria are justice (in terms of structures) and love, or charity (in terms of experiences).[31]

She continued to work with the International and its causes, and eventually took up the women's suffragist movement as well, even spending some time in jail in Washington, DC after a march for women's right to vote, which she chronicles in detail. To spend time in jail among the "least" and the ignored of society was a galvanizing experience for her, as it further exposed the injustices that inmates face on a daily basis—another form of suffering and inhumanity that she would later rally against. What she encountered in the prison, much as she discovered in Sinclair's *The Jungle* or in the slums of New York City, were experiences of suffering that do occur all around us, every day, and yet that we choose to ignore and pretend as if we are not implicated in these things, as if they are not part of our daily and increasingly global economies.[32] These are things which often cause us to turn away from the compassion we feel when we stop to take note of what is actually happening around us. Day, however, could not evade, ignore, or repress such situations.

While in jail, Day was left in isolation for a period of days, not even weeks, but it was enough for her to reconsider a good portion of her assumptions about life and about her own personal identity. The experience was one that rotated on the axis of justice in relation to worldly structures, and yet it penetrated deep into her comprehension of herself:

---

30. Day, *The Long Loneliness*, 135.

31. Perhaps, in very general and somewhat superficial terms, this is why Christianity, which focuses on the experiences of love, must forever be joined with Judaism, which focuses on the justice of (legal) structures. The former cannot exist without the latter.

32. Sweatshop labor, a very real part of today's global economy, functions in much the same way: if we saw the abuses incurred in manufacturing our clothing, computers, and phones, we might protest, or shop differently. But, mainly, we choose to ignore this reality, because it would be too painful to face.

> I lost all feeling of my own identity. I reflected on the desolation of poverty, of destitution, of sickness and sin. That I would be free after thirty days meant nothing to me. I would never be free again, never free when I knew that behind bars all over the world there were women and men, young girls and boys, suffering constraint, punishment, isolation and hardship for crimes of which all of us were guilty. The mother who had murdered her child, the drug addict—who were the mad and who the sane? Why were prostitutes prosecuted in some cases and in others respected and fawned on? People sold themselves for jobs, for the pay check, and if they only received a high enough price, they were honored. If their cheating, their theft, their lie, were of colossal proportions, if it were successful, they met with praise, not blame. Why were some caught, not others? Why were some termed criminals and others good businessmen? What was right and wrong? What was good and evil? I lay there in utter confusion and misery.[33]

The paradoxes of the world and its myriad injustices began to seep into the formation of Day's sense of self, and she, wonderfully, allowed it to alter her perception of who she was—a dislocation or de-realization experience indeed. The structural oppressions that brought about many of the world's "criminals" were real for her too, and they accordingly affected how she understood moral judgments and the selves such judgments construct. This experience would haunt Day throughout the years, and continue to motivate her search for both justice and charity: "Never would I recover from this wound, this ugly knowledge I had gained of what men were capable in their treatment of each other."[34]

While spending time in jail, Day had taken the time to ask for a Bible to read, perhaps because she recalled how the Psalms had once helped her in her youth to channel her feelings into words. Here, again, she began to read it as a way to respond to the situation in which she found herself. The effect was enormous at the time, though the struggle was also very real:

> I clung to the words of comfort in the Bible and as long as the light held out, I read and pondered. Yet all the while I read, my pride was fighting on. I did not want to go to God in defeat and sorrow. I did not want to depend on Him. I was like the child that wants to walk by itself, I kept brushing away the hand that held me up. I tried to persuade myself that I was reading for

---

33. Day, *The Long Loneliness*, 78.
34. Day, *The Long Loneliness*, 79.

literary enjoyment. But the words kept echoing in my heart. I prayed and did not know that I prayed.³⁵

Despite this profound experience, however, from the moment she left the prison, she began to forget about her experiences and the "echo" in her heart that the words had made (which is a wonderfully accurate way to express what the "language" of religion does in relation to our experiences), and to once again reject her own budding religious desires in favor of the political struggles that seemed to offer more significant yields in terms of justice.

After this rather harrowing time in her life, Day worked on occasion as a freelance journalist, but would also, on occasion, force herself to sit in the back of a Catholic Church, observing the foreign rituals and gestures from a distance, somehow still drawn to this place where people were able to connect their psychological need for reverence, worship, and adoration—all potentially dismissible factors that she refused to degrade.³⁶ She went into this "atmosphere of prayer" consciously, seeking a form of integrity that it would still take her some time to discover as a reality in her life. Justice from oppression, to her mind, continued to trump charity, "The true meaning of the word we did not know."³⁷

What Day was perhaps sensing at work in her life was the intimate interwoven nature of worship, gratitude, reverence, and adoration—falling down in awe and praise—and the essential element of finding justice in one's life as a true form of worship. From the Hebrew prophets onward, this latter dimension of worship has been a central tenet of Western religious practice and it is inseparable from other forms of worship, which can often seem at a certain remove from calls for social justice. Nonetheless, it was precisely the intimate merger of the two that set Day toward understanding her vocation and responding to it.

She felt an acute awareness of her sinfulness, and yet she was not sure how to alleviate this situation within her: "I just suffered desperately and desired to be freed from my suffering, with a most urgent and selfish passion. The instinct for self-preservation made me forget everything but a frantic desire for freedom, to get away from these depths into which I had fallen."³⁸ It would still be a while until she learned what "true" freedom, to her mind, was—something she only located at the time through the "echoes" she heard of her own struggles within the Catholic faith. She was clear, however, on the troubled state in which she dwelt: "The problem is,

35. Day, *The Long Loneliness*, 81.
36. Day, *The Long Loneliness*, 84.
37. Day, *The Long Loneliness*, 87.
38. Day, *The Long Loneliness*, 104–5.

how to love God? We are only too conscious of the hardness of our hearts, and in spite of all that religious writers tell us about *feeling* not being necessary, we do want to feel and so know that we love God."[39] And, yet, despite the difficulties, she was also acutely aware of the small ember of a desire *for* God that grew somehow steadily within her and which would give her cause to express sentiments parallel to Augustine: "it is true too that you love God if you want to love Him."[40]

In a very particular sense, her journey toward Catholicism occurred as a result of getting to know specific Catholic people, but also, in what would be for her vocational calling a very significant factor, due to the fact that the general mass of oppressed immigrants in America were Catholic, a fact she notes as what appealed to her greatly and "drew me to the Church."[41] There is thereby within her conversion story a particular *relational* reason why she became Catholic: her faith was relational from the start, and she does not apologize for this fact. She intuits that the only way to enter into a structural, organized, institutional religion is through the recognition that this is how and why religion matters to people in the first place—because they want to partake in the common life together.

> I had heard many say that they wanted to worship God in their own way and did not need a Church in which to praise Him, nor a body of people with whom to associate themselves. But I did not agree to this. My very experience as a radical, my whole make-up, led me to want to associate myself with others, with the masses, in loving and praising God.[42]

Tolstoy, in his autobiography, wonders how anyone could have faith in his day and age. Essentially, there is so much misery amongst those who have so much wealth and success, but lack in faith. But the peasants who worked for him and had almost nothing materially were some of the happiest and most religious people he had ever known. Henri Nouwen, as we will see in a moment, once asked himself a similar question when he traveled to South America about the people living there in poverty, yet who seemed to him much happier than many persons he knew living in affluence in the West. Tolstoy and Nouwen both recognized that these people grasped something about life and faith that they did not. Day, as with both of these authors, sought to understand what faith meant to such people and how their lives revolved around such a comprehension and practice of faith.

39. Day, *The Long Loneliness*, 139.
40. Day, *The Long Loneliness*, 139.
41. Day, *The Long Loneliness*, 107.
42. Day, *The Long Loneliness*, 139.

Without delving too far into this point, I will only indicate how such sentiments on the relational side of her understanding of faith will bring her to the place where, thanks to the help of the itinerant Frenchman Peter Maurin, personalism became a profound part of defining her theological worldview. As she will later remind us, "charity is personal," and the Catholic Worker movement would strive to embody such personal relations between people, taking each stranger into their houses of hospitality and trying to educate people on what it means to be present to each other.[43] "Personalism and communitarianism" were in fact the later rallying cries of the movement.[44]

Many life changes would also confront Day throughout this period in her life, including a more stable home life, a relationship with a man who would eventually drift away from her, and the birth of her daughter, Tamar. Throughout these various phases and important life events, she continued to ponder what religion and prayer meant to her, and to develop her calling to fuse the freedom she found through the love taught in the Catholic faith and her strong call to pursue justice on behalf of the poor. It was in this sense that she continued to find deep connections to the state of poverty, which occurred as a daily reality for her in both its material and physical senses. For example, she began to see a willingness to undergo a life of poverty as a calling in-itself that she could not ignore, just as she could not ignore the actually poor people gathering around her. As she read in a book by William James, and quotes in length in her autobiography as something with which she also found an "echo":

> Among us English-speaking peoples especially do the praises of poverty need once more to be boldly sung. We have grown literally afraid to be poor. We despise anyone who elects to be poor in order to simplify and save his inner life. If he does not join the general scramble, we deem him spiritless and lacking in ambition. We have lost the power even of imagining what the ancient realization of poverty could have meant; the liberation from material attachments, the unbribed soul, the manlier indifference, the paying our way by what we are and not by what we have, the right to fling away our life at any moment irresponsibly,—the more athletic time, in short, the fighting shape.[45]

A good many of us, especially in the more affluent parts of the world today, can perhaps resonate a good deal with the fear of being poor, and the

---

43. Day, *The Long Loneliness*, 179.
44. Day, *The Long Loneliness*, 195.
45. Day, *The Long Loneliness*, 119.

denial of the benefits which living "small," or more simply, might bring to us. Within the notion of poverty itself there is a powerful fusion of the material and the spiritual that moved Day to combine the various passions of her life and to develop them in conjunction with one another. Her struggles with prayer, with loneliness, with poverty, and with oppression were all integrated through the vocation she sought out, and as a testament to what the life of faith—any sense of a spiritual life really—must be about. Only in standing together in solidarity with the poor through our connection to our own compassion might we begin to even address the feeling of loneliness within ourselves. In this way, her efforts put toward achieving personal integrity, the bringing together of all these disparate parts of her life and desires that many people might see as unrelated or unnecessary to their own lives, became essential ingredients in making her life and faith what they were for her.

And so she began to cultivate a life of prayer that would bring the other elements of her life and her commitment to justice into play as well, as if prayer were the meeting place of these elements, the melting pot that ultimately formed the person she was becoming:

> I was surprised that I found myself beginning to pray daily. I could not get down on my knees, but I could pray while I was walking. If I got down on my knees I thought, "Do I really believe? Whom am I praying to?" A terrible doubt came over me, and a sense of shame, and I wondered if I was praying because I was lonely, because I was unhappy.[46]

Her experience of prayer, somewhat like Karr's, but not far removed either from moments in certain of Teresa's explanations, was a difficult one for her to understand. She suspected the worst in her motives, but as she would soon discover in her reflections, she wasn't approaching prayer due to some unhappiness in her life. She was happy in her life and in her movement toward the acceptance of what mattered to her most, and this is what led her to prayer. She was not able to put her finger on precisely what it was that continued to draw her to prayer at this in her existence, or why she found it so appealing in general, but it became a practice that she grew accustomed to undertaking. It was, in some ways, I would suggest, an acceptance of the mystery of life, and she began to make peace with this fact. She was still "restless," as she describes it, but she was nonetheless contented in some sense as well.

As time went on, she longed to share her spiritual life and the insights it yielded with her companion at the time, Forster, but he was unable to

---

46. Day, *The Long Loneliness*, 132.

reciprocate any interest, and continued to maintain a certain distance as a self-committed political activist. This did not stop Day, however, from pursuing a life within the Catholic Church—if anything, her resolve only grew stronger.

> I knew that I was going to have my child baptized, cost what it may. I knew that I was not going to have her floundering through many years as I had done, doubting and hesitating, undisciplined and amoral. I felt it was the greatest thing I could do for my child. For myself, I prayed for the gift of faith. I was sure, yet not sure. I postponed the day of decision.[47]

She herself was not baptized at this time, but she was drawn to having her child baptized. This is perhaps symbolic of how real her internal struggles were, and very much was indicative of the evolution of her life of faith. She would still ask many questions, and many theological thoughts would go unresolved throughout her long life, but she was at last in a position to unite what mattered most to her, and to bring any accompanying insights that went along with being in such a place of faith into her life.

Within a short span of time, she chose to become Catholic, started taking catechism classes, and learned more about what the Catholic faith was. Though her initial willingness to join the Catholic Church will appear to many as rather naïve, Day still maintained a critical position vis-à-vis the church which demonstrated, to my mind at least, that her approach was not naïve at all, but rather accepting at times, and critical at other times. That is, she was looking for something within religion that she found, and so was thereby able to formulate a critical approach in relation to this acceptance. As she describes her conversion, "Without even looking into the claims of the Catholic Church, I was willing to admit that for me she was the one true Church. She had come down through the centuries since the time of Peter, and far from being dead, she claimed and held the allegiance of the masses of people in all the cities where I had lived."[48] And, moreover, "I was in an agreeable and lethargic, almost bovine state of mind, filled with an animal content, not wishing to inquire into or question the dogmas I was learning. I made up my mind to accept what I did not understand, trusting light to come, as it sometimes did, in a blinding flash of exultation and realization."[49] As she says in hindsight about the choice she made then to become Catholic: "It may have been an unthinking, unquestioning faith, and yet the chance certainly came, again and again, 'Do I prefer the Church to my own will,' even

---

47. Day, *The Long Loneliness*, 136.
48. Day, *The Long Loneliness*, 139.
49. Day, *The Long Loneliness*, 143.

if it was only the small matter of sitting at home on a Sunday morning with the papers? And the choice was the Church."[50]

The tensions that she felt between Catholicism and social action mirror those between authority and freedom, as well as between the material and the spiritual. For Day, however, the tensions began to recede a bit into the integrity of the person becoming a recognition and acceptance of the complexity of the human person. (Perhaps this is similar in some ways to those moments when one accepts the "crazy things" their family does because of their love for them.) "It was through a whole love, both physical and spiritual, I came to know God."[51] I would suggest that it was the recognition of this permanent tension that also allowed her to unconditionally accept Catholicism while also maintaining a rigid critique of it—despite how paradoxical this might sound to our ears. Perhaps we hear in this a deep echo with Teresa of Ávila and her writings, which Day herself tells us she read and delighted in.[52] Such an apparent paradox might also simply signal how her critique of a hierarchical Catholic Church stemmed from the life of faith in solidarity with the poor with whom she was living.

It was for these reasons, among others, that the decision to embrace Catholicism made her feel as if she were pitting her newfound beliefs against her social activism, a tension she could not long abide without integrating them together in some way, even if that way was one that only maintained the tension, never resolving it. She went through the process of becoming Catholic, but, she notes, took no consolation from the sacraments, which she engaged "grimly, coldly."[53] As this reflection makes clear, hers was no sentimental longing after a nostalgic image of faith, but one that sought the hard, cold reality of the world underneath the love and comfort that one can also find within the spiritual life. In some sense, we might say that she saw the material reality and the spiritual, prayerful world as being in a tension that constitutes our very selves. Whereas some people romanticize their religious experience in order not to deal with their material reality, Day refused to exempt herself from the tension.

Day began to sense how joining the Catholic Church would have to happen along with a sort of "permanent dissatisfaction" with the

---

50. Day, *The Long Loneliness*, 139. As she will later say, and as it resonates with the above descriptions, "We have too little ritual in our lives," and, I believe, it is growing less and less each year" (200) and, "I felt that it was necessary for man to worship, that he was most truly himself when engaged in that act" (93).

51. Day, *The Long Loneliness*, 140.

52. Day, *The Long Loneliness*, 140 and 161.

53. Day, *The Long Loneliness*, 148.

Church—another way for a critical mechanism to reenter her field of vision.[54] She took to heart these words: "'Too often,' Cardinal Mundelein said, 'has the Church lined up on the wrong side.'"[55] For centuries, and especially in places globally of extreme poverty and exploitation, the Catholic Church has been on the side of those in power, and Day was intent on seeing this order of things reversed. She would even go so far as to critique the residences of bishops as palaces, which do a great injustice to the poor simply by existing, echoing some sentiments we have heard more recently from Pope Francis as well.

What Day does make clear is how she did not choose to become Catholic because of its more corrupt side, but because "I loved the Church for Christ made visible. Not for itself, because it was so often a scandal to me."[56] Her assessment of the Church in its historical manifestation was rather negative actually, and blunt: "There was plenty of charity but too little justice,"[57] though she was also quick to add that, in hindsight, there are so many good religious persons working for justice throughout the world.

In many ways, the presence of a diversity of opinions amongst those who lived at the Catholic Worker homes she was perpetually founding also generated a self-critical apparatus for her, as she herself notes when she claims that she wishes all Catholic Workers were pacifists, but is content that they have an ongoing conversation happening wherein everyone does not agree with each other.[58] So, as we see in this example, she is even willing to look to the organization that she herself founded and to see its faults and limitations, as her ability to critique herself is not diminished one bit by becoming religious—indeed, if anything, it took on new tones, while also allowing her to show herself some charity from time to time.

After making peace with the permanent tension that existed between her faith and her passion for justice, Day charted herself on a course that culminated with the creation of the Catholic Worker movement, one that still goes on to this day in numerous cities throughout the world. But it is her early story, I am contending, the one that brought her to faith in the first place, that reveals the unfolding of a journey to faith most directly. From this point onward, she runs downhill, you might say, inevitably following the path which leads her to integrate her life into one inclusive place. After a demonstration for worker's rights in Washington, DC, for example, she goes

54. Day, *The Long Loneliness*, 150.
55. Day, *The Long Loneliness*, 149.
56. Day, *The Long Loneliness*, 149–50.
57. Day, *The Long Loneliness*, 150.
58. Day, *The Long Loneliness*, 272.

to pray in a chapel at the Catholic University, and, as she tells us, "There I offered up a special prayer, a prayer which came with tears and with anguish, that some way would open up for me to use what talents I possessed for my fellow workers, for the poor."[59]

The Catholic Worker movement would become, for her and for many, a "permanent revolution," though in sharp contrast to the political revolutions that were ceaselessly occurring around the world.[60] It was, and still is, a movement focused on "the poor, the dispossessed, the exploited," and that is willing to live a life on the margins of society, with those in poverty, in order to find a better way to live more faithfully and more charitably toward others.[61] In many ways, as well, this was merely her reading of the life of Jesus, the life that continued to motivate her the most:

> He died between two thieves because He would not be made an earthly King. He lived in an occupied country for thirty years without starting an underground movement or trying to get out from under a foreign power. His teaching transcended all the wisdom of the scribes and pharisees, and taught us the most effective means of living in this world while preparing for the next. And He directed His sublime words to the poorest of the poor, to the people who thronged the towns and followed after John the Baptist, who hung around, sick and poverty-stricken at the doors of rich men.[62]

For Day, living at the margins of society was her way of faithfully responding to the call to live the life of Jesus she wanted to imitate. What she focuses our attention on to yet another degree is the role that poverty plays in making such a faith come to life—a consideration we cannot ignore any longer.

---

59. Day, *The Long Loneliness*, 166.
60. Day, *The Long Loneliness*, 186.
61. Day, *The Long Loneliness*, 204.
62. Day, *The Long Loneliness*, 205.

CHAPTER TEN

Henri Nouwen

Locating a Contemporary Spirituality

Although the city of Nijkerk is locally known for its scenic views of the Ijsselmeer inland bay, its place as the birth site of Henri Nouwen on January 24, 1932 would ensure that it would become well known far beyond the reach of the Netherlands. The famous poet, priest, and theologian was raised in a context where his Dutch heritage came second only to his family's Catholic identity and thus, it quickly became apparent to Nouwen that the priestly vocation was his chosen path. He was ordained in 1957 as a diocesan priest and in addition to his pastoral duties, he undertook the study of psychology at the Catholic University of Nijmegen.

The early 1960s presented Nouwen with an opportunity to further combine his passion for the well-being of his congregants with the continually developing techniques of clinical pastoral ministry at the Menninger Clinic in Topeka, Kansas. Upon completion of a graduate degree in religion and psychiatry, he was offered a teaching position at the University of Notre Dame, a post which led him to realize that his true passion was to be found in theology. Nouwen completed a doctorate in theology in 1971 and would spend the next fifteen years teaching at Harvard Divinity School, Yale, and making frequent ministerial trips to South America as the continent dealt with horrendous violations of human rights. In 1985, after a life changing meeting with Jean Vanier, Nouwen moved to L'Arche in Trosly, France, a community where people with developmental disabilities live with assistants. As he struggled with depression and his constant questions of vocation, Nouwen looked back on his time in Trosly as one of the most formational periods of his life. Nouwen would commit the rest of his life to the L'Arche model, specifically with a community in Toronto, where he died on September 21, 1996.

> The corpus that Nouwen left behind is as diverse as he was and spans genres ranging from the academic fields of psychiatry, and theology to poetry, correspondences with Thomas Merton, and his memoirs and spiritual journals. Among his most read works are The Wounded Healer *(1975)*, Reaching Out *(1975)*, Lifesigns *(1986), and* The Inner Voice of Love: A Journey through Anguish to Freedom *(1996)*.

If I had to suggest some of the twentieth century's greatest spiritual writers, I could perhaps do no better than to list Thomas Merton and Henri Nouwen, both of whom brought a balanced perspective on living the spiritual life to their work, and continue to inspire people to delve more fully into the life of faith after which many are seeking in our day. Both authors had their fair share of struggles to attend to in their own lives, but both also brought a refreshing honesty and sense of commitment to the Catholic tradition they were immersed in, in order to grow in personal integrity and faith.

Merton's autobiography of his conversion to Catholicism and his entrance into the monastic order of the Trappists at a monastery in Kentucky was, and still is, a major autobiographical story of faith from the mid-twentieth century, *The Seven Storey Mountain*. His choice to enter into a life of monastic silence, but to continue to develop his vocation as a writer, is a profound meditation too on the nature of ostensibly "removing" oneself from the world in order to actually find another (prayerful) way of entering back into it. For all of his enthusiasm for the faith, however, there is yet a strong tendency toward romanticizing his youthful faith in his autobiography that many converts, either inadvertently or consciously, develop in their perspective toward their newfound "home." In this sense, and despite its immense popularity, Merton's autobiography does not seek first to develop a self-critical perspective of his views on the divine; rather, he engages the reader more through the idealization of one's religious vocation, something that may perhaps be helpful for many to read at some point in their life, though, I would argue, it deviates from the general features that I believe describe the best type of such writing.

In what follows, and because it does indicate the trajectory of thought I am following more closely in the present study, I will be taking up a published journal of Henri Nouwen, which was written at a time in his life when he contemplated, and eventually went to live with, the members of the Toronto L'Arche community—a group founded originally in France by Jean Vanier that is focused on not just caring for those with physical and mental disabilities, but on living together and caring for one another *through* the faith that brought them together. I will pursue this path, for the most part, because Nouwen's attentiveness to his own potential for error is constantly corrected by his desire to "impoverish" himself through his fidelity to following God's call for him, a movement toward a life of poverty that allows a powerful dynamic of self-critical thought to resonate deeply within his reflections.

For Nouwen, who was a Catholic priest from the Netherlands and who had held teaching posts at some of the most prestigious universities in the world—including Harvard and Yale Universities—it was also a "conversion" to make the choice to live and work at L'Arche, or "the ark" that provides shelter from the storms of this world, as it allowed him to develop his personal life of faith and prayer in ways that exceeded his expectations and even his understanding. His desire to pray "Lord, show me where you want me to go, and I will follow you" had led him to this place in particular, though it was to take some time before he was fully able to accept the new home he felt God has called him to.[1]

Nouwen's personal narrative is in general very focused on his sense of vocation, a word which can be used in many ways: as entering a particular career path or a religious vocation or as a vocation for marriage. In Nouwen's story, we find that the idea of discerning a vocation is an ongoing task; it does not stop at some "final" destination. This is in many ways a common misconception: that you take vows and thus you are finished searching for your vocational path in life. But one's vocation is never actually a finished product having arrived at a terminal conclusion. This is the reason why Nouwen talks about vocation as a continuous process of conversion or transformation. One's vocation unsettles us as much as it may settle us in some way.

All too often, when people get married, after a long period of courtship and expectation, they lose their spark, so to speak, sometime afterwards, a sign of how the achieving of the vocation (of marriage in this instance) doesn't contain the "final" ends they were hoping it would. When you think the vocation (like marriage) is the end goal, and so that once you've achieved it you believe you're done, what can often result is a falsified point of view—a belief that there is nothing more to achieve, and the stagnation that results ends up creating further problems. Rather, the sense of vocation that Nouwen is trying to recover is one wherein you never fully settle. Rather, you enter into a marriage, or any vocation, with the sense that the commitment to one's vocation is just the beginning of a process of maturing and growing *within* an ongoing process of discernment. It is a commitment

1. Nouwen, *The Road to Daybreak*, 1.

to personal development and growth above all else in some ways. Indeed, discerning what a vocation even was to him (and despite the fact that he was already a priest who had in great measure already "found" his vocation) was an ongoing and major part of his life. In his words, "It became quite clear to me that idealism, good intentions, and a desire to serve the poor do not make up a vocation. One needs to be called and sent."[2] One must also be needed by others who are in need of one's gifts and talents. And yet, he continued to ask, "How does one follow Jesus unreservedly?"[3]

One of the most difficult things to discern in life perhaps, but also the very thing that should give us life abundant, is locating one's vocation, that to which one feels that their very being is "called." The first thing to consider, of course, when determining one's vocation is that it is not a static idea, but rather should be understood as a *continuous* conversion toward God, as Nouwen will put it, toward that which God calls one to, toward then that which one is—that is, the gifts and skills that one is given in order to do that which will yield the greatest results, and though such results will often be unknown to the one who listens and follows. Much like coming to faith, vocation is a complex series of probabilities and influences (as we saw earlier in the theology of John Henry Newman). Nouwen feels somehow drawn to this life, but he also feels anxious about it, and sorting through the complexity of one's vocational calling is part of the process of discernment. Nouwen's journals are in this sense the story of following a vocation, not of his priestly calling exclusively, but of the ways in which that initial calling was deepened and discerned over time.

His journal of this particular discernment, published as *The Road to Daybreak*, provides us with an intimate portrait of a person trying to discern what exactly God's calling might look like, and it is an honest and, I feel, accurate portrait of what exactly faith might look like when formed through such a process. As he himself foreshadows the answer to his own questions about embracing himself and God's will for him—and in ways that echo many of the authors we have been looking at already—"It is a screaming and kicking 'yes' that fills these pages. It is a 'yes' emerging from the recognition of my own brokenness and need for radical healing."[4] In a certain sense, you can only realize your vocation when you realize how broken you are. As this author of a book on ministry that aims to get people to look at their own brokenness before they can ably assist

---

2. Nouwen, *The Road to Daybreak*, 3.
3. Nouwen, *The Road to Daybreak*, 4.
4. Nouwen, *The Road to Daybreak*, 5.

others—appropriately titled *The Wounded Healer*[5]—Nouwen was seeking to couple his desire to follow God's calling for him with his desire for "a community of people who could lead me closer to the heart of God."[6] The myth we often foster is that we can only help others when we have our own lives together, that we can only help from a place of strength. But, for Nouwen, the truth is the opposite. We are only able to heal when we get in touch with our own wounds. If we rush in to help someone without self-awareness of our own brokenness, we can end up making things worse.

In dating, for example, when someone has just gotten out of a bad relationship, rushing in seemingly to fix everything that went wrong previously through a new relationship is in reality a terrible idea. Hurling oneself into the next relationship without looking at why the previous one failed is a bad pattern, however, that many people fall victim to in their search for love and intimacy. What Nouwen considered on a spiritual level, however, was how he needed to look within himself for healing before he would be able to assist others. In this way, the community of L'Arche had called him, thinking that he had something to teach them, but they ended up, in a paradoxical reverse, teaching him first. In truth, and as many at L'Arche communities around the world continue to recognize, this is how things should be.

Nouwen had been led to the community of L'Arche through the writings, theology, and personal faith of Jean Vanier, its founder, who had proposed living a simple life in a home in France with disabled persons who would be cared for and respected, as well as integrated into the spiritual life of the community. There would be no flashy glamor for this vocational calling, but rather a solid focus placed upon living life together in small communities, caring for the least among us, and discerning faith and spiritual growth in the midst of forms of physical poverty that society often neglects. As Nouwen will articulate its mission, "L'Arche is built upon the body and not upon the word."[7] The stress as such is placed upon our bodily being in this world, that which cannot be neglected, and which we often yet neglect—an aspect we have already seen highlighted in numerous spiritual paths we have looked at.

The body is essential for overcoming the "myth of autonomy" (Karr) that attempts to define us so completely that we become walled off from others and unable to complete the necessary task of translation that fosters all relationships leading to the establishment of faith. "The body thus becomes the way to know the word and to enter into relationship with the word. The

---

5. Nouwen, *The Wounded Healer*.
6. Nouwen, *The Road to Daybreak*, 7.
7. Nouwen, *The Road to Daybreak*, 150.

body of Jesus becomes the way to life. 'He who eats my body and drinks my blood will have eternal life.'"[8] In saying this, what Nouwen explicitly emphasizes is the manner in which the body of Christ who is the "Word of God," or the *logos* as it is put in Greek, becomes the ordering principle that gives shape to the chaos, not only of the world, but also within ourselves. This ordering principle, we are led to understand, is that which is embodied in the flesh, made *incarnate*, so that we might imitate him and bring this divine principle of order into our very selves. Nouwen's point is that there is simply no way to comprehend the figure of Christ without realizing the role that bodies—Christ's body and our bodies alike—play in the formation of one's faith. Despite the reality that we may never fully comprehend the complexities of their interaction, we should not fail to note their intertwined nature within one's spirituality.

What Vanier had realized, and had wanted to convey to the world through the care that could be demonstrated to the bodies of disabled persons, is that Christianity has a profound message for the world as a whole: "The body is not a prison to escape from, but a temple in which God already dwells."[9] Again, as Teresa had made clear in her keys to living the spiritual life, and as Augustine was overcome by the reality of, we cannot neglect our bodily dwelling on this planet. We cannot abstract ourselves from it and pretend it does not exist. We must embrace our bodily beauty (which is not to suggest any sense of a commercialized, idealized "body image") as well as the limitations of our having a body, and seek to develop ourselves in light of our bodily needs and desires, which are intimately connected to every other desire we have. This does not mean simply "giving in" to every bodily desire, but by acknowledging those desires, to work with them and to develop a faith that works in conjunction with them, at times perhaps limiting them, but at other times helping them to flourish.

In a very direct sense, Vanier's goal was simply "to be poor with the poor," though to take up a very different literal poverty than most might at first contemplate.[10] The form of poverty that Vanier addressed with his life was a physical form of it, and one that often goes ignored or neglected by society as a whole. This refocusing of the spiritual reality of embracing poverty was to have a significant impact upon the construction of Nouwen's spirituality.

> Here in Trosly France the saints are everywhere and the community for the handicapped is called L'Arche, a constant reminder of Noah's Ark, to which people and animals fled for shelter as

8. Nouwen, *The Road to Daybreak*, 151.
9. Nouwen, *The Road to Daybreak*, 163.
10. Nouwen, *The Road to Daybreak*, 13.

the flood covered more and more of the land. L'Arche is indeed the place where many vulnerable men and women who are threatened by the judgmental and violent world in which they live can find a safe place and feel at home.[11]

There is no better way to find one's faith than by practicing such a "preferential option for the poor," as the Catholic Church has put it. By immersing oneself in a life dedicated to helping the least among us in this particular context, Nouwen was entering into a deeper phase of his own personal life of faith, one that would intertwine humility and growth in important ways. For example, he would end up learning much from those often deemed as having little to contribute to society on the whole:

> During evening prayer we sang simple songs, we listened to Danny, one of the handicapped men from Cork, who with great difficulty read from Jean Vanier's book *I Meet Jesus*, and we prayed. Danny said, "I love you, Jesus. I do not reject you even when I get nervous once in a while . . . even when I get confused. I love you with my arms, my legs, my head, my heart; I love you and I do not reject you, Jesus. I know that you love me, that you love me so much. I love you too, Jesus." As he prayed I looked at his beautiful, gentle face and saw without any veil or cover his agony as well as his love. Who would not respond to a prayer like that?[12]

What Danny's story reveals to us, I believe, is how many of us believe our spiritual lives to be complex and of great depth, when, in actuality, when faced with such a simplicity of faith, we are forced to reconsider how many of our own spiritual needs and wants are just as, if not more, simple than Danny's. What Nouwen discovers in the simplicity of such prayers and lives of spiritual simplicity is that, despite his coming to L'Arche to be a sort of spiritual advisor to the community, he has far more to learn from the poverty in which the people there live, rather than having to teach others about a faith that is often detached from such forms of poverty. Just as Karr or Shapiro had to submit themselves to the broken people who make up AA, or as Tolstoy learned to step down from his elitism to the common masses who taught him of faith, so too does Nouwen have to reconsider his own journey to faith in light of the "broken" people of L'Arche who, precisely in their brokenness, exhibit a wholeness that many of us may never achieve. Rather than rejecting brokenness, one finds wholeness only in admitting their brokenness.

11. Nouwen, *The Road to Daybreak*, 9.
12. Nouwen, *The Road to Daybreak*, 11.

What Nouwen discovers above all else, you might say, is the beautiful "dislocation" of his former life as an intellectual, as a priest, as a person who thought he knew better than others what a life of faith is. In short, the lesson of faith he needed most was one he was only able to receive once his entire world was turned on its head. "As I walked home after having kissed everyone good-night, I felt a strange warm pain that had something to do with the many worlds I was trying to keep together."[13] What such sentiments accurately speak of is what he is realizing with great force, that "It makes no sense to preach the Gospel when I have allowed no time for my own conversion."[14] As he continues, this sense of conversion that he needs to recognize in his life was a major calling that he had been neglecting, hiding, in a sense, underneath what appeared to be a vocation already chosen.

Yet, he claimed soon after sensing this, "It struck me that selling what you own, leaving your family and friends, and following Jesus is not a once-in-a-lifetime event. You must do it many times and in many different ways. And it certainly does not become easier."[15] Simply being someone who has chosen a religious vocation does not guarantee you a boisterous life of prayer, a certitude free from all doubt, or a spontaneous sense of joy and warmth in the company of good friends. The dialectic between faith and doubt, between a bountiful spirituality and a deep dryness, is not something that suddenly disappears because one has made certain choices about themselves or their identity, as Wiman has already pointed out to us. Perhaps, in a particular way, choosing to enter into religious life or a community of faith presents an even more difficult path for the believer seeking to grow in faith—as Teresa's story has already made clear to us.

On a level that already includes his response to a calling to live a life of faith, but now which runs much deeper, Nouwen encounters in his situation at L'Arche the continuous process of "de-realization," wherein one's reality becomes unstable and things do not appear as we once thought they did, or should.[16] Again, we are confronted with a parallel formulation to Karr's sense of "dislocation," or Wiman's being "shattered," or Teresa's "violence" done to herself. What each individual encountered, I am suggesting, is a fundamental element in living the spiritual life, a process of realizing that we are not in control of our reality, and that God's reality at times "goes radically against our inclinations."[17] Rather than resist such moments, we

---

13. Nouwen, *The Road to Daybreak*, 12.
14. Nouwen, *The Road to Daybreak*, 20.
15. Nouwen, *The Road to Daybreak*, 46.
16. Nouwen, *The Road to Daybreak*, 113.
17. Nouwen, *The Road to Daybreak*, 154.

are advised to learn to see how God is challenging us to go deeper into the life of faith and to discern, along with both God and others we trust along the journey, that such experiences of disorientation may seem to herald the loss of a reality we had been living in, but they may also be a doorway to a new world we needed to encounter.

Such acts of "de-realization" are yet, from another angle, a form of poverty, an example of our not owning the means to control our own lives.[18] In such situations, no doubt, we might want to scream out that this is a terrible injustice being done to us, one that mirrors so many injustices being done to so many people throughout the world, even at this very moment (e.g., refugees, victims of abuse, those caught up in conflict or wars, etc.). But, we also need to stress, these "injustices" are not the same. The reality that Nouwen entered into was one that he himself chose and one that he sensed, despite his reluctance, would be a path toward the formation of a truer, better self (much as Teresa had earlier described the "compelling" state that God brought about within her).

In other situations, ones imposed externally by either circumstance or by those seeking to commit acts of violence, people who experience a lack of control in their lives may actually be called to take up forms of protest for the social injustices that litter our world, for themselves or on behalf of those who cannot protest. What is discovered, in such cases of necessary resistance, is that, in Nouwen's words, "The cross of horror became the cross of hope, the tortured body became the body that gives new life; the gaping wounds became the source of forgiveness, healing, and reconciliation."[19] This important triad of healing, forgiveness, and reconciliation are incidental neither to the story of Christianity nor to Nouwen's own life, for it is only through our ability to demonstrate all three things in an interconnected manner that we are able to grasp the significance of God's mercy. We are healed insofar as we are forgiven, insofar as we feel that forgiveness permeates us and transforms our lives, and this is the true source of reconciliation, amongst persons, but also within our own lives. We reconcile ourselves with others and with God when we realize that our sins do not bind us to being the "flawed" persons that we are—there is another way to hold ourselves in this world, and it is a way that can serve to unite us in relationship with others who are learning to live this way.

Nouwen, for his part, immerses himself in the quest of trying to discern the presence of "the God who is so deeply hidden that he can be

---

18. Nouwen, *The Road to Daybreak*, 168.
19. Nouwen, *The Road to Daybreak*, 161.

recognized only by the eye of faith."[20] In this locating of divine presence, he is moved profoundly by the other members of L'Arche and the ease with which the simplicity of spirituality comes to them and the way in which faith flows outward from such a spot with a burning intensity. "Here, too, God is hidden; here, too, is unceasing prayer of simply presence; here, too, is the utmost poverty."[21] Such an encounter with the depths of faith ultimately prompts him to rethink his entire understanding of faith and of prayer: "Why should I spend an hour in prayer when I do nothing during that time but think about people I am angry with, people who are angry with me, books I should read and books I should write, and thousands of other silly things that happen to grab my mind for a moment?"[22] As he explains, "The answer is: because God is greater than my mind and my heart, and what is really happening in the house of prayer is not measurable in terms of human success and failure."[23] Being faithful, then, is everything, a point he will drive home repeatedly throughout his journal of his experiences during his time at L'Arche: "The question as to whether it is helpful, useful, practical, or fruitful is completely irrelevant, since the only reason to love is love itself. Everything else is secondary."[24]

Love, in this fashion, has no practical utilitarian purpose. It is not practical, efficient, or productive. Love holds you back from being productive, and it can be a burden. A partner can be injured and the other gives up their job to be with that person for the sake of their love. It is at times perhaps a terrible weight, but that is also in the nature of love. Relationships should not be described in terms of who has the power or the upper hand. A relationship actually functions when you enter into it willingly looking to give up control, and the other person responds in kind rather than taking advantage of your apparent weakness. You end up thereby choosing to be trapped by love, and find yourself blossoming and growing as a result. This is how one's vocation actually works. What is destructive is entering a relationship seeking to get something out of it (attention, obedience, looking good to other people) and finding that you end up losing yourself instead of gaining all that you had thought was being made available to you. This paradoxical logic, I would argue, is exactly what Jesus meant when he spoke of losing your life in order to gain it (Luke 17:33).

20. Nouwen, *The Road to Daybreak*, 28.
21. Nouwen, *The Road to Daybreak*, 29.
22. Nouwen, *The Road to Daybreak*, 29.
23. Nouwen, *The Road to Daybreak*, 29–30.
24. Nouwen, *The Road to Daybreak*, 30.

Another way to say this is that relationships are started and deepened through inefficiency, that is, through wasting time together. This is why we make so many of our friends when we are young, when we have so little of great importance to do together, other than seemingly "hang out" and waste time together. And faith itself is a relationship, and needs to be accessed through inefficiency, in something like prayer, which one should be happy to report is a complete "waste of time." "Efficiency" in a relationship is a recipe for disaster. Perhaps the best thing you can find in a good relationship is someone who is not distracted by something else when they are wasting time with you. The longer it takes for the cell phone to come out in order to distract us, the better—and perhaps the quicker we will make a lasting relationship. For his part, Nouwen was being challenged to give up his sense of the world, his sense of efficiency, his personal use of time, and this was part of the learning curve of his vocation.

In the midst of such honest portrayals of his struggle to find his deeper calling within a vocation he was already called to, Nouwen is willing to admit the state he finds himself in, and which should appear to us as *nothing but* what the life of faith actually is: "So I am praying while not knowing how to pray. I am resting while feeling restless, at peace while tempted, safe while still anxious, surrounded by a cloud of light while still in darkness, in love while still doubting."[25] Such explicit self-realizations, as one might at this point expect as the norm of the developing spiritual life, are what allow him to develop that same self-critical awareness that we find to be a constituent part of the Christian faith.

In large part, L'Arche sees its communal identity as a vocation. This also allows it to be a transformational community. It is a form of poverty willingly embraced in order to encounter God and to challenge the "efficient" ways of the world. Jean Vanier therefore describes poverty similarly to how Karr describes prayer: a process of feeling small. Vanier says the process of finding God at L'Arche is a process of "becoming little." This also means, for Nouwen, becoming more self-critical. In Nouwen's words, "Maybe this is what is so important about quiet moments of meditation and prayer. They allow me to take a critical look at my moods and to move away from victimization to free choice."[26] Rather than feeling angry and blaming others, however, Nouwen realizes that he has choices to make.

Again, what we see unfold in such moments is the difference between living a spiritual life as a free choice, even when it evokes fierce resistance from us, versus an imposition made on someone that seeks to harm them

---

25. Nouwen, *The Road to Daybreak*, 134.
26. Nouwen, *The Road to Daybreak*, 138.

or turn them into a victim. This is often how people experience faith: as something forced upon them. But at some point, one needs to grow up and make the choice to see themselves and their actions more clearly. This can be hard for a young person especially, to ask yourself what choices you want to make and what having a spiritual life means to you, and not just as a reaction to something you were brought up with.

The age-old debate within Christian theology concerning free will and predestination often hinges upon this problematic understanding of victimization, for those who see God as controlling every aspect of this world often, in turn, feel victimized by God—a proposition that makes a good deal of sense too. What Nouwen is alerting us to, on the contrary, is the power of realizing that you have a choice in this life, even if that includes turning away from that which is good, or turning away from God, for example. We are no less held hostage by God than we are by our moods. The spiritual principle to be found here is that we must reach out to the fullest extent possible and take control of that which we *can* influence in order to put ourselves in a position where we are free to decide how our lives, and the lives of others too, will unfold. This is what we, ultimately, seek to do in relation to God, *with* God, not as a victim of God's choices and not as that which wholly works against God, though this may be a very difficult notion to digest if someone has experienced a trauma that they feel God bestowed upon them.

In point of fact, when people experience a trauma they feel God has imposed upon them, the question of theodicy—the problem of having faith in the face of suffering and evil within our world—arises as one of the biggest problem people encounter in constructing something like the life of faith. Nouwen, addressing this problem head on, points rather *toward* God working with us, not as someone who imposes himself upon us. God suffers *with* us, which is a very different way to frame the problematic. Such a realization of how God actually works in one's life may also bring with it a liberating sense of hope that there is a power that moves in our lives that works with us, in the places we find ourselves too.

Perhaps an analogy can be found in the Gospels where Jesus encounters people in the situations they are in in their lives, without saying a word about his possibly being God. In John's gospel, for example, Jesus meets a Samaritan woman drawing water at the well (John 4). He talks to her about her life and leaves it at that, not imposing a particular version of faith upon her Samaritan beliefs, but rather exposing the poverty of her situation in life and calling her to reexamine the very foundations of her identity. This, and nothing else, is what moves her to speak to others about the truth that she has found.

No longer choosing to feel "victimized" by others, for Nouwen, was actually what allowed him to make choices that freed him from that which had previously bound him. He is no longer afraid to be the "only person" who suffers from certain afflictions. He is able to open up and connect with others who have felt, or feel, similar to him. There is a liberation so profound in this movement that it can be recognized as one of the core features of what makes Christianity what it is: a balm to those who suffer even as it embraces and talks about the suffering that we all encounter in one form or another. "While our sufferings are so similar and our struggles so much a part of our shared humanity, we often live as if we are the only ones who experience the pain that paralyzes us."[27] But this isolated experience, we must eventually admit, is a lie that we tell ourselves, and this is precisely where God, you might say, takes the opportunity to "alienate our alienation," as Moltmann had put it, and to point us in a new direction entirely, one wherein we feel not so much alienated, as opened up to others who have gone through similar experiences.

Taking the time to battle such grounds for the fear of alienation is an explicit aim for Nouwen, and what motivates him not only to embrace those persons whom society often fears and isolates (such as the poor and disabled), but also to reflect upon how such core dynamics are at the heart of society's refusal to accept its own collective sins, opting instead to marginalize or scapegoat those whom it fears. Going through suffering can open one's eyes to the violences other people do to one another. This can make a person more compassionate to others. As he will explain the human heart as it works within such contexts: it is "compassionate—but ready to kill when afraid. Whether we become merciful people or killers depends very much on who tells us what life is about."[28]

The narratives that terrorists or other perpetrators of violence use to justify themselves often make little sense to us, but they make sense to those who perpetuate them because they have felt victimized and have been told that someone is to blame. In order to seek peace, as Nouwen will emphasize in multiple ways, we have to get in touch with our own vulnerability. For someone vested in demonstrating the radical mercy of the Christian narrative, Nouwen is quick to turn to the formative question that makes all the difference in terms of responding positively to the problems we repeatedly face: "Do I want to be seen by Jesus? Do I want to be known by him?"[29] This is the first step, so to speak, in becoming open to others, and of letting

---

27. Nouwen, *The Road to Daybreak*, 214.
28. Nouwen, *The Road to Daybreak*, 17.
29. Nouwen, *The Road to Daybreak*, 18.

things enter inside of us (the powerful act of translation that moves across our borders and boundaries), especially those things that we had previously resisted. It is as if we are asking ourselves repeatedly: Do you want to be seen, or do you want to hide? Finding faith, in this sense, is not an abstract thing. It is not just, "Do you want to know Jesus?" It is also "Do you want to be seen?," not only by God, but by other people?

This is what is so interesting about the Catholic practice of confession or reconciliation in many ways, which fundamentally means opening up to another human being. This is what Nouwen means too, I think, when he concludes that "If I do, then a faith can grow which proclaims Jesus as the Son of God. Only such a faith can open my eyes and reveal an open heaven."[30] Specifically, you cannot hide from people and still expect to be close. This happens at times in dating, when one person has a serious problem opening up and sharing who they are, for example, and so the relationship suffers, or perhaps does not continue forward into a deeper intimacy.

In other words, words more sensitive to those struggling with the essentials of the Christian message: "Thus, I will see when I am willing to be seen. I will receive new eyes that can see the mysteries of God's own life when I allow God to see me, all of me, even those parts that I myself do not want to see."[31] For those who want to see what God is doing now, Nouwen would say to take a look at yourself and see what you may be hiding. In relationships, some people do nothing but talk about themselves, and so they don't see the other person, and, in reality, they aren't truly open about themselves. If a person wants to see God in their life, I would also argue, they must allow themselves *to be seen*; if one wants friends in their life, be a friend to someone else, *be seen* by someone else.

In this suggestion, we find a reasonable response both to those who struggle to believe some of the Christian story (as one cannot know about that which they have not first seen or experienced themselves) and a guidepost toward encountering God (through a radical openness to the mysteries already present within one's life). Intermixed with both senses is the reality of how both acts are yet still centered on the act of confession, even the confession of one's brokenness or sin; we are able to be forgiven, to "receive new eyes," when we allow ourselves to be seen by God, another way of describing confession itself.

Nouwen has a wonderful passage in *The Road to Daybreak* where he talks about the resurrection, which I mentioned earlier. In it, he says not to worry if you struggle with the idea of the resurrection because the only

---

30. Nouwen, *The Road to Daybreak*, 18.
31. Nouwen, *The Road to Daybreak*, 18.

people who see Jesus after the resurrection are his intimate friends, and no one else. He does not show up to anyone who did not want to be seen themselves.[32] In this sense, it is a matter of interpersonal relationships and not mystical higher knowledge that allows someone to comprehend the resurrection of Jesus.

Nouwen, because he wants to be part of such an intimate communion, takes the time to look at himself and his desires during this time in his life, but also to realize and respond to those other persons that he needs to take a look at as well. His life had been so busy and so aimed at finding the solution to his *own* problems, that he had taken less time to simply sit, often inconveniently, with those deemed "less fortunate" by the world's standards. As he would soon discover, such a refocusing of his perspective makes all the difference in terms of developing one's faith.

His writing in this particular journal therefore begins to focus on the actual persons with whom he lives and works, and whose stories are very real and personal in his life, much as Day's life was frequently taken up with the various persons she was present to in her Catholic Worker homes.

> The simplicity, directness, and intimacy of their prayer often make me feel like a skeptical bystander. I even feel a certain jealousy of their special gift of prayer. But they do not want me to be jealous. They hugged and kissed me after the prayer, and Michael took me by the hand to the sacristy to show me the red stole he wants to wear.[33]

As he will learn when he picks the apples at the orchard too quickly, "efficiency is not L'Arche's most important word. Care is."[34] This is a terribly difficult thing to do for someone raised to be so terribly efficient, and so immersed in a global economy where accomplishing things in a particular manner often seems to be the only key to success. What Nouwen had to learn, however, is that taking the time to care, rather than to be efficient, makes all the difference in the world, both personally and in terms of one's relationships with others.

At L'Arche, "there is no urge to success; here time is filled with dressing, feeding, carrying, and just being with those in need. It is a very demanding and tiring way, but there is no rivalry, no degree to be acquired, no honor to be desired—just faithful service."[35] His faith develops, you might say, because he recognizes how his service to others is located in

---

32. Nouwen, *The Road to Daybreak*, 163–64.
33. Nouwen, *The Road to Daybreak*, 37.
34. Nouwen, *The Road to Daybreak*, 38.
35. Nouwen, *The Road to Daybreak*, 57.

taking the time to form relationships with others, not just doing things *for* them. Such a notion completely redefines what we typically think of as service, but also the person who "serves." Nouwen, for one, learns that he is no longer out to simply serve, but to "be with" others and this, in its truest sense, is what it actually means to serve. Rather than doing service *for* someone, as is often the version of service experienced by those who have required service hours in an educational program, for example, this vision of service involves being in relationship and friendship with actual people and their stories (the very heart of bio-graphy).

Again, emphasizing the differences between the world's economies—ones of competition and honor, much as Tolstoy had already seen—and those of the community in which Nouwen was now living, we begin to see the differences made much more concrete than many of us might have suspected a religious community was capable of providing. The truth is that living out one's vocation is inseparable from relationships and service. To suggest this divide, however, is no abstraction; it is a dealing with very real people, with very real bodies and in very dramatically differing ways than the world. It is not an ideological or idealist utopia. It is a messy reality that risks descending into poverty in order find oneself in another sense. "The handicapped people and the assistants need each other, though sometimes in different ways. Together they seek to form a true fellowship of the weak, always thanking and praising God for the fragile gift of life."[36] What such intentional practices run counter to—and this is a point well worth taking up from a number of angles—is that the typical motivational factors in our world, the ones that often bring "success" with them, are actually contrary to the Christian story. For example, as Nouwen lists them, "Human glory, based on competition, leads to rivalry; rivalry carries within it the beginning of violence; and violence is the way to death. Thus human glory proves to be vain glory, false glory, mortal glory."[37] L'Arche, though incredibly small in scale, promotes a series of values (and virtues) that run counter to this cyclical narrative of glory, competition, rivalry, and violence. The stress that Nouwen places is rather on humility, caring, inclusion of the other, and peace or love as the end fruits.

Such reflections on the nature of global rivalry and violence are what prompt him to reflect with great passion upon the Challenger space shuttle explosion in January of 1986, an event that caused a great trauma for many children watching it live on television (such as myself!), since an ordinary school teacher, Christa McAuliffe, was aboard this particular shuttle. This

36. Nouwen, *The Road to Daybreak*, 62.
37. Nouwen, *The Road to Daybreak*, 97.

tragedy became for Nouwen another way to consider what the space program is about at its roots and to critically examine its place in our world. "When I think about the fact that the United States space program is closely tied to the defense program and that this tragedy is at least in part the result of an international race for superiority and world domination, I cannot but wonder if the grief will lead to peace or a more determined preparation for war."[38] But, as I can testify, the fateful explosion did not necessarily lead for many, or even most, to a more determinate look at peace and preparations for war. It rather led to a focus on the spectacle itself (something which twenty-four-hour news coverage is now more than familiar with), sick jokes instead of a focus upon the pain ("What does NASA stand for? Need Another Seven Astronauts"), and a desire, perhaps more determined than before, to stand strong against the (often illusory) communist threat that seemed to assail American citizens from every direction.

What is revealed underneath these reflections that Nouwen was bold enough to pronounce is a profound meditation on the nature of violence, something that his life among the physically poor began to teach him with a renewed emphasis. Being in a situation where you are among those who cannot compete with the rest of the world, but who are pushed to the margins of our global economy and its goals, he realized, with great force, but also with great sadness, how indebted to models of competition and violence most of us truly are.

What was noticeably missing from the lives of those mourning this national tragedy, he felt, was a sense of where "real human grief" should be directed. This, I would add, is the focus that would actually, in the end, allow us to perceive our external "enemies" altogether differently—something as true after the American experience of 9/11 in 2001 as of the Challenger disaster in the 1980s. The national conversation around 9/11 was about who did it and how we could get back at them for what they had apparently done to us, rather than about what we had done to foster this antagonism or why it might have happened in the first place. When such things happen, the priority of "becoming little" becomes significantly and wrongly minimized.

Political rhetoric emphasized strength, which was the narrative most people wanted. Nouwen emphasizes a very different message. This singular insight was what Nouwen wished to lift up perhaps above all else in this context: "Real human grief means allowing the illusion of immortality to die in us.... If we do not allow this to happen, we will lose touch with reality, our lives will become increasingly artificial, and we will lose our human capacity

---

38. Nouwen, *The Road to Daybreak*, 129.

for compassion."³⁹ Practicing compassion becomes possible only at the cost of sacrificing the idea that we will live forever—the ultimate sign of trying to control one's life—a desire rendered that much more complex when we realize we typically couple it with fear and insecurity, as well as a willingness to do harm to others if they appear to threaten such a longing.

Nouwen's focus was quite the opposite of these motives. As he put it, "The national grief for the death of the seven astronauts will be fruitful if it helps us to die to our vainglory and our national desire to be the best and the most powerful at all costs, and stimulates us to search for a way of peace not dependent on military superiority."⁴⁰ This overtly political statement, one that seeks for a certain degree of national de-militarization, is one that is yet generated by his awareness that politics is in reality driven by fearful impulses and the desire for glory at its core—something wholly structural to most military codes of conduct. And so, in a heartfelt plea, he advises a society dealing with such tragedy:

> The real challenge now will be to help these children understand and accept without fear the brokenness and mortality of their parents, their teachers, their heroes, and themselves. If this tragedy gradually helps them to love themselves and the adults who guide them as precious, extremely vulnerable, mortal human beings, they may become peacemakers for whom solidarity and compassion are greater gifts than technical genius and the ability to dominate others.⁴¹

But, sadly, and frequently, getting in touch with such vulnerabilities is not what nation-states do in response to situations like these; in reality, the opposite is more often the case: strong ideological and patriotic sentiments take precedence over the necessary acts of grieving and mourning. It is in this same vein that we might often avoid teaching children about the horrible parts of our own past: the targeted extermination of Native Americans, the legacy of slavery in America, and so forth. The present story of trying to achieve superiority and dominance over others simply overpowers one's history. But telling these historical narratives is precisely what we need to do if we want to build peace.

The path that Nouwen foresees for the Christian is the opposite of fearful retaliation; it is a path toward humility that may at times involve forms of social and public humiliation. But, if Christ's death on the cross demonstrates anything, it is that this is the only path open to those who would pick

---

39. Nouwen, *The Road to Daybreak*, 130.
40. Nouwen, *The Road to Daybreak*, 130.
41. Nouwen, *The Road to Daybreak*, 130.

up their cross and follow him. Nouwen's commentary on this scene from the Gospel stories is consequently succinct and direct: "In his Gospel, John shows that God chose to reveal his glory to us in his humiliation. That is the good, but also disturbing, news. God, in his infinite wisdom, chose to reveal his divinity to us not through competition, but through compassion, that is, through suffering with us."[42] We must refocus our desires accordingly, and as a result find ourselves at odds with the world at many points, yet unafraid of what we might encounter, for

> Every time Jesus speaks about being glorified and giving glory, he always refers to his humiliation and death. It is through the way of the cross that Jesus gives glory to God, receives glory from God, and makes God's glory known to us. The glory of the resurrection can never be separated from the glory of the cross. The risen Lord always shows us his wounds.[43]

This is where the focus on poverty arises with renewed force in his life, and in the life of faith in general. To be a Christian, for Nouwen, means to make the movement toward a form of humility that will end with the "death" of a human being to the world in some sense—the ultimate expression of the principle of poverty, you might say. Those who are unrecognized by society—the marginalized, impoverished persons of the world, no matter their name or religion—are the very persons Christians are called to stand by, witness to, care for, love and act charitably toward in all manner of ways. "If we truly want to see the glory of God, we must move downward with Jesus. This is the deepest reason for living in solidarity with poor, oppressed, and handicapped people. They are the ones through whom God's glory can manifest itself to us. They show us the way to God, the way to salvation."[44] We are not only called to look out for such persons, but actually to learn from them about the way toward achieving our own salvation, which may be little more than seeing with "new eyes" the realities of this world that are already there before us. Such persons move and motivate us to take life seriously from another angle altogether, and, from Nouwen's perspective, we must imitate Jesus and heed this call.

Now, at this culminating point, we can begin to comprehend Nouwen's desire to "become poor" like those he lives with, for such a "calling" is motivated by the core of the story of Jesus. As Nouwen will cry out, "Come, Lord Jesus, and be with me where I feel poorest."[45] As if directly spoken to himself

---

42. Nouwen, *The Road to Daybreak*, 98.

43. Nouwen, *The Road to Daybreak*, 98.

44. Nouwen, *The Road to Daybreak*, 98.

45. Nouwen, *The Road to Daybreak*, 102, de-emphasized from the original.

at the same moment, he prays to be shown his poverty and to embrace it as the only way forward. He wants to "learn" of his "weakness, powerlessness, unworthiness,"[46] but also of "humility," "hiddenness," and "littleness."[47] His faith, like Teresa's, is one that is continuously on the lookout for self-deceptions and false humilities, for a trust placed in himself that should not be there, and for a lack of transparency and honesty that only allows sin to multiply and spread within him.[48] It is, for this reason, a critical, self-aware faith (truly a personal, ongoing *confession*) that guides him forward to (re)consider his faith anew time and again.

What is his goal in formulating and maintaining his faith through such a process? In his words, "To give, not from my wealth but from my want, as the widow of Jerusalem who donated her last coin, that is the great challenge of the Gospel."[49] To give from our place of poverty, and not after we have stored up a vast amount of wealth. This is where true faith, as true transformation or conversion, happens. This is also why poverty is such an important factor in faith development, as the book of James in the New Testament makes abundantly plain as well.

This poverty, we must understand, can also be a poverty of the heart and of one's own moral life, which is not to be intentionally sought out, of course, but which still provides a platform for allowing God's love to take hold in a unique way, as Karr's narrative, among others, made clear to us: "God does not require a pure heart before embracing us."[50] No matter what drives us to God, God still takes us in, and it is this charitable act that moves us so deeply from within, in whatever place we find ourselves struggling. It is acceptance and love that transforms us, but also what we often push away from that we desire above all else, because we have been lured away by that which seems to offer much more (but which is really much less).

> It is so easy to be swept off one's own feet by the glitter of the world, seduced by its apparent splendor. And yet the only place I can really be is the place of poverty, the place where there is loneliness, anger, confusion, depression and pain. I have to go there in the name of Jesus, staying close to his name and offering his love.[51]

---

46. Nouwen, *The Road to Daybreak*, 117.
47. Nouwen, *The Road to Daybreak*, 118.
48. Nouwen, *The Road to Daybreak*, 178.
49. Nouwen, *The Road to Daybreak*, 71.
50. Nouwen, *The Road to Daybreak*, 72.
51. Nouwen, *The Road to Daybreak*, 186.

Even if others do not recognize the name of Jesus, he seems to be suggesting, it is to this name that he must go because of his commitments, and this is as things should be. People of faith do not need to be "honored" as Christians for doing spectacular "Christian" deeds. Indeed, no one should care as to who does what, so long as this story of love united in suffering through the poverty of our humility reaches up to transform the lives of those around us. It is a calling that extracts everything you once thought meaningful from you, and yet which we cannot ignore if we are seeking something much "nobler" than ourselves and our so often misguided desires.

This reversal of values, as Vanier would put it, is what L'Arche strives to accomplish, on the most particular and specific of scales, and which is the only way that Jesus communicated. We must get involved and "get messy" at this level, and never stop being involved as such. "Jesus did not say, 'Happy are those who serve the poor,' but 'Happy are the poor.'"[52] And, as Nouwen adds, "Being poor is what Jesus invites us to, and that is much, much harder than serving the poor. The unnoticed, unspectacular, unpraised life in solidarity with people who cannot give anything that makes us feel important is far from attractive. It is the way to poverty. Not an easy way, but God's way, the way of the cross."[53] Again, quoting Jean Vanier, Nouwen proclaims the directive he seeks in this new life to follow: "Jesus always leads us to littleness. It is the place where misery and mercy meet. It is the place where we encounter God."[54]

Much as we have already seen in the life of Karr, in particular, becoming small before God—a gesture often physically enacted in the process of getting down on one's knees—is a necessary step toward embracing the poverty that we are called to take up for ourselves, much as Jesus did. To live life in this manner is not an abstracted vision of living a life of faith, it is the key to living an *embodied* life of faith—the only kind of faith that truly exists. As Vanier tells him at one point throughout his stay at the France L'Arche community, "Often I go off in dreams about living and being with the poor, but what the poor need are not my dreams, my beautiful thoughts, my inner reflections, but my concrete presence. There is always the temptation to replace real presence with lovely thoughts about being present."[55] Or, as Augustine had put it, this is to be in love with the idea of love, and not the actual person standing before you. These temptations toward abstraction in order to "connect" with what appears to transcend our world are, however, *not* how we encounter the

---

52. Nouwen, *The Road to Daybreak*, 84.
53. Nouwen, *The Road to Daybreak*, 84.
54. Nouwen, *The Road to Daybreak*, 88.
55. Nouwen, *The Road to Daybreak*, 83.

divine. The only way to encounter God is, as Jesus did, through our humanity, in its particularity and embodied being.

In this, there is an inseparableness to the way in which prayer (as thought and theory) merges with action (as concrete practices in one's life). It is the Christian's prayer asking for courage and faith to follow in taking up their cross that brings about those faithful actions that run counter to the workings of the world. From the other perspective, Nouwen states, "I now see clearly why action without prayer is so fruitless. It is only in and through prayer that we can become intimately connected with Jesus and find the strength to join him on his way."[56] Such an insight also coincides with James's comprehension of how faith and works must be joined inseparably together (James 2:14-26).

What we witness in the world of L'Arche that Nouwen brings alive for us is a spiritual growth that is at odds with much of the world's ways. But, lest we be mistaken on this matter, it is also a challenge to the church itself, or *any* religious institution, which has for far too long been immersed in ways of "living together" that have been a distraction from what God actually calls us to (i.e., more focused on its self-definition than on the transformative acts of translation that bring faith to life). As another one of L'Arche's founders puts it, in Nouwen's relating of things,

> Père Thomas is convinced that much of the crisis in the life of the Church today is connected with a lack of knowledge of the heart. Much Church discussion today focuses on the morality of human behavior: premarital sex, divorce, homosexuality, birth control, abortion, and so on. Many people have become disillusioned with the Church because of these issues. But when the moral life gets all the attention, we are in danger of forgetting the primacy of the mystical life, which is the life of the heart.[57]

Living a devout religious life is not just about making the right moral decisions—just as it is not about perpetually discussing immense "theological" issues and abstractions. It is about cultivating an interior life of meaning, one that even a child can sense at times working within themselves.[58]

---

56. Nouwen, *The Road to Daybreak*, 89.

57. Nouwen, *The Road to Daybreak*, 48.

58. See the remarkable story told by Leo Tolstoy of three monks of faith and their interactions with a bishop who misperceives their faith at first, seeing as how they don't know the creeds or even the "Our Father" by heart, until they miraculously walk on water and point the way toward another sense of faith, as an illustration of this simplicity of living the life of faith as retold in Nouwen, *The Road to Daybreak*, 49–50.

What Nouwen is seeking access to is a form of poverty that becomes even, I would suggest, a poverty of the religious, opening us up perhaps to other religious traditions or the secular world around us in ways that would probably astound us if we genuinely were open to such acts of translation. The handicapped persons he saw at the L'Arche in India were bringing together peoples of various religious traditions through the primacy of their poverty. "They are truly a uniting force."[59] Or, as he would put it eventually,

> Do we really need to belong to one country or one culture? In our world, where distances are becoming less each day, it seems important to become less and less dependent on one place, one language, one culture, or one style of life, but to experience oneself as a member of the human family, belonging to God and free to be wherever we are called to be. I even wonder if the ability to be in so many places so quickly and so often is not an invitation to grow deeper in the spirit and let our identity be more rooted in God and less in the place in which we happen to be.[60]

There are real, and serious, implications for an authentic religious pluralism within this sentiment, which is, I think, the real poverty of faith or "poverty of theology" that we have not yet begun to access, but which certainly seems to stem from a Christian perspective on matters of the divine. What would it mean to so care for others and to practice love to the extreme, in the face of suffering, that we care not as much for how we identify ourselves, or how we shape our theologies, as we do about practicing the life of prayer that Jesus indicated? The task that Nouwen puts before us, and which is very much generated by the Christian story, is to cultivate an interior life of meaning, which is possible within a number of religious traditions, but which must also take poverty and suffering seriously—truths that the Christian message points to as universal parts of being human, finding redemption, and showing love to others.

We see such an inner life of meaning unfold in a personal story Nouwen takes us through, one involving the death of a young man in San Francisco. In many ways, and this will help to point to the heart of the issue, this story is not just one of a dying young man, but also of Rose, the mother, whose son, John, died of AIDS after a protracted struggle. Concerning his impending death, Rose held, in Nouwen's words, "No condemnation, no accusation, no rejection, but love as only a mother can give."[61] And from such love, even in the face of death, good things would start to come forth,

---

59. Nouwen, *The Road to Daybreak*, 173.
60. Nouwen, *The Road to Daybreak*, 209.
61. Nouwen, *The Road to Daybreak*, 53.

especially for those who were around her son and were caring for him. Nouwen himself administered the "last rites" for the dying son: "I asked him to accept death when it came, and not to hasten it."[62] As Rose described the involvement of those who volunteered to cleanse her dead son's body, "These people are so loving, so caring, so good . . . they may not all believe in God, but they surely help me to do so."[63] And suddenly, the importance of faith is revealed in a new way, even one that shines from the apparently "godless" back to those who hold religious "belief." As Nouwen himself would reflect upon the death of this young man: "I thank God for having known John and having come to know in a new way the inexhaustible mystery of human suffering and human love."[64]

Suffering and love—two inextricable elements of the human life captured perfectly in the stories of so many searching for redemption, including Jesus' own life. For Nouwen, suffering and love come together in such a marvelous way as to point toward the life of faith, as it is relevant to all persons, whether believers or not, even those who have "lost faith" in God while yet searching for a profound connection between love and suffering. "Your eyes, O Lord, see in one glance the inexhaustible love of God and the seemingly endless agony of all people who have lost faith in that love and are like sheep without a shepherd."[65]

Through all of this, Nouwen does not lose sight of what is important: the person who stands before him, whether John, or his mother Rose, or the disabled persons of L'Arche. As he describes the entire focus he wants to cultivate further in his life: "I discovered once again that what is most personal is most universal."[66] And, related to this: "Friendship is more important than the work we do together."[67] Faith, but also theology, is grasped here as a form of relationality, and thereby as that which points directly toward the position of the autobiographical within any formulation of the theological. This is what lingers on his mind as Nouwen approaches the Easter vigil during that year in particular, and which we should take note of as it permeates and develops his theological insights and personal sense of vocation:

> I felt very close to the Easter event. It was not a spectacular event forcing people to believe. Rather, it was an event for the friends of Jesus, for those who had known him, listened to him,

62. Nouwen, *The Road to Daybreak*, 53.
63. Nouwen, *The Road to Daybreak*, 54.
64. Nouwen, *The Road to Daybreak*, 54.
65. Nouwen, *The Road to Daybreak*, 56.
66. Nouwen, *The Road to Daybreak*, 69.
67. Nouwen, *The Road to Daybreak*, 93.

and believed in him. It was a very intimate event: a word here, a gesture there, and a gradual awareness that something new was being born—small, hardly noticed, but with the potential to change the face of the earth.[68]

This is what Nouwen seeks at L'Arche, in his vocational calling in life, and in the development of his faith as a theology of relationships. One must be wholly immersed in this life of intentional poverty, for only such a willingness as this can bring about the profound relationships of faith that matter most.

---

68. Nouwen, *The Road to Daybreak*, 164.

Chapter Eleven

Diana Eck

The O/other Already Before Us

Diana Eck was born on July 5, 1945 in Bozeman, Montana. She was raised within the Methodist denomination, though a college trip to India would open up a whole new world of possibilities in her mind. Her initial interactions with non-Christians would develop into a career of studying world religions and participating in interreligious dialogue, most tangibly present in her work with the Pluralism Project and her publications, both academic and popular. Among these renowned works are India: A Sacred Geography *(2012),* A New Religious America: How a "Christian Country" Has Become the World's Most Religiously Diverse Nation *(2001), and the focus of this chapter,* Encountering God: A Spiritual Journey from Bozeman to Banaras *(1993). She received her BA in religious studies from Smith College, her MA in South Asian history from the University of London, her doctorate in the comparative study of religion and Indian studies from Harvard University, and holds a postgraduate diploma from Banaras Hindu University. In addition to her aforementioned publications, Eck has also been involved in the interfaith dialogue program of the World Council of Churches for almost forty years and currently chairs their Interfaith Relations Commission. She is also a full professor of Comparative Religion and Indian Studies at Harvard Divinity School and holds the Frederic Wertham Chair of Law and Psychiatry in Society at Harvard University.*

Diana Eck has given us a remarkable book on the nature of interreligious dialogue, mainly because it is written as part autobiography and part comparative religious analysis. For this reason, the book can only strike its readers as an honest appraisal of our global religious atmosphere alongside its profound understanding of religion as a form of relationship, friendship even, that alters the manner by which we perceive religious belonging entirely. By taking up her story immediately in the context of Nouwen's emphasis upon the poverty of faith and how such a viewpoint opens the person of faith up to other religious traditions, I am hoping to more fully flush out some of the more significant and provocative implications for theological thought in an autobiographical context, ones that might contain enough force to alter theological methodologies entirely.

Growing up in a Methodist Church in the state of Montana, Eck was an active leader in her church, as well as the Methodist Youth Fellowship she was raised in, eventually coming to study religion as her passion in life, though never really deviating from her Christian roots, which had made her faith meaningful and relevant to her. Christianity, in this sense, was her "language," what she was raised to speak, and she continued to speak it. Concerning her childhood faith, and the church community that had raised her, she confesses: "It was a faith nourished, as all faith finally is, by people—energetic, loving, committed, visionary people."[1] But it was also, as geography and the American religious scene at the time dictated, a somewhat isolated experience, offering few chances to encounter religious diversity.

Many years later, in the 1960s, she went to the holy city of Banaras, India on a study trip while she was a college student at the University of Wisconsin. Very literally, this was her first encounter with people of a religious tradition that was not her own, and the numerous experiences she had while in India were enough to push her in the direction of becoming a scholar who tries to deal with the complexity and difficulties of interreligious dialogue. But, as she will also describe things, she was challenged in India, not necessarily by "ideas" alone, but, more significantly, by specific people, by the Hindus who took their faith very seriously and served as role models of faith for her.

On one occasion, for example, she met a wonderful man who had fought nonviolently for India's independence and who was a man of "simple, self-giving love." She was deeply moved by his life of faith, and challenged, like Rachel Held Evans was, at the same time to confront many of her assumptions about her almost exclusively Christian worldview.

> He was a man whose life was a witness to love and justice. He was very much like the people I had most loved and admired as a teenager. But he was not a Christian. He did not find an example and a companion in Christ, as I did. To my surprise, it

---

1. Eck, *Encountering God*, 7.

did not seem to me that he somehow ought to be a Christian. What did this mean about some of the biblical claims of my own tradition?[2]

Eck thereby began the self-critical journey of encounter and dialogue, as well as an examination of her own most fundamental religious beliefs, through her friendship with this man who continued to motivate her inquiries into faith. Such an encounter and a taking seriously of the faith of others was, and remains, central to how she perceives the pulse of faith in a person's life.

Theological reflection begins, in a sense, with our encounter with "otherness" and the translations such an encounter entails, no matter whether that other is God, the religiously "other," the stranger, or even a certain otherness within ourselves. Encountering an O/otherness that challenges you is essentially how encountering God works, in scriptural narratives as in real life. In some ways, all kinds of otherness scare us, especially in terms of racial, gendered, sexual, ethnic, or even political and religious differences. But it is necessary that we encounter such differences in order to be challenged and to grow. At times, it is even hard to tell the difference: between encountering God, others, or the otherness within ourselves. Often people are scared of others because of something that scares them within themselves. From this angle, encountering the religious other, among the many others it is possible to meet, can in some ways too be an encounter with God, if we let the experience speak directly to us.

By entering into relationship with such otherness, we are prodded to the challenges of growth in our experience and expression of faith, and such is what Eck began to see more clearly in a way that would help her to reformulate her entire definition of religion.

> Our experience with people of other faiths may be difficult or rewarding, or both. In any case, our "interfaith dialogue" does not usually begin with philosophy or theory, but with experience and relationships. Individually and collectively, our experience has now begun to challenge traditional religious thinking and to contribute decisively to the reformulation of our theologies.[3]

To suggest as much is somewhat similar to speaking about faith as the language of lovers, rather than as a strict moral code or set of propositions. In this switch of linguistic register, the messy complexity of relationships becomes a way to understand the most fundamental characteristics of religion.

---

2. Eck, *Encountering God*, 8.
3. Eck, *Encountering God*, 2.

The challenges to her faith that would persist throughout multiple visits to India, as well as in her present understanding of religious belief, as with all encounters with otherness, do not cease over time—if anything they continue to inspire and guide our most elementary religious desires. In this sense, it would be accurate to say that we never "figure it all out" in terms of how to handle our relationships—something will always remain "other" about those we love. Rather, we continually grow and learn about such otherness. Indeed, and perhaps most importantly, our engagement with otherness is what allows us to alter our perceptions of religion altogether.

> For many people religion is a rigid concept, somewhat like a stone that is passed from generation to generation. We don't add to it, change it, or challenge it; we just pass it along. But even the most cursory study of the history of religions would undermine such a view. Religious traditions are far more like rivers than stones.[4]

There is an otherness *even within* each religious tradition that opens that particular tradition up to other traditions, and which is ignored by those within a given tradition at the cost of excluding some while including others. For instance, though many people would rather not notice, some texts and stories in the Christian and Hebrew Bibles are directly derived from ancient Egyptian and other Ancient Near Eastern traditions. In this way, religion is like a language, always incorporating words from other languages in order to construct its present system of meaning. A religious tradition that sees itself as static and unchanging over time, uninfluenced at its roots by other religious faiths, is, on the contrary, a dead faith, not one that thrives and evolves over time with the people who comprise it. As Eck will formulate this situation, "All of us contribute to the river of our traditions. We do not know how we will change the river or be changed as we experience its currents."[5] Using the language I have already stressed of finding ourselves between structure and experience in terms of identifying our place within the complexity of faith, we at times focus, wrongly, on the dichotomies of exclusion/inclusion, sameness/difference, or authority/freedom *only*, as if these were the only options before us, and as if we need only to identify with one side of the spectrum in order to find ourselves. What Eck discovered, much like Day, is that it is only by returning to each side in the equation, over and again, in the contexts in which we experience them, and insofar as we seek justice on both sides, that we are able to gather a sense of self.

4. Eck, *Encountering God*, 2.
5. Eck, *Encountering God*, 2.

On one of her visits to India, for example, she met J. Krishnamurti, a person devoted to avoiding the labels and boundaries that typically define our world and the people located in it. In her words, "he observed the way in which we fearfully, anxiously, shape our whole lives by religious, political, cultural, and personal labels and names—all of which function as a buffer zone of security between ourselves and the experience of life."[6] Though it often makes us upset if we can't figure out how to label something, Eck began to see this absence of labels as a profound encounter with a permanent sense of transformative otherness through the translations of faith that were constantly encircling her. Transcending these borders and boundaries in order to more genuinely engage with those around us—to form more and more authentic relationships at the heart of our religious longing through the act of translation—Krishnamurti tried to expose the flaws in our religious logic that is really a political logic, one of drawing up identity markers for ourselves when the divinity we worship truly acknowledges no boundaries such as these. The challenge of "otherness" that she received from him was one that she would continue to respond to with her life and, later, through her own teaching.

For Eck, such moments of discovery in relation to religious faith, and which are also always already self-discovery too, were monumental signposts along the way to reformulating her worldview, including the core assumptions of her Western religious sensibilities.

> What I discovered and confronted in the course of my work was my own distinctively Western habit of thought, grounded primarily in the Western tradition of monotheism: the expectation of singularity and uniqueness, and the valuing of such singularity and uniqueness. It is a way of thinking equally pervasive in the three great monotheistic traditions of the West—Judaism, Christianity, and Islam. In monotheistic consciousness, the singular is the proper number for questions of Truth: There is One God, one Only-Begotten Son of the Father, one Seal of the Prophets, one Holy Book, one Holy Catholic and Apostolic Church. It might be called "the myth of monotheism": that there is one and only one holy story to be told, to be reflected upon by theologians, and to be participated in by the faithful.[7]

There is a long history of "myth" (in its often "polytheistic" forms, and hence frequently labeled as "idolatry") being contrasted with a "purer" religious faith of monotheism, though there is also a more recent, modern critique of

6. Eck, *Encountering God*, 8.
7. Eck, *Encountering God*, 59.

monotheism as "just another myth." What Eck is offering us instead of these polarizing views is a way to look at the "myth" within monotheism, a myth *of* monotheism, then, in that it often takes itself to be the sole, "true" religion—a point that Evans confronted in her own life, as we have seen.

In many ways, throughout history, this has been the foundational understanding of monotheism, and the way in which people have read its objection to "other" gods and "other" religious "truths," though this view and way of holding monotheistic traditions has been challenged in more recent times and is starting to wear thin with people who live in an actual multicultural, pluralistic world. In many ways, what Eck is pointing us toward is something like an understanding of the poverty of faith, a view that is capable of renouncing the superiority of one's faith over other faiths while at the same time maintaining one's ties with a particular religious tradition, not simply succumbing to a relativistic view of things.

To see monotheism as the only "true" faith is, of course, the opposite of the Indian, Hindu mentality, which is inherently pluralistic and open to other stories, other religious traditions. "Plurality is not given up in favor of oneness, nor oneness in favor of plurality. Both viewpoints are held—and are understood to be held—simultaneously."[8] In this context, there is no problem seeing both plurality and oneness. Such a realization of her own Western limitations was a remarkable engagement with an ongoing self-critical understanding that she would never master per se, but would rather continue to extend all the way down to the core of her sense of being a Christian.

She was so moved by Krishnamurti and his presence-filled teachings that she began to question her own learning process, and how many presuppositions underlay it as well: "Were we taking down notes? Why? Were we hoping to seize what he had to say? Were we comparing his ideas to those of Teilhard de Chardin or Zen Buddhism? Were we judging his thoughts with our likes and dislikes? Why couldn't we just listen? Is simple presence and attention so impossible?"[9] What continuously moved her within this journey of self-exploration was the way in which certain spiritual guides "embodied their faith" with their lives. Witnessing their commitment to the presences of otherness all around them, she was motivated to question many, if not all, of her preconceived representations of faith as well as of the divine.

The question that I believe we must continue to ask, which is also the question that Eck continued to ask herself, concerned what she was to make of her own religious—that is, American Christian—identity. What was she, as a Christian, to make of all of this religious diversity? How was she to

---

8. Eck, *Encountering God*, 63.
9. Eck, *Encountering God*, 9.

contemplate religious faith and belonging in the globalized age in which we live, where so many beliefs are juxtaposed in close proximity to one another? Should she simply drop the label of Christian, so worn out from centuries of abuse, and clearly not a label that would indicate the deep wealth of insight she was experiencing in dialogue with people in India? Should she sell everything and sit at the feet of a guru, soaking up all he has to offer, and refuse to engage with labels of any sort? It seems that for many today, apathy is the answer, which is really no answer at all.

What Eck would conclude—and I think her reaction underscores the essential nature of trying to locate oneself between the traditions that identify us, and that we identify with, and the experiences that reposition such traditions—was that her dialogue with otherness must prompt her to repeatedly go back and revisit the Christianity she was raised with in order to reexamine, and re-own, you might say, her faith. A genuine encounter with otherness, as she was to learn, often sends us back to our home traditions, with a new, critical eye. What Eck would reconsider, in this new light, was in particular how "Jesus engaged fully and openly with the people of this world and his time, regardless of tradition, culture, ethnicity, or social status. Our Christian faith requires no less of us."[10] And furthermore, she reminds us, "I would even say that it is Christ who enables Christians—in fact, challenges us—to recognize God especially where we don't expect to do so and where it is not easy to do so."[11] Her experiences of otherness did not drive her away from Christianity, but back toward it, in order to reconceive of it entirely anew, and as a challenge to many Christians who are locked in a static understanding of what their own faith tradition is, or could be.

Part of the uniqueness of Christianity that Eck began to see unfolding before her, and which she chose to highlight especially, is the believed reality of how the divine came down into *humble* circumstances, completely into human form, which Hinduism does not reciprocate among its own teachings. Such a realization not only put a certain distance between her childhood faith and what she experienced in certain religious traditions in India, but it also gave her the ability to critique the very experiences she was having, much as Evans had done while on her trip to India as well. The God found in the person of Jesus is not looking to justify the sufferings of this lifetime in order to place one higher up the caste in the next life: "God does not justify our suffering, God participates in it."[12] Christianity, indeed,

---

10. Eck, *Encountering God*, 12.
11. Eck, *Encountering God*, 79.
12. Eck, *Encountering God*, 111.

contains within itself a radical critique of suffering and injustice that cannot be pushed to one side and ignored.

This critical examination is what also allowed her to redefine Christianity in a certain sense as well, pushing it beyond where many Christians might be comfortable:

> Indeed, the God whom Jesus reveals is not a tribal god or a stingy one, but has surely sought and loved the sheep of every fold. And the humanity which Jesus reveals is not narrow, arrogant, or dogmatic, but boldly open to claiming the stranger as neighbor. Both sides of this double revelation—the Godward and the human—must push Christians beyond the narrow obsession with uniqueness as singularity.[13]

The "myth of monotheism" is again exposed and critiqued, and it is the force of this critique that opens up new vistas of creative faith for Eck.

The vision of Christianity that was now laid open to Eck is profoundly different than her childhood faith—it was not as naïve, not as willing to overlook the realities of suffering all around her, and it was a faith that she felt she could commit herself to despite her inability to know if this is the "one true" religion among all the other world religions. "Faith in Christ rests on two remarkable affirmations: Jesus Christ reveals to us the face of God, which is love. And Jesus Christ reveals to us the meaning of the human, which is love. This double revelation is enough. I do not need to know that it is the only true story on earth to affirm that it is worth giving my heart to."[14] In the midst of her rediscovery of her Christian faith, she continued to press questions of religious identity, including her own, and to redefine the very nature of theological inquiry, which is no small thing in the context of trying to merge one's own autobiographical narrative and the "absolute truth" of God. Of this, however, she is sure: "theological questions are not merely theoretical; they are the life and death questions of real people who do not think of themselves as theologians, but who struggle with real questions of faith in the world in which we live."[15] Seeing things as such meant, for her, trying to produce a theology for oneself that takes seriously the reconsideration of one's own faith, and not simply an abstracted theology that pretends it does not require concrete persons to sustain its theoretical edifice—a major defining feature of theological inquiry that we cannot afford to ignore under any circumstances.

---

13. Eck, *Encountering God*, 89.
14. Eck, *Encountering God*, 89.
15. Eck, *Encountering God*, 15.

Eck wishes to utilize those critical theologies (e.g., feminist, liberation theologies) that probe the depths of Christian truth claims and that push the boundaries of what we consider Christianity to be in the first place, to be more inclusive and focused on the emancipatory potential of the Christian message. Such messages are relevant, she will also find, for other global contexts beyond the Christian or American ones, though we must always be cautious not to imperialistically impose our beliefs onto other cultures and nations. This is the mistake so many Western Christian missionaries have made throughout the past and that we should certainly seek to avoid in the present. Eck therefore promotes forms of dialogue that aim toward "relationship, not domination," that are concerned with "mutuality, not of power."[16] This means that even the promulgation of the Christian message must be severed from its sovereign political claims in some sense and willing to engage in relating with the otherness around it, even its *own* otherness, in order to arrive at some semblance of truth.

There has been a long history within the monotheistic West of linking God's sovereignty, glory, and power to the king or political ruler's sovereignty, glory, and power. In fact, it has been very difficult to disentangle these concepts from one another and to say with any sort of clarity which exactly belongs exclusively to whom. It is clear perhaps only that Christianity, in particular, has had a hard time letting go of its claims to political power, and this is certainly true today as well as in recent history.[17]

One of the first realizations that Christianity, among other faiths, must make in order to humble itself and its claims to truth, is to admit the real nature of the religious language that we use. In Eck's estimation, our use of relational language to describe the divine is "Like most theological language . . . more poetry than metaphysics."[18] As with the other authors we have already looked at who have criticized the overemphasis in Christianity throughout the centuries on its doctrinal content rather than its perpetually subversive edge—theologian Moltmann's notion of a "permanent iconoclasm"—this realization she is pushing for is one that opens faith up to those around it, including them in what meaning one might find within their life, the passion and relationships that matter most: "Faith, as we have seen, is not about propositions, but about commitment. It does not mean that I intellectually subscribe to the following list of statements, but that I give my heart to this reality."[19] It is in such a manner that Eck finds herself

16. Eck, *Encountering God*, 19.
17. Kirwan, *Political Theology*.
18. Eck, *Encountering God*, 136.
19. Eck, *Encountering God*, 95.

continuously "challenged to deeper faith"[20] as well as willing to recognize that "Today there is perhaps too much certainty, too little pondering, among both the religious and the irreligious."[21] In this sentiment, we hear strong echoes with Wiman, Evans, Augustine, and Shapiro.

This is also something inherent to Christianity that is permanently open to the other and even otherness itself, and this cannot be overlooked or undervalued. Christianity began as a movement within Judaism that sought to recognize the otherness of God and from this place to reach out to the strangers and foreigners (even Gentiles) that appeared—to some, perhaps, but not all Jews even—to be outside the fold of Israel. Comprehending this foundation is central to comprehending the identity (or non-identity) of Christianity. Indeed, this is why it is often so baffling when Christians reject otherness. Eck found that her religious tradition in some ways failed to entirely remove its own otherness (and that, in the end, proved to be a good thing). At the same time, she encountered Hindus whose religion had also failed them. In this manner, she not only makes a connection between the two faiths, but goes back to Christianity to learn how to fail better at it, to expose otherness more clearly and learn to receive it as a transformative gift.

In order to stimulate our thinking about the various religions of the world and the myriad ways in which they encounter each other, Eck reminds us as well of the significance of the original World's Parliament of Religions that first took place in Chicago in 1893, and which was the first time historically that many Westerners had engaged in-depth conversations with people of other religious traditions. Many religious groups and persons were omitted, to be sure, but it was the first time in the history of humanity that such an endeavor had been attempted—a fact which tells us how little time we have actually had to work through the implications of religious plurality in our world. In other words, our global dialogue with otherness is really just beginning. As Eck provides commentary on this situation,

> What is new today is not the diversity of our religious traditions nor the task of interpretation. What is new is our sharply heightened awareness of religious diversity in every part of our world and the fact that today everyone—not just the explorers, the missionaries, the diplomats, and the theologians—encounters and needs to understand people and faiths other than their own.[22]

---

20. Eck, *Encountering God*, 21.
21. Eck, *Encountering God*, 103.
22. Eck, *Encountering God*, 43.

To see things thus changes not only one's understanding of other religions, but of their own as well, a point that Eck was determined to take seriously in the context of her own life.

Such religious diversity is part of our daily lives, and yet we have such trouble trying to understand the implications of such otherness for the construction of our own identities. We continue to identify ourselves in singular ways, as if there were no way to be a multiple-belonger to more than one religious tradition, or as if the truth of one religious group precluded other truths in other groups. In many ways, once again, our sense of political belonging and economic possession perhaps say more about how religious people understand themselves (in terms of self-definition) than does the core of most of our religious traditions.

This route, in short, is an economic language of exclusivity. In political terms, we can and do talk about patriotism or citizenship, but this, too, can be a language of exclusivity that ignores complex, living realities, such as the phenomenon of dual citizenship or children raised in households with parents of differing religious traditions. Precisely what we see before us are much more complex realities than we can often grasp with labels. For this reason, Eck wants us to think about identifying ourselves differently than through such exclusionary perspectives.

> To the native peoples of the Pacific Northwest and the Great Plains, the ownership of God was as unimaginable as the ownership of nature. The claims of the missionaries who came in the wake of conquest preaching exclusive access to the true God were as astonishing to the Suquamish and the Blackfeet as the claims of homesteaders and miners to land, forests, minerals, and water.[23]

For many people, God becomes "yet another possession" capable of granting a person some exclusive access to something that they cannot name, but that they have sought after with everything within them, much like money or financial gain, I would add.[24] Some people find the idea of believing in God something that grants them security, the way that money might. They view religion, and its often-associated notion of salvation, as something to be possessed. Such a logic is easily undermined, however, by grasping the political resonance that such divisions (saved/damned, heaven/hell) often maintain, or by pointing to the way in which true love and true compassion can reveal the prejudice at work in the forming of such divisions. The Zen Buddhist writer D. T. Suzuki, for example, once said that if he had a choice between going to heaven or to hell, he would choose

23. Eck, *Encountering God*, 45.
24. Eck, *Encountering God*, 51.

to go to hell, because that was where he might help alleviate the suffering of others—a radical challenge to those who would discard the "other" to a realm beyond any reach or compassion. The real nature of the divine, whatever such a thing may be to us, is forever beyond our possession, a point that Eck illustrates quite adamantly:

> Whatever we may think of God, the referent of that word, that symbol, is a mystery. God is finally beyond our grasp. God is not ours—even with the grace of God's revealing. There are, however, Christians and people of other faiths who seem to have no trouble speaking of God's ultimacy with one breath and staking out a private territory of God's activity and grace with the next. But what if we presuppose, as do both the inclusivist and the pluralist, that God's activity and grace abound?[25]

That is, what if we assume that God's grace is larger than our historically constructed religious schemes? We have learned and passed along our various conceptualizations of the divine, but we must also, eventually, take responsibility for the conceptualizations of God that we hold, and the impact that such representations have upon other people, especially those "others" whom we exclude from our religious institutions and groupings.

Providing us with a comprehensive model by which to comprehend the various approaches one might take with regard to global, religious diversity, Eck unfolds three possible scenarios of religious belief and interaction that will be helpful to illustrate the complexity of negotiating identity in our world today. First there is the exclusivist position, which holds that there is only one view of the divine and our religion possesses it. A good deal of fundamentalism espouses such a view, but so do many others as well. Second, there is the inclusivist position, which maintains that one's religion possesses the truth, but other faiths have partial views that can be included within one's own. This was the position that developed around Vatican II in the Catholic Church through the theology of Karl Rahner who developed the idea of an "anonymous Christianity," which tried to identify those who worship the same God even though they do not see themselves as Christian, for example. Third, there is the pluralist position, which claims that every religion has a limited view on the divine, as God transcends any single religious viewpoint. This is, in a sense, ultimately a negative theological perspective that leaves one permanently open to the possibility of otherness.[26]

What Eck will conclude when faced with these three options is that, in order to be intellectually honest, we should strive for the pluralist position,

---

25. Eck, *Encountering God*, 46.
26. Eck, *Encountering God*, 50.

but we may have to settle for the inclusivist viewpoint at times insofar as it is the bedrock language with which we comprehend and discuss our world.[27] We need labels and representations, as inaccurate as they will be, in order to make sense of our world and communicate something about it to others. We should strive for pluralism, but will always be pulled back into inclusivism in some manner. This is an inevitable and very realistic portrait of living in a world where multiple religious traditions abound.

The inevitability of this compromised position is a reflection of the linguistic and cultural reality in which we dwell. As she puts it, "As long as we hold the religious insights of our particular traditions, cast in our particular languages, to be in some sense universal, we cannot avoid speaking at times in an inclusivist way. It is important to recognize this."[28] What is yet somewhat unsettling in this solution to the problem, however, is that, according to Eck, we are entirely bound to only one language "to make definitive claims about the whole of reality."[29] This is a reality too which is presumably much larger than any single language. There is an obvious contradiction, or paradox, in holding this position, but it is one that we simply cannot do without—and despite the fact that we tend to prefer our religious claims to appear as "absolute," something they will never be able to be as we might like them to.[30] If a person uses one language or religion to try to describe all of reality, it is of course particularly limiting—yet we continue to do this as we *must* do this. This is the cost of having language and why we have definition and clarity at all in our world. Analogous to what I am here articulating, using the language of lovers, it is pathetically and comically a failure when you try to fully describe to your beloved why you love them, though we *will* try again and again to do just that, to use words to declare our love. This is an inevitable and inescapable reality that is always bound for failure, but which we cannot avoid.

The "danger of inclusivism" recognized by many is that it does not hear or take seriously those marginalized voices of dissent that speak of alternative languages and ways of communicating.[31] We might notice, moreover, how inclusivism is the perspective taken from the point of view of someone

---

27. Eck, *Encountering God*, 170.

28. Eck, *Encountering God*, 180.

29. Eck, *Encountering God*, 184.

30. We should recall here Jacques Derrida's presentation of an antinomy of language that continues to shape us: that we only ever speak one language, but also that we never speak only one language. Derrida, *Monolinguism of the Other*. This is a tension that we are continuously bound up within and which we cannot escape. But it is also the signal of the limitation of our linguistic selves. See also Smith, *Derrida and Autobiography*.

31. Eck, *Encountering God*, 185.

within a given tradition (holding that definitions do and must mean something), and how pluralism is the point of view taken from someone who most directly experiences the complexity within our world (advocating the necessity of translation). If Eck's position were merely that of the "insider" inclusivist, she would not have sought out a model of interreligious dialogue that begins by taking our personal relationships seriously. She would have instead tried to promote a sensitive inclusivism that does not seek to become friends with the other, to listen to the other, their stories and their life. In this sense, a "sensitive inclusivist" is tolerant of the other but doesn't enter into relationship. For Eck, "When the inclusivist really begins to listen to the voices of others, speaking in their own terms, the whole context of theological thought begins to change along the continuum toward pluralism."[32] And so, the inclusivist (searching for definition) is continuously challenged by the pluralist position (which ceaselessly makes translations), and opened up by it as much as it also is open to it. To engage with an authentic pluralism means that we recognize our inclusivist tendencies, but that we do not entirely succumb to them. We remain open to what will always lie beyond our own desire to label and identify ourselves. Yet, in her words, "This does not mean we cease speaking in our own language and adopt some neutral terminology, but it does mean that we cease speaking only to ourselves and in the terms of our own internal Christian conversation. We will speak in the context of interreligious dialogue."[33]

What might she take as a model within the history of Christianity to help understand why this might be the way to go about things? We might think here of Jesus' own Jewishness, or the first Christians, who weren't even called "Christians" at first but were Jews searching the limits of their own identities. Including others in Jewish religious identity *is* the Christian story of translation and of transformation in many ways. This understanding of identity, a radical openness to that which transforms us through the act of translation, is at the heart of what it means to be Christian, but which also always already exceeds the boundaries of what it means even to be Christian. The church established itself by being open to otherness, though subsequently the ways in which the church constructed itself over time drifted far from this intention (in many ways the correcting intention behind the Reformation). The sense that otherness teaches us about our own identity is the central thing we cannot miss here—it is the pivot around which all forms of self-critique turn. As Jean Halperin put it, and which Eck freely quotes, "We not only need

---

32. Eck, *Encountering God*, 185.
33. Eck, *Encountering God*, 187.

to understand one another, we need one another to understand ourselves."[34] This is a very realistic portrait of faith, as it is also a very realistic portrait of our lives formed by those around us.

Lest one become convinced that being open to the diversity of difference in otherness that pluralism remains open to leads directly to relativism, Eck contends that pluralism differs from relativism in that it is engaged in openness and commitment, not just a never-ending sense of openness.[35] The goal of pluralism, she finds, is "to find ways to be distinctively ourselves and yet be in relation to one another."[36] The aim, then, is not to dissolve faith to a "lowest common denominator," as relativism has sought to do, but to be passionately committed to a particular faith tradition and also open to the otherness that must come within one's own life of faith, not simply remain external to it. Pluralism doesn't lead one to relativism, which isn't a position one can embody; rather, it leads you back to an inclusivist point of view.

It is intriguing as well, though she does not develop this analogy in an in-depth manner, that she briefly mentions a parallel between pluralism and ecology, which also seeks to comprehend "the interrelated household of living and non-living beings" on our planet.[37] Just as many environmental activists have argued, and which resonates a good deal with Eck's analysis, we all exist in relationship with one another, symbiotically even, so that we each have an effect upon the other, though we often live our lives as if this reality weren't true either (the "myth of autonomy" once again). In fact, you might say that trying to realize how we can only define our life of faith in relation to the "others" around us is about as difficult as trying to understand how we are all members, together, of an ecosystem whose complexity we will perhaps never fully fathom. I do not think it is a coincidence, therefore, that new age spiritualities have often tried to connect an abstracted spiritual reality with certain perceptions of nature. The different relationships and probabilities that make up our life of faith are like an ecosystem. The quest of each is to realize our interdependency, and to act from that place of understanding: "Being able to feel the hurt of one another and to speak out on behalf of one another is one of the greatest spiritual challenges of an interdependent world."[38]

It is also one that we are still very much struggling to take part in. We will always be human, but we need to learn to live in relationship with that

34. Eck, *Encountering God*, 189.
35. Eck, *Encountering God*, 193.
36. Eck, *Encountering God*, 197.
37. Eck, *Encountering God*, 204.
38. Eck, *Encountering God*, 220.

which surrounds us. Human beings have not treated the environment respectfully; we have used a possession model (its economic dimension) and have protected what we want to the exclusion of others, including the environment (its political dimension). What Eck essentially argues is that we need to recognize this complexity of interrelationship in religious terms as well, causing our definitions of religious faith to expand into territories almost wholly unexplored in the history of religious identities and definitions.

In the end, Eck makes clear a notion that has been guiding us from the start: truth emerges in our lives from the seedbed of dialogue, from being in relationship with one another, and not from some abstract, *a priori* universal truth—this is what pluralism seeks to uncover as the reality of our world and religious truth claims.[39] Putting this realization in dialogue with the (linguistic, cultural, economic, social, political, and religious) traditions that are often geared toward either an exclusive or inclusive bent is the way forward for us as a civilization, and a quest that we are not a moment too soon in taking up. It is a humble attitude, one that is willing to embrace the poverty of its inclusivist (definitional) thinking that opens us up to an otherness that can truly transform (translate) us into the faithful people we are called to be.

---

39. Eck, *Encountering God*, 221.

Conclusion

Somewhat recently, Pope Francis has placed before Christians a particular viewpoint for understanding faith—the ultimate focus of theological inquiry—as a relationship, a point that I have taken up in this book as one of the main reasons helping to explain why autobiographical writings have multiplied over the years and why taking a closer look at them within a theological setting would be a good idea. In his words, "I would not speak about 'absolute' truths, even for believers. . . . Truth is a relationship. As such, each one of us receives the truth and expresses it from within, that is to say, according to one's own circumstances, culture, and situation in life."[1] What grips us in this statement is that truth is not defined as a series of doctrinal propositions, but as something that is brought to bear on us as a relationship, something that may seem "less than serious" in terms of its propositional or doctrinal content. What I believe the Pope is trying to articulate, however, is something vastly different from what we normally think of when we refer to truth: it is the "weak" claim that truth actually resides, for many of us, in the already established relationships that we have in our lives. This is not something to be downplayed or cast aside as so incredibly "weak" that such claims must be discarded; rather it is, as John Henry Newman put it, the "weakness" of faith that is inherent to the nature of faith.[2] Faith rests contented on evidence that will always seem "weak" to the claims of reason, and this is how it should be. We come to faith because a variety of "weaker" probabilities have swelled to such proportions that we are pushed over the edge toward a certainty in faith,

---

1. Pope Francis, "Letter to a Non-Believer."
2. Newman, *Fifteen Sermons Preached before the University of Oxford Between A.D. 1826 and 1843*.

though this process is more akin to the highly personal act of falling in love than it is to scientific discovery.[3]

To understand the proper context in which theology is performed, as I have argued, is to learn to take autobiography more seriously as a methodological issue than it has ever been taken before. To repeat a claim we already saw in Wiman's recent autobiography:

> There is no clean intellectual coherence, no abstract ultimate meaning to be found, and if this is not recognized, then the compulsion to find such certainty becomes its own punishment. This realization is not the end of theology, but the beginning of it: trust no theory, no religious history or creed, in which the author's personal faith is not actively at risk.[4]

In other words, there is no systematic or abstract reflection upon faith that will give us a clean "proof" for God's existence, or the Christian faith as the only "true faith" (as a claim analogous to scientific proofs). One may come to conclude that the Christian faith—or another faith—*is* the only true faith, but this is only possible after one enters oneself into the fray of tradition and theology, and puts oneself "at risk" in the search for faith. There is no other authentic way to do it, and certainly not as a detached, purely rational, or abstract exercise performed at a complete remove from religious ritual, the life of prayer, personal confession, and so forth. Likewise, realizing that one's tradition contains something of the truth—whatever such a claim means to the individual believer—does not remove the challenges that other religions bring, but actually dictates that one engage other religious traditions more openly than ever before. The act of translation, as I have argued throughout, must be brought to bear upon every definition that we conceive. There is simply no other way for a living faith to become intelligible to others and passed along through the ages.

There is no doubt that those who have written theologically, especially in a historical sense, have often been loath to engage their own life story, perhaps in a quest to be more "universal" or "transcendent" of any historically particular context (and, theologically speaking, trying perhaps to mirror those qualities they perceive to be praised in a God that so many people worship). There are no doubt too many contemporary theologians who would join in such a legacy to talk about God, the sacred, the Infinite, the universal, etc., without taking account of their own personal life and involvement in the subject.[5] Yet the last fifty years or so have also witnessed

---

3. Latour, *Rejoicing*.
4. Wiman, *My Bright Abyss*, 75.
5. Cf. the call for the use of "I" in academic, formal writing in Vattimo, *Belief*.

an increased focus in autobiographical studies on the particular contexts that we inhabit, not as a refusal to engage in the most universal topics of human experience, but, if anything, as a turning *to* the relevance of one's life story, drawing out its detail and confessing one's rootedness in it as the only way to truly bring out the universal truth we have been searching for, something that may end up looking more like the expression of faith as a relationship and less like a creedal statement of belief.[6] This turn to the autobiographical context has the potential to produce a major change in the tone of theological work—as it would for any academic discipline, and yet so few theologians have actually taken autobiographical work seriously, excepting the occasional well-known theologian who would pen some portion of their own life story.

As I hope I have demonstrated in the present series of reflections, taking account of our own social and political location as an essential part of what we write, mining our personal stories for the ways in which God has taken root in an individual's everyday life, can be a powerful and productive force for a more honest articulation and understanding of those selves we are pining to describe in more complex and elaborate detail.[7] To center ourselves on such insights is to reimagine theology as more concerned with the relationships that comprise one's faith than the belief systems that have often dominated religious life—though this is not to say that one's beliefs drop out of the bottom altogether. I am thinking rather of Diana Eck's more than appropriate comment, which bears repeating, that "We do not enter into dialogue with the dreamy hope that we will all agree, for the truth is we probably will not. We do not enter into dialogue to produce an agreement, but to produce real relationship, even friendship, which is premised upon mutual understanding, not upon agreement."[8] Such a refocusing of our desires toward relationship, toward friendship even, rather than solely on almost entirely abstracted, theoretical, rational, truth-based, or doctrinal agreement, is what theology truly should be about, though, in an age where scientific, logical certainty seems to be the gold standard against which all other things are judged, this seems more often to be less than we were bargaining for.

As has already been suggested, and which must be developed further, I am calling for a dialogue to occur between the historical structures of faith (the "doxography of faith") and one's own personal experience of the divine,

---

6. Eakin, *Fictions in Autobiography*; Stanley, *The Auto/biographical I*; Smith, *Subjectivity, Identity, and the Body*; Bjorklund, *Interpreting the Self*.

7. Lejeune, *On Autobiography*; Bourdieu, *Language and Symbolic Power*.

8. Eck, *Encountering God*, 197.

or even lack thereof—something which theology often does not know what to do with, but which in fact it should.[9] Such a dynamic dialogue between these two poles is not to become a "preoccupation" with "one concern" or with becoming "irrefutable"—the tempting and yet destructive quest for certainty in religious terms—but rather with "a conceptually abridged and condensed narrative of a life's story bio-graphy in God's presence."[10] This, I am suggesting, is what it means to stand before God, with all of our ugliness and humanity and to *confess* that this is indeed who we are, no better, but also no worse. This is where we admit that in the telling of our life's story before those members of faith that define our relations and our community we find something essential to our lives, to our story, and to the establishment of our faith.

The task for the theologian Johann Baptist Metz, and here I am merely following his lead, is to put one's "mystical" experience in dialogue with the Christian doxological tradition, and not simply to favor one over the other—perhaps the indirect downfall of so many who seek to become "spiritual but not religious" as they lose touch with any structure altogether and so eventually lose all spirituality as well. Though I find Metz's effort in this instance to distance such a theological dialectic from the everyday autobiographical contexts of ordinary Christians might lean a tad too far toward the "extraordinary" than is perhaps necessary, there is a certain truth in what he says that I would want to develop further. Not just any autobiographical account will be an "edifying discourse," to borrow Kierkegaard's phrasing.[11] Yet, despite this caution, Metz is clear on the benefits of such a dialectic between the biographical and the dogmatic:

> Who, after all, is in greater need of a biographical form of dogmatic theology than the Christian who finds it very difficult to feel part of theological teaching as a whole, to be affected by it or involved in it and to identify himself or his experience with the mysticism of theology because it is so often concealed from itself?[12]

The genre of spiritual autobiography is just now beginning to draw the attention it well deserves, and it is my sincerest hope that it continues to blossom as a genre, but also that theologians attentive to the needs of the average believer begin to take it more seriously than they have thus far, offering up not only a

---

9. Metz, *Faith in History and Society*.

10. Metz, *Faith in History and Society*, 200.

11. Barbour, *The Conscience of the Autobiographer*; Couser, *Altered Egos*; Smith, *Derrida and Autobiography*; Gilmore, *The Limits of Autobiography*.

12. Metz, *Faith in History and Society*, 221.

willingness to engage with such writings, but to place them under careful and critical study so that we might further our understanding of what makes the presence of God so unique in a person's life. By turning to spiritual autobiographies we might actually learn to place our emphasis where it matters most, not on the abstractions and speculations that, while necessary for theological discourse, have also frequently clouded its vision on the true subject of theology, but on the people whose lives of faith move us deeply and cause us to reexamine our own lives in light of their witness.

Bibliography

Adams, Timothy Dow. *Telling Lies in Modern American Autobiography*. Chapel Hill: University of North Carolina Press, 1990.
Agamben, Giorgio. *The Time that Remains: A Commentary on the Letter to the Romans*. Translated by Patricia Dailey. Stanford, CA: Stanford University Press, 2005.
Aguilar, Mario I. *Contemplating God, Changing the World*. New York: Seabury, 2008.
Augustine. *Confessions*. Translated by Henry Chadwick. Oxford: Oxford University Press, 1991.
Barbour, John D. *The Conscience of the Autobiographer: Ethical and Religious Dimensions of Autobiography*. London: Macmillan, 1992.
———. *Versions of Deconversion: Autobiography and the Loss of Faith*. Charlottesville, VA: University Press of Virginia, 1994.
Basil the Great. *On the Holy Spirit*. Translated by David Anderson. Yonkers, NY: St. Vladimir's Seminary Press, 1980.
Berrigan, Daniel. *Testimony: The Word Made Fresh*. Maryknoll, NY: Orbis, 2004.
Bjorklund, Diane. *Interpreting the Self: Two Hundred Years of American Autobiography*. Chicago: University of Chicago Press, 1998.
Boitani, Piero. *The Bible and its Rewritings*. Translated by Anita Weston. Oxford: Oxford University Press, 1999.
Bourdieu, Pierre. *Language and Symbolic Power*. Edited by John B. Thompson. Translated by Gino Raymond and Matthew Adamson. Cambridge, MA: Harvard University Press, 1991.
Butler, Judith. *Giving an Account of Oneself*. New York: Fordham University Press, 2005.
Bynum, Caroline Walker. *Christian Materiality: An Essay on Religion in Late Medieval Europe*. Cambridge, MA: Zone, 2011.
Caputo, John D., and Gianni Vattimo. *After the Death of God*. Edited by Jeffrey W. Robbins. New York: Columbia University Press, 2007.
Caputo, John D. *On Religion*. New York: Routledge, 2001.
———. *The Weakness of God: A Theology of the Event*. Bloomington, IN: Indiana University Press, 2006.
Cary, Phillip. *Augustine's Invention of the Inner Self: The Legacy of a Christian Platonist*. New York: Oxford University Press, 2000.
Comstock, Gary L. *Religious Autobiographies*. Belmont, CA: Wadsworth, 1995.

Couser, G. Thomas. *Altered Egos: Authority in Autobiography.* Oxford: Oxford University Press, 1989.

Day, Dorothy. *The Long Loneliness.* San Francisco: Harper and Row, 1981.

Derrida, Jacques. *Circumfession.* In Geoffrey Bennington and Jacques Derrida, *Jacques Derrida,* 3–315. Chicago: University of Chicago Press, 1993.

———. *Monolinguism of the Other: Or, The Prosthesis of Origin.* Translated by Patrick Mensah. Stanford, CA: Stanford University Press, 1998.

Dunning, Benjamin H. *Aliens and Sojourners: Self as Other in Early Christianity.* Philadelphia: University of Pennsylvania Press, 2009.

Eakin, John Paul. *Fictions in Autobiography: Studies in the Art of Self-Invention.* Princeton, NJ: Princeton University Press, 1985.

Eckhart, Meister. *The Complete Mystical Works of Meister Eckhart.* Translated by M. O'C. Walshe. New York: Crossroad/Herder and Herder, 2008.

Elie, Paul. *The Life You Save May Be Your Own: An American Pilgrimage.* New York: Farrar, Straus and Giroux, 2003.

Evans, Rachel Held. *Evolving in Monkeytown: How a Girl Who Knew All the Answers Learned to Ask the Questions.* Grand Rapids: Zondervan, 2010.

Gilmore, Leigh. *The Limits of Autobiography: Trauma and Testimony.* Ithaca, NY: Cornell University Press, 2001.

Gilmour, Peter. *The Wisdom of Memoir: Reading and Writing Life's Sacred Texts.* Winona, MN: Saint Mary's Press, 1997.

Ginsberg, Elaine K., ed. *Passing and the Fictions of Identity.* Durham, NC: Duke University Press, 1996.

Girard, René. *Violence and the Sacred.* Translated by Patrick Gregory. Baltimore: Johns Hopkins University Press, 1997.

Graham, Elaine L. *Making the Difference: Gender, Personhood, and Theology.* Minneapolis: Fortress, 1996.

Guibert of Nogent. *Monodies and On the Relics of Saints: The Autobiography and a Manifesto of a French Monk from the Time of the Crusades.* Translated by Joseph McAlhany. New York: Penguin, 2011.

Hauerwas, Stanley, and William H. Willimon. *Resident Aliens: Life in the Christian Colony.* Nashville: Abingdon, 1989.

Hess, Cynthia. *Sites of Violence, Sites of Grace: Christian Nonviolence and the Traumatized Self.* Lanham, MD: Lexington, 2009.

Ignatius of Loyola. *Reminiscences, or Autobiography of Ignatius Loyola.* Translated by Joseph A. Munitiz and Phillip Endean. New York: Penguin, 1996.

Justin Martyr. *First Apology and Dialogue with Trypho.* Edited by Thomas B. Falls. Washington, DC: Catholic University of America Press, 1948.

John of the Cross. *The Collected Works of St. John of the Cross.* Translated by Kieran Kavanaugh and Otilio Rodriguez. Washington, DC: Institute of Carmelite Studies, 1991.

Karr, Mary. *The Art of Memoir.* New York: Harper Collins, 2015.

Kasper, Walter. *Mercy: The Essence of the Gospel and the Key to the Christian Life.* Mahwah, NJ: Paulist, 2014.

Kearney, Richard. *The God Who May Be: A Hermeneutics of Religion.* Bloomington, IN: Indiana University Press, 2001.

Kierkegaard, Søren. *Either/Or, Part II.* Translated by Howard V. Hong and Edna H. Hong. Princeton, NJ: Princeton University Pres, 1987.

———. *Works of Love*. Translated by Howard V. Hong and Edna H. Hong. Princeton, NJ: Princeton University Pres, 1998.
Kirwan, Michael. *Political Theology: An Introduction*. Minneapolis: Fortress, 2009.
Kort, Wesley A. *Textual Intimacy: Autobiography and Religious Identities*. Charlottesville, VA: University of Virginia Press, 2012.
Latour, Bruno. *Rejoicing: Or the Torments of Religious Speech*. Translated by Julie Rose. Cambridge: Polity, 2013.
Leigh, David J. *Circuitous Journeys: Modern Spiritual Autobiography*. New York: Fordham University Press, 2000.
Lejeune, Phillippe. *On Autobiography*. Translated by Katherine Leary. Minneapolis: University of Minnesota Press, 1989.
Lyotard, Jean-François. *The Confession of Augustine*. Translated by Richard Beardsworth. Stanford, CA: Stanford University Press, 2000.
MacKendrick, Karmen. *Divine Enticement: Theological Seductions*. New York: Fordham University Press, 2012.
Malabou, Catherine. *Plasticity at the Dusk of Writing: Dialectic, Destruction, Deconstruction*. New York: Columbia University Press, 2010.
Martin, James. *The Jesuit Guide to (Almost) Everything: A Spirituality for Real Life*. New York: HarperCollins, 2010.
McClendon, James Wm, Jr. *Biography as Theology: How Life Stories Can Remake Today's Theology*. Eugene, OR: Wipf and Stock, 2002.
Medwick, Cathleen. *Teresa of Avila: The Progress of a Soul*. New York: Image, 1999.
Metz, Johann Baptist. *Faith in History and Society: Toward a Practical Fundamental Theology*. Translated by J. Matthew Ashley. New York: Crossroad, 2007.
Miles, Jack. *Christ: A Crisis in the Life of God*. New York: Alfred A. Knopf, 2001.
———. *God: A Biography*. New York: Alfred A. Knopf, 1995.
Miller, Adam S. *Speculative Grace*. New York: Fordham University Press, 2013.
Moltmann, Jürgen. *The Crucified God: The Cross of Christ as the Foundation of Christian Theology*. Minneapolis: Fortress, 1993.
———. *The Trinity and the Kingdom*. Minneapolis: Fortress, 1993.
Newman, John Henry. *Apologia Pro Vita Sua*. New York: Modern Library, 1950. (1854.)
———. *An Essay in Aid of a Grammar of Assent*. Cambridge: Cambridge University Press, 2010.
———. *Fifteen Sermons Preached Before the University of Oxford Between A.D. 1826 and 1843*. 3rd ed. Notre Dame, IN: University of Notre Dame Press, 1997.
——— *A Letter Addressed to the Duke of Norfolk: On Occasion of Mr. Gladstone's Recent Expostulation*. London: Aeterna, 2015.
Norris, Kathleen. *Amazing Grace*. New York, Riverhead, 1998.
Nouwen, Henri. *The Road to Daybreak*. New York: Doubleday, 1988.
———. *The Wounded Healer*. New York: Doubleday, 1972.
Olney, James. *Memory and Narrative: The Weave of Life-Writing*. Chicago: University of Chicago Press, 1998.
———. *Metaphors of Self: The Meaning of Autobiography*. Princeton: Princeton University Press, 1972.
Olney, James, ed. *Studies in Autobiography*. Oxford: Oxford University Press, 1988.
Patel, Eboo. *Acts of Faith*. Boston: Beacon, 2007.
Plekon, Michael. *Saints as They Really Are: Voices of Holiness in Our Time*. Notre Dame, IN: University of Notre Dame Press, 2012.

Pontifical Council for Justice and Peace. *Compendium for the Social Doctrine of the Church*. Washington, DC: United States Conference of Catholic Bishops, 2005.
Pope Francis. *Letter to a Non-Believer*. https://w2.vatican.va/content/francesco/en/letters/2013/documents/papa-francesco_20130911_eugenio-scalfari.html
Ricoeur, Paul. *On Translation*. New York: Routledge, 2006.
Rodriguez, Richard. *Darling*. New York: Viking, 2013.
Sentilles, Sarah. *Breaking Up with God*. New York: HarperCollins, 2011.
Shapiro, Dani. *Devotion: A Memoir*. New York: HarperCollins, 2011.
Smith, Robert. *Derrida and Autobiography*. Cambridge: University of Cambridge Press, 1995.
Smith, Sidonie. *Subjectivity, Identity, and the Body: Women's Autobiographical Practices in the Twentieth Century*. Bloomington, IN: Indiana University Press, 1993.
Stark, Rodney. *The Rise of Christianity: How the Obscure, Marginal Jesus Movement Became the Dominant Religious Force in the Western World in a Few Centuries*. San Francisco: Harper, 1997.
Stanley, Liz. *The Auto/biographical I: The Theory and Practice of Feminist Auto/biography*. Manchester: Manchester University Press, 1992.
Stone, Albert E. *Autobiographical Occasions and Original Acts: Versions of American Identity from Henry Adams to Nate Shaw*. Philadelphia: University of Pennsylvania Press, 1982.
Teresa of Ávila. *The Life of Saint Teresa of Ávila by Herself*. Edited by J. M. Cohen. New York: Penguin, 1957. (Orig. sixteenth century.)
Tolstoy, Leo. *A Confession and Other Religious Writings*. Translated by Jane Kentish. New York: Penguin, 1987.
Turner, Léon. *Theology, Psychology and the Plural Self*. Burlington, VT: Ashgate, 2008.
Vattimo, Gianni. *Belief*. Translated by Luca D'Isanto and David Webb. Stanford, CA: Stanford University Press, 1999.
Walshe, M. O'C., trans. *The Complete Mystical Works of Meister Eckhart*. New York: Crossroad/Herder and Herder, 2008.
White, Carolinne, ed. *Early Christian Lives*. New York: Penguin, 1998.
———. *Lives of Roman Christian Women*. New York: Penguin, 2010.
White, Thomas Joseph, ed. *The Analogy of Being: Invention of the Antichrist or Wisdom of God?* Grand Rapids: Eerdmans, 2010.
Wiman, Christian. *My Bright Abyss*. New York: Farrar, Strauss, and Giroux, 2013.
Winner, Lauren F. *Girl Meets God*. New York: Random House, 2003.
Yagoda, Ben. *Memoir: A History*. New York: Riverhead, 2009.

Selected spiritual (auto)biographies and other related literature

Abbey, Edward. *Desert Solitaire*. New York: Simon & Schuster, 1990. (1968)
Abelard, Peter. *The Story of My Misfortunes*. Glencoe, IL: Free, 1958. (Orig. twelfth century.)
Abū Ḥāmid Muḥammad ibn Muḥammad al-Ghazālī. *The Deliverer*. (Orig. twelfth century.)
Ackerley, J. R. *My Father and Myself*. New York: New York Review of Books, 1968.

Adiele, Faith. *Meeting Faith: The Forest Journals of a Black Buddhist Nun*. New York: W. W. Norton, 2004.
Adler, Janet. *Arching Backward: The Mystical Initiation of a Contemporary Woman*. Rochester: Inner Traditions, 1995.
Ælfric of Eynsham. *Lives of the Saints*. Charleston, SC: Nabu, 2011.
Aherne, Brian. *A Proper Job*. Boston: Houghton Mifflin, 1969.
Ali, Ayaan Hirsi. *Infidel*. New York: Free, 2008.
Allen, Diogenes. *Steps Along the Way*. New York: Church, 2002.
Allen, Jimmy Raymond. *Burden of a Secret: A Story of Truth and Mercy in the Face of AIDS*. Nashville: Moorings, 1995.
Allende, Isabel. *Paula*. San Francisco: HarperCollins, 1994.
———. *The Sum of Our Days*. New York: HarperCollins, 2014.
Angelou, Maya. *I Know Why the Caged Bird Sings*. New York: Random House, 1969.
Armstrong, Karen. *The Spiral Staircase: My Climb Out of Darkness*. New York: Anchor, 2005.
———. *Through the Narrow Gate: A Memoir of Spiritual Discovery*. New York: St. Martin's, 1994.
Asad, Muhammad. *The Road to Mecca*. Louisville: Fons Vitae, 2000.
Athanasius. *The Life of Antony and the Letter to Marcellinus*. Mahwah, NJ: Paulist, 1980.
Augustine. *Confessions*. Translated by Henry Chadwick. Oxford: Oxford University Press, 1991.
Barbour, John D. *The Conscience of the Autobiographer: Ethical and Religious Dimensions of Autobiography*. London: Macmillan, 1992.
Bass, Diana Butler. *Strength for the Journey: A Pilgrimage of Faith in Community*. New York: Jossey-Bass, 2002.
Beak, Sera. *Red Hot and Holy: A Heretic's Love Story*. Louisville, CO: Sounds True, 2013.
Beck, Edward. *God Underneath: Spiritual Memoirs of a Catholic Priest*. New York: Crown, 2002.
Bernardin, Joseph. *The Gift of Peace: Personal Reflections*. Chicago: Loyola, 1997.
Besa. *The Life of Shenoute*. Translated by David N. Bell. Kalamazoo, MI: Cistercian, 1983.
Beveridge, William. *Private Thoughts upon Religion*. London: A. Bettesworth, 1719. (Orig. 1709.)
Bolen, Jean Shinoda. *Crossing to Avalon: A Woman's Midlife Pilgrimage*. San Francisco: HarperSanFrancisco, 1994.
Bolz-Weber, Nadia. *Pastrix: The Cranky, Beautiful Faith of a Sinner and Saint*. Nashville: Jericho, 2013.
Bonazzi, Robert. *Man in the Mirror: John Howard Griffin and the Story of Black Like Me*. Maryknoll, NY: Orbis, 1997.
Boyett, Micha. *Found: A Story of Questions, Grace, and Everyday Prayer*. Brentwood, TN: Worthy, 2014.
Brigance, O. J., and Peter Schrager. *Strength of a Champion: Finding Faith and Fortitude through Adversity*. New York: New American Library, 2013.
Briggs, Carolyn S. *Higher Ground: A Memoir of Salvation Found and Lost*. Lanham, MD: Rowman & Littlefield, 2011.
Brody, Leslie. *Daughters of Kings: Growing Up as a Jewish Woman in America*. Boston: Faber and Faber, 1997.

Brooks, Joanna. *The Book of Mormon Girl: A Memoir of an American Faith*. New York: Free, 2012.
Brown, Christy. *My Left Foot*. London: Mandarin, 1954.
Buechner, Frederick. *Now and Then: A Memoir of Vocation*. San Francisco: HarperSanFrancisco, 1991.
———. *The Sacred Journey: A Memoir of Early Days*. San Francisco: HarperSanFrancisco, 1991.
Bullitt-Jonas, Margaret. *Holy Hunger: A Memoir of Desire*. New York: A. A. Knopf, 1999.
Bundesen, Lynne. *So the Woman Went Her Way: A Personal Journey*. New York: Simon & Schuster, 1993.
Bunyan, John. *Grace Abounding to the Chief of Sinners*. Oxford: Clarendon, 1962. (Orig. 1666.)
Burgess, Anthony. *Little Wilson and Big God: Being the First Part of the Confessions of Anthony Burgess*. New York: Random House, 2012.
Butterfield, Rosaria Champagne. *The Secret Thoughts of an Unlikely Convert: An English Professor's Journey into Christian Faith*. San Diego: EChristian, 2013.
Byrne, Lorna. *Angels in My Hair*. New York: Doubleday, 2009.
Call, Susan. *A Search For Purple Cows: A True Story of Hope*. New York: Guideposts, 2013.
Cameron, Sharon. *Beautiful Work: A Meditation on Pain*. Durham, NC: Duke University Press, 2000.
Campbell, Colleen. *My Sisters the Saints: A Spiritual Memoir*. New York: Doubleday Religion, 2012.
Carroll, James. *Practicing Catholic*. New York: Houghton Mifflin Harcourt, 2010.
Casals, Pablo. *Joys and Sorrows: Reflections*. New York: Simon and Schuster, 1970.
Caspary, Anita Marie. *Witness to Integrity: The Crisis of the Immaculate Heart Community of California*. Collegeville, MN: Liturgical, 2003.
Castro, Joy. *The Truth Book: Escaping a Childhood of Abuse Among Jehovah's Witnesses: A Memoir*. New York: Arcade, 2011.
Chaudhuri, Nirad C. *The Autobiography of an Unknown Indian*. Berkeley, CA: University of California Press, 1968. (1951)
Chesterton, G. K. *The Autobiography of G. K. Chesterton*. San Francisco: Ignatius, 2006. (Orig. 1936.)
Ciszek, Walter. *With God in Russia*. San Francisco: Ignatius, 1997.
Collier, Sophia. *Soul Rush: The Odyssey of a Young Woman of the '70s*. New York: Morrow, 1978.
Collins, Judy. *Singing Lessons*. New York: Simon and Schuster, 1998.
Comstock, Gary L. *Religious Autobiographies*. Belmont, CA: Wadsworth, 1995.
Corbett, Jim. *Goatwalking*. New York: Viking, 1991.
Crapsey, Algernon Sidney. *The Last of the Heretics*. Newcastle Upon Tyne: Cambridge Scholars, 2007. (Orig. 1924.)
Crisp, Quentin. *The Naked Civil Servant*. New York: Holt, Rinehart and Winston, 1968.
Crittenden, Lindsey. *The Water Will Hold You: A Skeptic Learns to Pray*. New York: Harmony, 2007.
Cyril of Scythopolis. *Lives of the Monks of Palestine*. Translated by R. M. Price. Kalamazoo, MI: Cistercian, 1991.
Czeslaw, Milosz. *Native Realm: A Search for Self-Definition*. Garden City, NY: Doubleday, 1969.

Daly, Mary. *Outercourse: The Be-Dazzling Voyage*. New York: HarperCollins, 1992.
Day, Dorothy. *The Duty of Delight: The Diaries of Dorothy Day*. Edited by Robert Ellsberg. New York: Image, 2011.
———. *The Long Loneliness*. San Francisco: Harper & Row, 1981.
De Vinck, Christopher. *The Power of the Powerless*. New York: Doubleday, 1988.
Dear, John. *A Persistent Peace: One Man's Struggle for a Nonviolent World*. Chicago: Loyola, 2008.
Delbrel, Madeline. *We, the Ordinary People of the Streets*. Grand Rapids: Eerdmans, 2000. (1966).
Dillard, Annie. *Pilgrim at Tinker Creek*. New York: Harper Perennial Modern Classics, 2013. (Orig. 1974.)
Dobson, Ed. *Seeing Through the Fog: Hope When Your World Falls Apart*. Colorado Springs: David C Cook, 2012.
Doddridge, Philip. *Rise and Progress of Religion in the Soul*. Philadelphia: R. Aitken & Son, 1788. (Orig. 1745.)
Donofrio, Beverly. *Looking for Mary: Or, the Blessed Mother and Me*. New York: Viking Compass, 2000.
Drain, Lauren. *Banished: Surviving My Years in the Westboro Baptist Church*. New York: Grand Central, 2013.
Dubner, Stephen J. *Choosing My Religion: A Memoir of a Family Beyond Belief*. New York: Harper, 1998.
Dubus, Andre. *Meditations from a Movable Chair*. New York: Knopf, 1998.
Eck, Diana. *Encountering God: A Spiritual Journey from Bozeman to Banaras*. Boston: Beacon, 1993.
Erikson, Richard M. *Late Have I Loved Thee: Stories of Religious Conversion and Commitment in Later Life*. New York: Paulist, 1995.
Eugippius. *Life of St. Severin*. Washington, DC: Catholic University of America Press, 1964.
Eusebius. *Life of Constantine*. Translated by Averil Cameron. Oxford: Oxford University Press, 1999.
Evans, Rachel Held. *Evolving in Monkey Town: How a Girl Who Knew All the Answers Learned to Ask the*
———. *Searching for Sunday: Loving, Leaving, and Finding the Church*. Nashville: Thomas Nelson, 2015.
Feld, Merle. *A Spiritual Life: A Jewish Feminist Journey*. Albany, NY: State University of New York Press, 1999.
Finers, Carol. *At the Root of this Longing: Reconciling a Spiritual Hunger and a Feminist Thirst*. San Francisco: HarperSanFrancisco, 1998.
The Fourteenth Dalai Lama. *Freedom in Exile—The Autobiography of the Dalai Lama*. New York: Harper Perennial, 1991.
———. *My Land and My People*. London: Weidenfeld & Nicholson, 1962.
Frank, Anne. *The Diary of a Young Girl*. Garden City, NY: Doubleday, 1952. (Orig. 1947.)
Gallagher, Nora. *Things Seen and Unseen: A Year Lived in Faith*. New York: Vintage, 1998.
Gandhi, Mahatma. *The Story of My Experiments with Truth*. Washington, DC: Public Affairs, 1948. (Orig. 1929.)
Gaustad, Edwin S., ed. *Memoirs of the Spirit*. Grand Rapids: Eerdmans, 1989.

Gennadius and Jerome. *Lives of Illustrious Men*. London: Aeterna, 2016.
Gilbert, Elizabeth. *Eat, Pray, Love: One Woman's Search for Everything Across Italy, India and Indonesia*. New York: Viking, 2006.
Gilmour, Peter, and Patricia O'Connell Killen, eds. *Journeys in Ministry: Nine Memoirs from Around the World*. Chicago: Loyola University Press, 1989.
Gohn, Pat. *Blessed, Beautiful and Bodacious: Celebrating the Gift of Catholic Womanhood*. Notre Dame, IN: Ave Maria, 2012.
Grant, Jennifer. *Love You More: The Divine Surprise of Adopting My Daughter*. Nashville: Thomas Nelson, 2011.
Green, Graham. *A Sort of Life*. New York: Random House, 2011.
Gregory of Nyssa. *The Life of Moses*. Translated by Abraham Malherbe. Mahwah, NJ: Paulist, 1978.
Gregory, Dick. *Nigger*. New York: Pocket, 1964.
Guibert of Nogent. *Monodies* and *On the Relics of the Saints*. Translated by Joseph McAlhany and Jay Rubenstein. New York: Penguin, 2011. (Orig. eleventh-twelfth century.)
Haile, Ahmed Ali. *Teatime in Mogadishu: My Journey as a Peace Ambassador in the World of Islam*. Harrisonburg, PA: Herald, 2011.
Haines, Jennifer. *Bread and Water: A Spiritual Journey*. Maryknoll, NY: Orbis, 1997.
Halifax, Joan. *A Buddhist Life in America: Simplicity in the Complex*. New York: Paulist, 1998.
Hampl, Patricia. *Virgin Time: In Search of Contemplative Life*. New York: Ballantine, 1992.
Hartzler, Aaron. *Rapture Practice: A True Story*. New York: Little Brown, 2013.
Hauerwas, Stanley. *Hannah's Child: A Theologian's Memoir*. Grand Rapids: Eerdmans, 2010.
Hayworth, Jenny. *Inside/Outside: One Woman's Recovery From Abuse and a Religious Cult*. North Charleston: CreateSpace, 2013.
Idliby, Ranya. *Burqas, Baseball, and Apple Pie: Being Muslim in America*. New York: Palgrave Macmillan, 2014.
Ignatius of Loyola. *Reminiscences, or Autobiography of Ignatius Loyola*. Translated by Joseph A. Munitiz and Philip Endean. New York: Penguin, 1996. (Orig. sixteenth century.)
Isaacs, Susan E. *Angry Conversations with God: A Snarky but Authentic Spiritual Memoir*. New York: FaithWords, 2009.
Jackowski, Karol. *Divine Madness: Why I'm Still a Nun*. Notre Dame, IN: Ave Maria, 1996.
Jackson, Phil. *Sacred Hoops*. New York: Hachette, 2012.
Jacobs, Harriet Ann. *Incidents in the Life of a Slave Girl Written By Herself*. New York: Oxford University Press, 1968. (Orig. 1861.)
Jay, Frances. *Walking with God Through 12 Steps: What I Learned About Honesty, Healing, Reconciliation, and Wholeness*. Chicago: ACTA, 1996.
Jerome. *Three Biographies: Malchus, St. Hilarion, and Paulus the First Hermit*. N.p.: CreateSpace, 2013.
John of the Cross. *Dark Night of the Soul*. Edited by T. N. R. Rogers. New York: Dover, 2003. (Orig. sixteenth century.)
Johnson, Mary. *An Unquenchable Thirst: One Woman's Extraordinary Journey of Faith, Hope, and Clarity*. New York: Spiegel & Grau, 2011.

Jones, Mary Harris. *Autobiography of Mother Jones*. New York: Arno, 1969. (Orig. 1925.)
Julian of Norwich. *Revelations of Divine Love*. Collegeville, MN: Liturgical, 2003. (Orig. 1400.)
Jung, Carl. *Memories, Dreams, Reflections*. New York: Vintage, 1965.
Kamenetz, Rodger. *The Jew in the Lotus: A Poet's Rediscovery of Jewish Identity in Buddhist India*. San Francisco: HarperSanFrancisco, 1994.
Karr, Mary. *Lit*. New York: Harper Perennial, 2010.
Katz, Jon. *Running to the Mountain: A Journey of Faith and Change*. New York: Villard, 1999.
Kavanagh, P. J. *The Perfect Stranger*. London: Chatto and Windus, 2015. (Orig. 1966.)
Keen, Sam. *To a Dancing God*. New York: Harper & Row, 1970.
Kelty, Matthew. *Flute Solo: Reflections of a Trappist Hermit*. Kansas City: Andrews and McMeel, 1979.
Kempe, Margery. *The Book of Margery Kempe*. Oxford: Oxford University Press, 2015. (Orig. 1501.)
Kidd, Sue Monk. *The Dance of the Dissident Daughter: A Woman's Journey from Christian Tradition to the Sacred Feminine*. San Francisco: HarperSanFrancisco, 1996.
King, Heather. *Redeemed: A Spiritual Misfit Stumbles Toward God, Marginal Sanity, and the Peace That Passes All Understanding*. New York: Viking, 2008.
Kourdakov, Sergei. *The Persecutor*. Old Tappan, NJ: Fleming H. Revell, 1973.
Kuehn, Heinz R. *Mixed Blessings: An Almost Ordinary Life in Hitler's Germany*. Athens, GA: University of Georgia Press, 1988.
Lee, Jarena. *Religious Experience and Journal of Mrs. Jarena Lee, Giving An Account of Her Call to Preach the Gospel*. Philadelphia: Pantianos, 1836.
Lehmann, Rosamond. *The Swan in the Evening: Fragments of an Inner Life*. New York: Houghton Mifflin, 2015. (Orig. 1967.)
Leonardi, Lillie. *In the Shadow of a Badge: A Spiritual Memoir*. Tarentum: Word Association, 2011.
Levi, Primo. *If This Is a Man*. New York: Orion, 1959. (Orig. 1947.)
Lewis, C. S. *Surprised by Joy: The Shape of My Early Life*. New York: Harcourt, Brace & World, 1955.
Mairs, Nancy. *Ordinary Time*. Boston: Beacon, 1993.
Malcolm, Boyd. *Gay Priest: An Inner Journey*. New York: St. Martin's, 1986.
Malcom X with Alex Haley. *Autobiography of Malcom X*. New York: Ballantine, 1973. (Orig. 1965.)
Manning, Richard. *It Runs in the Family: A Memoir*. New York: St. Martin's, 2013.
Marchione, Margherita. *The Fighting Nun: My Story*. New York: Cornwall, 2000.
Martin, James. *My Life with the Saints*. Chicago: Loyola, 2006.
Martyr, Justin. *First Apology* and *Dialogue with Trypho*. Edited by Thomas B. Falls. Washington, DC: Catholic University of America Press, 1948.
Mayberry, Georgette. *It Could Happen to You: A Testimony of Overcoming a Chronic Illness*. Bloomington: AuthorHouse, 2012.
McSorley, Richard T. *My Path to Peace and Justice: An Autobiography*. Marion: Rose Hill, 1996.
Merton, Thomas. *The Seven Storey Mountain*. New York: Harcourt, Brace and Company, 1948.
Miles, Sara. *Take This Bread*. New York: Ballantine, 2007.

Miller, Donald. *Blue Like Jazz: Nonreligious Thoughts on Christian Spirituality.* Nashville: Thomas Nelson, 2003.
Moon, Sun Myung. *As a Peace-Loving Global Citizen.* Washington, DC: The Washington Times Foundation, 2010.
Murray, Margaret. *My First Hundred Years.* New York: W. Kimber, 1963.
Murray, W. J. *My Life Without God.* New York: WND, 2012.
Mussolini, Benito. *My Autobiography: With the Political and Social Doctrine of Fascism.* Mineola, NY: Dover, 2006. (Orig. 1928.)
Nabokov, Vladimir. *Speak, Memory.* New York: Putnam, 1966.
Neihardt, John G. *Black Elk Speaks.* Lincoln, NE: University of Nebraska Press, 2014. (Orig. 1932.)
Niebuhr, Reinhold. *Leaves from the Notebook of a Tamed Cynic.* San Francisco: Harper & Row, 1980. (Orig. 1929.)
Norris, Kathleen. *Amazing Grace.* New York: Riverhead, 1998.
———. *The Cloister Walk.* New York: Riverhead, 1996.
———. *Dakota: A Spiritual Geography.* Boston: Houghton Mifflin, 1993.
Nouwen, Henri. *The Road to Daybreak.* New York: Doubleday, 1988.
———. *The Wounded Healer.* New York: Doubleday, 1972.
Okoro, Enuma. *Reluctant Pilgrim: A Moody, Somewhat Self-Indulgent Introvert's Search for Spiritual Community.* Nashville: Fresh Air, 2010.
Omar, Manal M. *Barefoot in Baghdad.* Naperville, IL: Sourcebooks, 2010.
Orwell, George. *Such, Such Were the Joys.* New York: Penguin, 2014. (Orig. 1953.)
Palladius. *Dialogue on the Life of John Chrysostom.* Translated by Robert T. Meyer. Mahwah, NJ: Newman, 1985.
Passes All Understanding. New York: Viking, 2008.
Patel, Eboo. *Acts of Faith: The Story of an American Muslim, the Struggle for the Soul of a Generation.* Boston: Beacon, 2007.
Paul, Christi. *Love Isn't Supposed to Hurt: A Memoir.* Carol Stream, IL: Tyndale, 2012.
Pick, Alison. *Between Gods: A Memoir.* New York: HarperCollins, 2015.
Pontius the Deacon. *Vita Cypriani.* Translated by Robert Ernest Wallis. Cambridge, MA: Charles River, 2012.
Questions. Grand Rapids: Zondervan, 2010.
Radhanath Swami. *The Journey Home: Autobiography of an American Swami.* San Rafael, CA: Mandala, 2010.
Ram Goel, Sita. *How I Became a Hindu.* New Delhi: Voice of India, 1993.
Recinella, Dale S. *Now I Walk on Death Row: A Wall Street Finance Lawyer Stumbles into the Arms of a Loving God.* Grand Rapids: Chosen, 2011.
Richmond, L. *Healing Lazarus: A Buddhist's Journey from Near Death to New Life.* New York: Pocket, 2002.
Ricoeur, Paul. *On Translation.* New York: Routledge, 2006.
Roberts, Bernadette. *The Experience of No-Self: A Contemplative Journey.* Sunspot: Iroquois House, 1982.
Rodriguez, Richard. *Darling: A Spiritual Autobiography.* New York: Viking, 2013.
———. *Days of Obligation.* New York: Viking, 1992.
Rousseau, Jean-Jacques. *The Confessions.* New York: A. & C. Boni, 1928. (Orig. 1782.)
Ruskin, John. *Praeterita.* Keele: Ryburn, 1994. (Orig. 1885.)
Ruttenberg, Danya. *Surprised By God: How I Learned to Stop Worrying and Love Religion.* Boston: Beacon, 2008.

Samson, Lisa, and Ty Samson. *Love Mercy: A Mother and Daughter's Journey From the American Dream to the Kingdom of God*. Grand Rapids: Zondervan, 2010.
Sanchez, Ricardo. *It's Not Over*. Lake Mary, FL: Charisma, 2012.
Schullenberger, Bonnie. *A Time to Be Born*. Cambridge, MA: Cowley, 1996.
Schwehn, Kaethe. *Tailings*. Eugene, OR: Cascade, 2014.
Scot, Barbara J. *Prairie Reunion*. New York: Farrar, Straus and Giroux, 1995.
Scott, Thomas. *The Force of Truth*. New York: Williams and Whiting, 1810. (Orig. 1779.)
Sei Shōnagon. *The Pillow Book*. Translated by Ivan Morris. New York: Columbia University Press, 1991.
Senter, Ruth Hollinger. *The Season of Friendship: A Search for Intimacy*. Grand Rapids: Zondervan, 1982.
Sentilles, Sarah. *Breaking Up With God*. New York: HarperCollins, 2011.
Shannon, James P. *Reluctant Dissenter*. New York: Crossroads, 1998.
Shapiro, Dani. *Devotion: A Memoir*. New York: HarperCollins, 2010.
———. *Slow Motion: A Memoir of a Life Rescued by Tragedy*, New York: Harper, 1998.
Smith, Tracy K. *Ordinary Light*. New York: Knopf Doubleday, 2015.
Soelle, Dorothee. *Against the Wind: Memoir of a Radical Christian*. Minneapolis: Fortress, 1999. (1995)
Spong, John Shelby. *Here I Stand: My Struggle for a Christianity of Integrity, Love, and Equality*. New York: HarperCollins, 2000.
Stanford, Shane. *A Positive Life: Living with HIV as a Pastor, Husband, and Father*. Grand Rapids: Zondervan, 2010.
Stanford-Rue, Susan M. *Will I Cry Tomorrow?* Old Tappan, NJ: Revell, 1990.
Staples, Brent. *Parallel Time*. New York: Pantheon, 1994.
Strayed, Cheryl. *Wild: From Lost to Found on the Pacific Crest Trail*. New York: Knopf, 2012.
Sulpicius Severus. *The Life of St Martin*. Translated by Alexander Roberts. Buffalo, NY: Christian Literature, 1894.
Taylor, Barbara Brown. *Leaving Church: A Memoir of Faith*. San Francisco: HarperSanFrancisco, 2007.
Thérèse of Lisieux. *Story of a Soul: The Autobiography of St. Thérèse of Lisieux*. Translated by John Clarke. Washington, DC: ICS, 1996. (Orig. 1898.)
Thompson, Deanna A. *Hoping for More: Having Cancer, Talking Faith, and Accepting Grace*. Eugene, OR: Cascade, 2012.
Thompson, Mark. *Gay Body: A Journey Through Shadow to Self*. New York: St. Martin's, 1997.
Tietjen, John H. *Memoirs in Exile*. Minneapolis: Fortress, 1990.
Tippett, Krista. *Speaking of Faith: Why Religion Matters—and How to Talk About It*. New York: Penguin, 2008.
Tirabassi, Becky. *Being a Wild Wonderful Woman for God*. Grand Rapids: Zondervan, 1994.
Tolstoy, Leo. *A Confession*. Mineola, NY: Dover, 2005. (1879)
Vanier, Jean. *From Brokenness to Community*. New York: Paulist, 1992.
Vattimo, Gianni. *Belief*. Translated by Luca D'Isanto and David Webb. Stanford, CA: Stanford University Press, 1999.
Velthouse, Lisa. *Craving Grace: A Story of Faith, Failure, and My Search for Sweetness*. Carol Stream, IL: SaltRiver, 2011.

Vincent, Leah. *Cut Me Loose: Sin and Salvation After My Ultra-Orthodox Girlhood.* New York: Penguin, 2014.
Wakefield, Dan. *Returning: A Spiritual Journey.* New York: Doubleday, 1988.
Weil, Simone. *Waiting for God.* New York: G. P. Putnam's Sons, 1951.
Weisenfled, Judith, and Richard Newman, eds. *This Far by Faith: Readings in African-American Women's Religious Biography.* New York: Routledge, 1996.
White, Carolinne, ed. *Early Christian Lives.* New York: Penguin, 1998.
———. *Lives of Roman Christian Women.* New York: Penguin, 2010.
White, Mel. *Stranger at the Gate: To be Gay and Christian in America.* New York: Simon and Schuster, 1994.
Whitefield, George. *A Short Account of God's Dealings with the Reverend George Whitefield.* Edinburgh: T. Lumisden and J. Robertson, 1741.
Wiesel, Elie. *All Rivers Run to the Sea.* New York: Alfred A. Knopf, 1995.
———. *Night.* New York: Avon Books, 1960.
Willis, Jan. *Dreaming Me: Black, Baptist, and Buddhist: One Woman's Spiritual Journey.* Somerville, MA: Wisdom, 2008.
Wiman, Christian. *My Bright Abyss.* New York: Farrar, Straus and Giroux, 2013.
Winner, Lauren F. *Girl Meets God: A Memoir.* New York: Random House, 2003.
Yogananda, Paramahansa. *Autobiography of a Yogi.* Los Angeles: Self-Realization Fellowship, 1971. (1946)
Zichterman, Jocelyn. *I Fired God: My Life Inside—and Escape From—the Secret World of the Independent Fundamentalist Baptist Cult.* New York: St. Martin's, 2013.

Subject Index

absence (of God), 71–72, 90–93, 96–97, 168, 176n53
abstraction, 1, 5, 32, 34, 44, 51–53, 60–62, 69–70, 85, 94, 98, 130, 163, 168, 175, 203, 211, 218–19, 230, 237–38, 240–41, 243
academic, 1–2, 3, 46, 180, 199, 223, 240n5, 241
adult, adulthood, 5–7, 127, 139, 164, 183
analogy of being, 53–54
apophatic theology, 52
atheism, 13, 135, 138
authenticity, 6–7, 21, 31, 66n6, 76, 107, 110, 123, 125, 131, 171, 188, 227
authority, 53, 64, 122, 149, 157, 184, 187, 195, 226

Bible, 23, 28, 43, 57n41, 59, 81, 122, 125, 189, 226
bios, 26–27
beauty, 12, 46, 51, 55, 146, 203
belief, 47, 58, 68, 72–73, 85–86, 89–90, 92–94, 96, 101, 106–8, 113, 118–19, 124–25, 129–30, 133, 135, 168, 185, 195, 209, 221, 225–26, 229, 231, 234, 241
body, 38, 44, 60–61, 70, 74–75, 98, 111, 129–30, 142, 153, 163, 175, 176n53, 202–3, 206

brokenness, 9, 20, 31, 37, 41–42, 44–45, 47–48, 50, 63, 77, 81, 96–97, 129, 137, 201–2, 204, 211, 215

certainty, 4, 51, 58–59, 93, 95, 124, 127, 143, 147, 232, 239–42
childhood, childlike 5–6, 17, 57, 87, 102, 119, 127, 139, 141, 163–64, 182–84, 215, 219, 224, 229–30
church, 2, 4–5, 16, 26–27, 31, 36, 50, 64–65, 69–70, 81, 87, 89, 94, 106–7, 109n7, 119–20, 124, 126, 129, 137, 149, 151, 157–59, 162, 166, 171–72, 181, 186–87, 191, 194–96, 219, 224, 227, 236
communion, 32, 64, 90, 97, 100, 103, 109, 145, 175, 212
community, 7, 16, 29, 72, 75, 81, 89, 97, 123, 125, 129, 161–62, 169, 172–73, 181–82, 184, 198–99, 202–5, 208, 213, 224, 242
compassion, 99, 180–81, 188, 193, 210, 215–16, 233–34
confession, 14, 47–48, 53–54, 62, 65, 69, 89, 107, 120, 131, 133, 146–47, 150–51, 162–63, 166, 168–69, 181, 211, 217, 240–42
conscience, 49, 184
contingency, 87, 95, 99–101, 103–4, 138

SUBJECT INDEX

conversion, 21–22, 28, 33, 40, 63, 88, 100, 135, 143, 148–49, 166–67, 179, 191, 194, 199–201, 205, 217
crisis, 6–7, 129, 137, 139
critique, 16, 37, 67, 72, 90, 92, 107, 114, 119, 148, 153, 183, 187, 195–96, 227, 229–30
cross (of Jesus), 33, 37–39, 44, 91–92, 96–97, 99, 168, 176n53, 206, 215–16, 218–19
curiosity, 49

death, 4, 27–28, 31–32, 37, 54, 60–61, 79, 83, 87, 95, 99, 107, 110–13, 115–16, 128, 149, 151–52, 155, 157, 213, 215–16, 220–21, 230
　death (of God), 92
　death (of Jesus), 32, 34–35, 37–38, 45, 72, 91–92, 96–97
　death (of the self), 37–39
deconstruction, 14
desire, 7, 12–15, 17, 35, 37, 39–41, 48–50, 55–56, 58–60, 70, 72, 74, 87, 91, 111, 118–19, 124, 128, 131, 133, 136, 139–40, 142–43, 149, 154, 156–57, 163, 168–69, 170, 175–76, 181–82, 187, 190–91, 193, 200–203, 212–18, 226, 236, 241
devil, 114, 148, 150–52, 154–55, 157, 171–72
devotion, 28, 64, 176n53
dialogue, 9, 61, 71, 76, 85, 157, 162, 223–25, 229, 231–32, 236, 238, 241–42
discernment, 9, 23, 57–58, 66–67, 72, 78, 80, 82, 89, 96, 120, 129, 143, 147, 151–52, 154–57, 159, 168, 173, 185, 200–202, 206
discipline, 33, 49n6, 69–70, 73, 170, 175
division (of self), 41–42, 92, 98
doctrine, 9, 11, 23, 27, 34, 49, 59, 65n6, 85, 90, 94–96, 106, 108, 158, 231, 239, 241
doubt, 4, 73, 86, 107, 109, 124, 129–30, 132–33, 139, 193–94, 205, 208

embodiment, 4–5, 8, 34, 36, 43–45, 61, 70, 74–75, 82, 86, 130, 132, 163, 177n53, 178, 203, 218–19, 228, 237
Eucharist, 8, 82, 153

fragility, 3, 19, 55, 95, 134–35, 138, 213
freedom, 49, 55, 65–66, 83, 187–88, 190, 192, 195, 226
friendship, 3, 5–6, 13, 16, 32, 40, 44, 52, 71, 74, 99, 103, 118, 205, 208, 211–13, 221, 224–25, 236, 241
fundamentalism, 10, 124–25, 128, 130, 134, 153, 234

Gospel, 1, 26, 29, 32, 73, 205, 216–17
gospel, 27, 42, 64, 128, 131, 157, 174, 209
grace, 8, 48, 50–51, 94, 131, 165–66, 234
graphe, 26–27
gratitude, 77, 80, 102, 190

hagiography, 36
heresy, 14, 26, 46–47, 62, 100, 107–8, 119, 151, 157
holiness, 26, 33, 36, 51–52, 56, 62, 133, 143, 148, 154, 163, 170
holy place, 152, 157
Holy Spirit, 33, 157–58
hope, 19, 27, 31, 37, 39, 75, 80, 87, 100, 118, 129–30, 177, 206, 209
hospitality, 102, 180, 192
humility, 52–53, 80, 86, 101, 131, 154, 162, 164–65, 169–71, 173–77, 204, 213, 215–18

identity, 13, 17, 21–22, 29, 37–40, 42–43, 45, 47, 64–65, 95, 120, 124–25, 130, 135, 139, 143, 148, 157, 164, 188–89, 198, 205, 208–9, 220, 227–28, 230, 232, 234, 236
immanence, 69n16, 94, 100, 104
incarnation, 5, 34, 60–61, 91, 99, 130, 175, 203

intimacy, 2, 4–5, 10, 23, 31–32, 45, 50–52, 54, 69, 74, 89, 98, 102, 131, 202, 211–12, 219, 222

journey, 1, 11–12, 16–17, 66, 82–83, 85, 94, 97, 106, 121, 123–24, 127, 133–34, 139, 147, 160, 165, 191, 196, 204, 206, 225, 228
justice, 87–88, 180, 186–90, 192–93, 196, 206, 224, 226, 230
   social justice, 30–31, 35, 180, 190, 206

kataphatic theology, 52
knowledge, 44, 51, 58n41, 90, 101, 107–8, 114, 146–47, 154, 163, 165, 189, 212, 219

language, 6, 8–9, 22–23, 52, 54, 64, 66, 70, 85, 87–89, 159, 164, 183, 190, 220, 224–26, 231, 233, 235–36
   language of lovers, 28, 31, 52, 56, 68, 70n16, 136, 225, 235
liberation, 132, 135, 187, 192, 209–210
liberation theology, 132, 231

marginalization, 23–24, 29, 31–32, 42, 99, 104, 115, 131, 137, 210, 216, 235
meditation, 75, 141–42, 146, 208
metaphysical, 51, 89, 231
ministry, 34, 46, 187, 198, 201
miracle, miraculous, 32, 34, 36, 45, 77, 82, 147, 158, 171, 219n58
modern, modernity, 1–2, 4, 10, 36, 47n1, 64–65, 83, 85–87, 93–94, 97, 103, 106–7, 123, 127, 134, 160, 227
morality, 29, 109, 111, 119, 124, 130–31, 148, 183, 189, 217, 219, 225
mystery, 12, 57–59, 82, 86, 89–90, 95, 96, 143, 182, 193, 211, 221, 234
mystic, mysticism, 5, 87, 89, 98, 141, 161–63, 173, 219, 242
myth, 64–66, 70, 202, 227–28, 230

myth of autonomy, 66, 70, 72–73, 82, 110, 163, 202, 237
mythology, 23, 30

narrative, 1, 4, 10, 14–15, 21, 23–24, 26–28, 31–34, 36–38, 45, 66–68, 71, 91, 95–96, 125, 128, 136, 150, 152, 180–81, 200, 210, 213–15, 225, 230, 242
neighbor, 5, 230

obedience, 78–80, 118, 167, 207
omnipotence (of God), 13, 18–19, 51, 68, 77
omniscience (of God), 13, 18–19, 51, 68
orthodoxy, 5, 107, 115, 122
otherness, 13, 90, 225–29, 231–34, 236–38

pain, 14, 17, 51, 69, 96, 99, 112, 128, 170, 205, 210, 214, 217
Paul (Apostle), 20, 27, 31–32, 35–42, 44–45, 53, 59, 77, 79, 98, 116, 130, 175, 178
perichorisis, 91
philosophy, 59, 61, 65, 112, 163, 179, 225
piety, 131, 146, 148–49, 183, 185
Platonic thought, 51, 61
pluralism, 11, 220, 228, 232, 234–38
poetry, poetic, 10–11, 22, 60–61, 63–65, 84–90, 109, 199, 231
poverty, 70, 75, 93, 97, 113, 120–21, 131–32, 145–46, 148, 161, 168, 174–75, 177n53, 180, 187, 189, 191–93, 196–97, 200, 202–4, 206–9, 213, 216–18, 220, 222, 224, 228, 238
prayer, 17, 26–27, 49–50, 71–73, 75–78, 83, 118, 133, 136–37, 141–42, 148–49, 162–66, 169–70, 172–78, 190, 192–93, 195–96, 199–200, 204–5, 207–8, 212, 219–20, 240
projection (of God), 13, 15, 17–19, 37, 52, 69

SUBJECT INDEX

reason, 3–6, 9, 45, 53, 58, 70, 74–75, 78, 80, 93, 110–11, 113–16, 127, 147, 171, 173, 239
relationality, 9, 13, 16, 23, 36, 76, 132, 191–92, 221, 231
resurrection (of Jesus), 24–25, 32, 34, 38, 45, 60, 211–12, 216
revelation, 1, 16, 59, 72, 78, 88, 91, 96, 126, 131, 154, 165, 230
ritual, 6, 11, 50, 89, 106, 108, 134, 136, 138, 140, 159, 182, 184, 190, 195n50, 240

sacrament, 8, 34, 47, 82, 195
salvation, 18, 48, 79–80, 128–29, 149, 216, 233
scripture, 10, 22–29, 51, 57n41, 58–59, 72, 88, 100, 120, 125, 162
secular, 45, 103, 128, 220
secularization, 93
self-critique, 12, 33, 40, 56, 120, 128, 147, 162, 171–73, 181, 196, 199–200, 208, 225, 228, 236
    self-critical (faith), 12, 107, 124, 146, 163
silence, 12, 71–72, 101, 103–4, 199
sin, 6, 9, 38–40, 46–48, 54, 56, 59, 63, 89, 96, 98, 146–47, 150–54, 162–66, 176n53, 178, 181, 190, 206, 210–11, 217
sovereignty, 118, 137, 231
speculative (thought or theology), 1, 51, 53, 59, 61–62, 69, 169, 175, 243
substitution (logic of), 3, 66–67
suffering, 18–19, 31–34, 60, 75, 87, 98–100, 114–16, 129, 137–38, 149, 168, 170, 174–75, 177n53, 180–81, 188–90, 209–211, 216, 218, 220–21, 229–30, 234
symbol, 34, 64, 152, 159, 194, 234

temptation, 1, 55, 109n7, 128, 150, 155, 164, 170, 175, 187, 218
theodicy, 19, 137–38, 209
theology, 1–2, 21, 23, 28, 38, 40–41, 49n6, 51–52, 59, 62, 64, 70, 81–82, 84, 98, 103–4, 119–20, 130–33, 151, 158–59, 163, 173, 198–99, 201–2, 209, 220–22, 230, 234, 240–43
theological discourse, 1–2, 52, 104, 131, 243
tradition, 2, 4, 7–9, 11, 14–15, 19, 23, 32, 36–38, 40, 43, 47, 49, 61–62, 65–67, 72, 75, 78, 80, 82–83, 88–90, 103, 106, 119–21, 122–23, 126–27, 134–35, 139–41, 143, 157–60, 162, 182–83, 188, 199, 220, 224–29, 232–33, 235–38, 240, 242
transcendence (spiritual or divine), 59, 61, 69–70, 92–94, 133, 162–63, 218, 234, 240
transformation, 21–22, 95, 100, 116–17, 130, 145, 186, 200, 217, 236
translation, 1, 6–9, 12, 18, 21–23, 26–27, 32, 35, 38, 40–45, 66–67, 71, 85, 88, 91–93, 95, 102, 116, 118, 129, 135, 137, 143, 147, 153, 157, 159, 202, 211, 219–20, 225, 227, 236, 240
    in tension with definition, 5, 7–9, 18, 21–23, 38, 40, 71, 82, 89, 91, 93, 95, 116, 120, 124–25, 129, 135, 148, 156, 159, 219, 235–36, 238, 240,
trauma, 9, 209, 213
trinity, 5, 59, 90–92

violence, 29n5, 110, 120, 167–68, 173, 205–6, 210, 213–14
vision, 29, 154–55, 157, 164–65, 173
vocation, 63, 150, 157–58, 168, 184–85, 187, 190–91, 193, 198–202, 205, 207–8, 213, 221–22
vulnerability, 3, 6, 24, 31, 45, 62, 75, 93, 97, 102, 111, 134–35, 141, 181, 210

weakness, 3–4, 14, 18, 20, 31, 37, 42–44, 53, 55, 58, 68, 77, 80, 92–93, 107, 113, 116, 131, 167, 175, 207, 213, 217, 239

Author Index

Armstrong, Karen, 2
Augustine, 46–62, 68, 70, 72, 86–88, 90, 92, 97–98, 101–2, 111, 118–19, 133, 144–46, 149–50, 162, 170, 174, 182, 191, 203, 218, 232

Bolz-Weber, Nadia, 2
Boyle, Greg, 2

Cairns, Scott, 2
Cassier, Ernst, 64

Day, Dorothy, 119, 171, 179–97, 212, 226

Eck, Diana, 223–38, 241
Eckhart, Meister, 89, 95, 141
Evans, Rachel Held, 122–43, 159, 224, 228–29, 232

Francis (Pope), 143, 196, 239

Gallagher, Nora, 2
Gilbert, Elizabeth, 2
Guibert of Nogent, 144–60

Ignatius of Loyola, 81, 120, 144–60, 164, 172, 177n53

John of the Cross, 77, 92, 163, 167

Kamenetz, Roger 2
Karr, Mary, 10, 21, 49–50, 61, 63–83, 85–88, 98, 107, 109–110, 112, 118, 136–37, 142, 162, 164, 167–69, 175, 193, 202, 204–5, 208, 217–18
Kierkegaard, Søren, 142, 165, 242

Lamott, Anne, 2
Levine, Stephen, 2
Lewis, C. S., 2

Merton, Thomas, 2, 136, 199
Metz, Johann Baptist, 242
Miles, Jack, 2
Miles, Sara, 2
Moltmann, Jürgen, 98, 168, 210, 231

Newman, John Henry, 3–4, 23, 49, 74, 80, 93, 126, 201, 239
Norris, Kathleen 2, 5–8
Nouwen, Henri, 32, 75, 131, 142, 156, 191, 198–222, 224

Patel, Eboo, 10–12

Rahner, Karl, 234
Ricoeur, Paul, 9
Rodriguez, Richard, 35

Sentilles, Sarah, 14–19, 136, 138

Shapiro, Dani, 122–43, 145, 159, 204, 232

Taylor, Barbara Brown, 2
Teresa of Ávila, 92, 141–42, 146, 152, 156, 160, 161–78, 183, 193, 195, 203, 205–6, 217
Tillich, Paul, 139
Tolstoy, Leo, 105–121, 123, 127, 131, 135, 162, 175, 186, 191, 204, 213, 219n58

Vanier, Jean, 75, 198–99, 202–4, 208, 218

Weil, Simone, 87
Wiman, Christian, 15, 59, 84–104, 116, 118, 124, 126, 135, 138–39, 141–42, 145, 162, 167–68, 170, 177n53, 205, 232, 240
Winner, Lauren, 2, 13–14

Scripture Index

Exodus

3:6   24

Deuteronomy

10:18   31

Ruth

1:16–17   28

1 Samuel

3   72

Isaiah

58:5–9   33

Jeremiah

1:4–10   29–30

Zechariah

7:10   31

Matthew

5:3   174
22:23–33   25

Mark

9:24   73
14–16   34

Luke

6:17–49   34
9:23–25   39
17:33   87, 207
24:13–35   32

John

4   209

Acts

2   158
3:13–15   26

Romans

1:20	53
6:5–11	38
7	178
7:15	59

1 Corinthians

1:22–23	44
1:22–24	77
1:6–7	77
2:2	40, 44
3:1–6	41
4:16	35
9:19–23	42
11:1	35
12:1	77
13	130

Galatians

3:28	41
5:16–26	40–41

Philippians

3:17	35

1 Thessalonians

2:8	27
2:17–20	31–32
3:10	32

Hebrews

2:8	33
11:4—12:13	33
12:1–6	33

James

1:22–27	43
2:14–26	44, 219

2 Maccabees

	91

www.ingramcontent.com/pod-product-compliance
Lightning Source LLC
Chambersburg PA
CBHW030822230426
43667CB00008B/1333